# CHATS ON
# JAPANESE
# PRINTS

HIROSHIGE: THE BOW-MOON.

Size 15×7. Signed *Hiroshige, hitsu.*

*Frontispiece.*

# CHATS ON JAPANESE PRINTS

BY

ARTHUR DAVISON FICKE

WITH A PREFACE BY

GLADYS B. FICKE

RUTLAND, VERMONT

CHARLES E. TUTTLE COMPANY

TOKYO, JAPAN

*Representatives*
*For Continental Europe: BOXERBOOKS, INC., Zurich*
*For the British Isles: PRENTICE-HALL INTERNATIONAL, INC., London*
*For Australasia: PAUL FLESCH & CO., PTY. LTD. Melbourne*

*Published by the Charles E. Tuttle Company, Inc.*
*of Rutland, Vermont & Tokyo, Japan*
*with editorial offices at Suido 1-chome, 2-6*
*Bunkyo-ku, Tokyo, Japan*

*Library of Congress Catalog*
*Card No. 58-11117*

*First printing, 1958*
*Second printing, 1960*
*Third printing, 1966*

Printed in Japan

TO

# FREDERICK WILLIAM GOOKIN

AND

## HOWARD MANSFIELD

CUSTODIANS, APPRAISERS, AND LOVERS OF BEAUTY

As chosen guests we may partake
Of this strange hostel's ancient wine.
For thirst no common drink can slake
Tapsters of lineage divine
Here pour sweet anodyne.

The hurly-burly of the road,
The turmoil of the carters' feet,
Intrude not to this still abode
Where travellers from the world-ends meet,
And find the gathering sweet.

Hence may perhaps some secret gleam
Follow along our onward way,
From evening feast with lords of dream,
As we go forth into the grey
To-morrow's cloudy day.

# PREFACE

*by Gladys B. Ficke*

THIS book was first published in 1915; in the course of these many years new discoveries have outdated certain data found here, but these are factual matters such as the exact date of issuance of a given design, the number of copies known, or the collections in which they are, or were, held. Some of the great collections of that day are now dispersed or are placed in museums; and in consequence the public is better acquainted with Japanese prints than it was when this book was written. There is new information about some of the artists, such as, for example, that Shunko was born in 1743 and died in 1812, dates unknown forty years ago, though the approximate time was known. And more biographical details are known in some cases. Such facts are of importance to specialists in the field and should be checked by them in recent authentic books; but for an understanding of the prints themselves this book, among the many that have been concerned with the art, has remained perennially the book of print lovers; and a novice who reads it is likely to have the pleasant experience of finding that his reactions to the prints, his diffused feelings, his uncertain perceptions, his undefined intuitions, have become more articulate because they have been discussed in illuminating language. The author was especially well fitted to supply this need, being a lover of the art and a poet prepared to express his feelings in words. No one can say wholly what an art is, but a broad gate to understanding is opened when one moves freely in discussion. Furthermore, Arthur Ficke was not only a writer, he was a great conversationalist, and the flavor of conversation with an easy flow of thought runs through the book, imparting a sense of intimacy, of participation with the author in examining these rare and beautiful pictures. In both prose and poetry he tells us about them, interprets them as a musician interprets a score, and there is always room for another version by another lover of the art. It is this quality of delight in the subject that engages anyone with the least curiosity to look, and to see, and to know.

And once one knows and has become a true lover the image is ineradicably stamped upon the memory. "I can never lose them, they are a part of my vision," he, my husband, said. I have gone with him to a presale exhibition, seen him suddenly stare across the gallery, then approach a print and, taking a small magnifying glass from his pocket, examine it carefully. "Yes, I thought so. I bought it in Japan in 1904, the merest penny picture then, a work of art worth hundreds of dollars now. I hated to put it in my sale." This could happen even if, to my eyes, an identical print was near by—but not *the one*.

And he said, "The aristocracy were repelled by the plebeian and vulgar nature of these mundane subjects, but it was due almost as much to the barriers of class as to any aesthetic verdict. All the garish, novel, exuberant vitality of Yedo with its expanding industries and popular arts would receive small official approval from those to whom the secluded formal gardens of old Kyoto, the long-treasured paintings of Chinese masters, the reserved and stately simplicity of the ancient tea-ceremony were the criteria of aesthetic perfection. Quite to the contrary, it is the courtesan of gay Yedo who is the central figure of the print art—even more than the actor; it is her promenades in festival streets, her daily occupations within the enclosure of her matted rooms, her merry boating parties, her picnics in gardens where the cherry blossoms are not more luminous than she, that recur forever in these sheets with a brilliant monotony. But, though it is the most commonplace of daily occupations and popular life which the prints purport to depict, it is in fact the classic and unchanging aspect of these things which they perpetuate—the immemorial attitudes, the gestures as old and as significant as life itself, the hereditary permanences in the 'floating world.' "

We looked at the sheets, brilliant indeed, finding none monotonous. He said of landscapes by Hiroshige and Hokusai that, "The wholly artificial aspect of even the most natural Japanese landscape is a thing impossible for the stranger to Japan to take sufficiently into account when viewing the landscape prints. Just in this incredible and theatrical fashion hills *do* jut up toward enamel skies; precisely thus pine-trees *do* twist their labyrinthine silhouettes over the sea; the rice fields, the winding road, the little rivers, and the mists along the bases of mountains exist in this unreal, exaggeratedly picturesque and quite unbelievable fashion. All is pictorial and the painter who reports the truth takes on for us the aspect of a consummate deceiver showing an imaginary fairy-land."

Even to this day after the havoc of war, visitors return from Japan marvelling at the spectacular beauties both of the natural world and the cultivated gardens, all treated with care and reverence by every citizen. Love of nature is a special and happy development of their culture. It is impossible to imagine, in our country, poems of admiration written to and hung upon flowering trees, not as an advertisement, not as a prank, not for profit, not for anything but an expression of delight.

But one thing, my husband reminded me, we never find in the whole range of Japanese prints: there is no reflection of either Buddhism or of Shintoism, the commingled religions of Japan in that day, and largely in this. When there is any slight allusion it is to a great prophet or to a great dogma, but done lightly and for the decorative quality. For this world of the print is a human world only, a world of beauty and light and love such as each of us in his prime may know and leave at last with regret.

Although the prints were made cheaply for transient pleasure, both chance and their own intrinsic beauty have worked to preserve a great many of them. Some were mounted in albums and, thus guarded from light and air, they come to us in perfect condition. Then there are others modified by time whose effect has been to soften some of the colors into combinations of peculiar harmony. But time is not always merciful, and many prints are faded and darkened to a monotone of chocolate color. It is against these, whose value is negligible, that the novice should be warned. On the other hand chemical changes may work little miracles. The oxidation of orange woodwork or skies or drapery, as well as the modification of blues and purples to a kind of wavering gradation, gives a charm as definite and unique as the patina of bronze or the iridescence of old glass, and they are the source of some of the rarest and most haunting beauties in this art.

In the original edition acknowledgments were given by Ficke to friends who had aided him in preparing the book: Mr. F. W. Gookin, Mr. Howard Mansfield, Mr. W. S. Spaulding, Mr. J. T. Spaulding, Mr. Judson Metzgar, Mr. C. H. Chandler, Mr. J. S. Happer, Col. Henry Appleton, Mrs. Arthur Aldis, Mr. E. Oberholtzer, and Mr. C. A. Ficke. And he acknowledged indebtedness to the writings of Von Seidlitz, Bing, Huish, Anderson, Strange, Binyon, Gookin, Kurth, Morrison, Happer, Koechlin, Vignier, Succo, Field, De Goncourt, Okakura, Edmunds, Perzynski, Wright, Fenollosa, and De Becker. There were thanks given to collectors for permission to use certain prints of theirs for illustration. These were from the Spaulding collection, Boston; the Gookin collection, Chicago; the Mansfield collection, New York; the Chandler collection, Evanston, Illinois; the Metzgar collection, Moline, Illinois; and the Ainsworth collection, Moline, Illinois. Four of the poems appeared first in the *Little Review;* a number of others are from the author's book *Twelve Japanese Painters.*

April, 1958

# CONTENTS

13

# ILLUSTRATIONS

15

# 16 ILLUSTRATIONS

# GLOSSARY

**Beni.**—A delicate pink or red pigment of vegetable origin.

**Beni-ye.**—A print in which *beni* is the chief colour used. The term is generally employed to describe all those two-colour prints which immediately preceded the invention of polychrome printing.

**Chuban.**—A vertical print, size about 11 × 8, sometimes called the " medium size " sheet.

**Diptych.**—A composition consisting of two sheets.

**Gauffrage.**—Printing by pressure alone, without the use of a pigment, producing an embossed effect on the paper.

**Hashira-ye.**— A very tall narrow print, size about 28 × 5, used to hang on the wooden pillars of a Japanese house; a pillar-print.

**Hashirakake.**—See *hashira-ye.*

**Hoso-ye.**—A small vertical print, size about 12 × 6.

**Kakemono.**—A painting mounted on a margin of brocade; hung by its top when in use, and rolled up when not in use.

19

**Kakemono-ye.**—A very tall wide print, size about 28 × 10.

**Key-block.**—The engraved wooden plate from which the black outlines of the print were produced.

**Kira-ye.**—A print with mica background.

**Koban.**—A vertical print slightly smaller than the *Chuban* (q.v.).

**Kurenai-ye.**—A hand-coloured print in which *beni* is chiefly used.

**Mon.**—The heraldic insignia used by actors and others as coat-of-arms ; generally worn on their sleeves.

**Nagaye.**—See *hashira-ye.*

**Nishiki-ye.**—Brocade picture—a term used at first to describe the brilliant colour-inventions of Harunobu, but now loosely applied to all polychrome prints.

**Oban.**—A large vertical print, about 15 × 10—the normal full-size upright sheet.

**Otsu-ye.**—A rough broadsheet painting, of small size, on paper ; the precursor of the print.

**Pentaptych.**—A composition consisting of five sheets.

**Pillar-print.**—See *hashira-ye.*

**Sumi.**—Black Chinese ink.

**Sumi-ye.**—A print in black and white only.

**Surimono.**—A print, generally of small size and on thick soft paper, intended as a festival greeting or memento of some social occasion

**Tan.**—A brick-red or orange colour, consisting of red oxide of lead.

**Tan-ye.**—A print in which *tan* is the only or chief colour used. Such prints, in which the *tan* was applied by hand, were among the earliest productions.

**Triptych.**—A composition consisting of three sheets.

**Uchiwa-ye.**—A print in the shape of a fan.

**Urushi.**—Lacquer.

**Urushi-ye.**—A print in which lacquer is used to heighten the colour. The term is generally employed to describe only the early hand-coloured prints in which lacquer, colours, and metallic dust were applied to the printed black outline.

**Yokoye.**—A large horizontal print, about 10 × 15—the normal full-size landscape sheet.

# I

# PRELIMINARY
# SURVEY

## THE GENERAL NATURE OF JAPANESE PRINTS

## GROWTH OF INTEREST IN THEM

## THE TECHNIQUE OF THEIR PRODUCTION

## THEIR ÆSTHETIC CHARACTERISTICS

Bring forth, my friend, these faded sheets
Whose charm our laboured utterance flies.
Perhaps our later search repeats
The groping of those scholars' eyes

Who, ere the dawned Renaissant day,
With duskèd sight and doubtful hand,
Bent o'er the pages of some grey
Greek text they could not understand ;

Drawn by the sense that there concealed
Lay key to spacious realms unknown ;
Held by the need that be revealed
Forgotten worlds to light their own.

# CHAPTER I

## PRELIMINARY SURVEY

The general nature of Japanese prints—Growth of interest in them—
The technique of their production—Their æsthetic characteristics.

THAT sublimated pleasure which is the seal of all the arts reaches its purest condition when evoked by a work in which the æsthetic quality is not too closely mingled with the every-day human. Poetry, because of its close human ties, is to a certain extent a corrupt art; its medium is that base speech which we use for communicating information, and few are the readers whose minds can absolve words from the work-a-day obligation of conveying, first of all, mere tidings. Music, on the other hand, employing a medium wholly sacred to its own uses, starts with no such handicap; its succession of notes awakens in the listener no expectation of an eventual body of facts to carry home. Between the two extremes lie the graphic arts. These are perhaps most fortunate when they deal with material not familiar to the spectator, for it is then that he most readily accepts them as designs and harmonies, without looking to them for a literal record of things only too well known to him.

25

The graphic art of an alien race has therefore an initial strength of purely æsthetic appeal that a native art often lacks. It moves free from the demands with which unconsciously we approach the art of our own people. It stands as an undiscovered world, of which nothing can logically be expected. The spectator who turns to it at all must come prepared to take it on its own terms. If it allures him, it will do so by virtue of those qualities of harmony, rhythm, and vision which in these strange surroundings are more perceptible to him than in the art of his own race, where so many adventitious associations operate to distract him. Like a man whom Mayfair bewilders with its fashions, he may find that fundamental verity, that humanity which he seeks only among the Gipsy beggars.

Perhaps this theory best explains the impulse that has of late led many lovers of beauty to turn to the arts of Persia, China, and Japan for their keenest pleasure. Here, in unfamiliar environment, the fundamental powers of design stand forth free. Here the beautiful is discoverable for its own sake, liberated from the oppression of utility.

Toward Japan this impulse has in our own day been strongly directed. The handicrafts of the Japanese people have charmed the Western world, possibly to an undue extent. On the other hand, the great classical schools of Japanese painting have unfortunately been difficult of access. But between the two, half craft and half art, lies the Japanese colour-print—a finer product than mere dexterous artizan work, and more accessible than the paintings of the classic masters. In the print many a Western mind has found its clearest intimation of the universal principles of beauty.

During a period of a little more than a hundred years, roughly delimited by 1742 and 1858, there were produced in Japan large numbers of wood-engravings, printed in colours; these have of late come to occupy an almost unique place in the esteem of European art-lovers. So great is the importance now attached to these works that the Japanese public of earlier days, for whose delectation they were designed, would be astounded could they witness it. Just as obscure Greek potters moulded for common use vases that are to-day treasured in the museums as paradigms of beauty, so the coloured broadsheets, whose immediate purpose was to give pleasure to the crowds of the Japanese capital, have taken in the course of years a distinguished rank among the beautiful things of all time.

The day is passing when the love of these sheets can be looked upon as the badge of a cult, the secret delight of far-searching worshippers of the strange and exotic. Even did the collector desire, he could not long hide this light under a bushel; and the Japanese print is swiftly becoming a general treasure. This is proper and natural. An understanding of the origin of this form of art makes its present popularity in Europe seem like the felicitous rounding of a circle begun on the other side of the world.

It was in Yedo, the teeming capital of Japan, that the art of the colour-print flourished; and the patron sought by the artists was primarily the common man.

No art more purely national or more definitely
popular and exoterical in its inception has ever
existed. The subjects of the prints are alone
enough to make this fact evident. In them appear
the forms and faces of the popular actors in their
admired rôles, fashionable courtesans decked in all
the splendour of their unhappy but far-famed days
and nights, legendary heroes, dancers, wrestlers, and
popular entertainers. In the matter of landscape,
the scenes shown are the festival-crowded temples
of Yedo, the sunlit tea-gardens and gay midnight
boating-parties of the Sumida River, the great high-
roads of national travel, the famous spots of popular
recreation. Only rarely are there episodes from
aristocratic life; and the occasional occurrence of
these has precisely the significance of a photograph
of a royal house-party shown in a penny paper.
The Yoshiwara, as the licensed quarter of Yedo is
called, appears in these prints more often than do
the garden-parties of noble ladies; the vulgar theatre
is shown, but not the classic Nō drama of the
aristocracy; it is a Japanese Montmartre, not a
Japanese Faubourg St. Germain, that is revealed.
The artist's sense of beauty subdues these riotous
pleasures of the populace to the severe demands of
a beautiful pattern; but it is a whimsical vulgar
world, a world of the people, a world of passing
gaiety, that he portrays.

The purposes of these pictures were various. " To
some extent," says Mr. Frederick W. Gookin, " they
were used as advertisements. Incidentally they
served as fashion plates. Some were regularly pub-

lished and sold in shops. Others were designed
expressly upon orders from patrons, to whom the
entire edition, sometimes a very small one, was
delivered. The number struck from any block or
set of blocks varied widely. Of the more popular
prints many editions were printed, each one, as
might be expected, inferior to those that preceded
it. . . . Most of the prints were sold at the time of
publication for a few *sen*. The finer ones brought
relatively higher prices, and such prints as the great
triptychs and still larger compositions by Kiyonaga,
Yeishi, Toyokuni, Utamaro, and other leading artists
could never have been very cheap. In general, however, the price was small, and they were regarded as
ephemeral things. Many were used to ornament the
small screens that served to protect kitchen fires
from the wind, and in this use were inevitably soiled
and browned by smoke. Others, mounted upon the
sliding partitions of the houses, perished in the fires
by which the Japanese cities have been devastated ;
or, if in houses that chanced safely to run the
gauntlet of fires, typhoons, cloudbursts, and other
mishaps, their colours faded, and their surfaces were
rubbed until little more than dim outlines were left."

The plebeian origin of the prints explains why the
cultivated Japanese have not, as a rule, looked upon
them with much enthusiasm. Only now, when the
greatest print treasures have gone out of Japan, are
a few Japanese collectors beginning to buy back at
high prices works which they allowed to leave the
country for a song. The admiration of Europe and
America has awakened them to a realization of the

distinction of the prints, in spite of the undistinguished nature of their subjects ; and the day will
come when the Japanese themselves will be the most
formidable bidders at the sales of great Western
collections.

The interest of Western collectors in Japanese
prints is of comparatively recent origin.  As late as
1861 it was possible for a writer on Japan to regard
them with blank indifference.  There is a rare little
book by Captain Sherard Osborne, printed in that
year in London, called "Japanese Fragments."  It
contains six hand-coloured reproductions of prints
and a number of uncoloured cuts, all from prints
which Captain Osborne had purchased in Japan.  In
the following words he makes reference to Hiroshige,
who is now generally ranked as one of the supreme
landscape artists of all time : "Even the humble
artists of that land have become votaries of the
beautiful, and in such efforts as the one annexed
strive to do justice to the scenery.  Their apprecia-
tion of the picturesque is far in advance, good souls,
of their power of pencil, but our embryo Turner
(i.e. Hiroshige) has striven hard . . ." etc.  In 1861,
perhaps, few people would have believed it possible
that to-day many serious judges might question
whether any product of European art has ever
matched the designs of these "humble artists."

The earliest of European collectors was, according
to Mr. Edward F. Strange, a certain M. Isaac
Titsingh, who died in Paris in 1812.  M. Titsingh
had for fourteen years served the Dutch East India
Company in Nagasaki ; and among his effects were

"nine engravings printed in colours." Doubtless he had acquired them merely as curiosities, without any perception of their artistic importance. Mr. Strange notes that four prints were reproduced in Oliphant's "Account of the Mission of Lord Elgin to China and Japan" (1859); and, as we have seen, Osborne devoted some desultory attention to prints in 1861. These are, perhaps, the chief evidences of early European interest.

Subsequently such events as the International Exhibition in London, 1862, the Paris Exposition of 1867 and that of 1878, and the Centennial Exhibition in Philadelphia, 1876, served to bring a few prints to the notice of Western amateurs. Particularly in Paris was intense interest in them aroused among painters and literary men. From 1889 to 1891, S. Bing was bringing out in Paris his magazine *Le Japon Artistique*, whose pages contain many fine reproductions of notable prints. In 1891, Edmond de Goncourt issued his volume on Utamaro. Other books followed rapidly. In 1895, Professor Anderson issued his small but important monograph on "Japanese Wood Engraving." In 1896, Fenollosa's epoch-making catalogue, "Masters of Ukioye," was published in New York, establishing for the first time the foundations of all our present knowledge of this field, and pronouncing judgments from which the consensus of later opinion has, in the main, never departed. The same year brought forth de Goncourt's "Hokusai." Mr. Strange's "Japanese Colour Prints" appeared in 1897. In the same year, Von Seidlitz issued his "Geschichte des japanischen Far-

benholzschnittes" (published in England as "A
History of Japanese Colour Prints" in 1900), which
remains to-day the most comprehensive and accurate
single treatise on the subject.

Of recent years, the growth of interest and the
increase of books has been rapid. Eager collectors
have scoured the world to bring to light new masterpieces; Japan has been ransacked so thoroughly that
the would-be purchaser can perhaps more wisely go
to London or Paris or New York than to Tokyo or
Kyoto in his search for prizes; and the places of
honour accorded these sheets in the portfolios of
discriminating collectors and great museums leaves
no doubt as to the esteem with which they are
regarded. Values have been multiplied by tens
and hundreds, so that to-day the supreme rarities
among prints are beyond the reach of the ordinary
purchaser.

All this is due neither to accident nor to any
strange freak of whimsical tastes. It has come
about because the prints are in fact artistic treasures. Commonplace and trivial as the subjects of
most of them are, they rise by virtue of the quality
of their execution to a very high point—masterpieces
of composition, triumphs of colour, monuments of
the power of human genius to impose its sense of
rhythm, form, and harmony on the appearances
of the seen world.

But as is true in the case of any art, the content
of the colour-prints is not to be grasped at a first
glance by the casual passer-by. Familiarity with
the aims selected, the conventions employed, and

the achievements possible is necessary before the specific charm of these works makes itself manifest. It is the experience of most print-lovers that, starting with perhaps a mere casual liking for a certain landscape design, they progress gradually, in the course of years, to an unmeasured delight in the whole body of prints, and eventually find in them a unique source of repose and exaltation.

There are certain peculiarities, common not only to prints but to Japanese art as a whole, that require a special effort of the Western mind before they become acceptable. The first and most vital of these is the absence of realism. " Throughout the course of Asian painting," writes Mr. Laurence Binyon, " the idea that art is the imitation of Nature is unknown, or known only as a despised and fugitive heresy. . . . A Chinese critic of the sixth century, who was also an artist, published a theory of æsthetic principles which became a classic and received universal acceptance, expressing as it did the deeply rooted instincts of the race. In this theory, it is rhythm that holds the paramount place; not, be it observed, imitation of Nature, or fidelity to Nature, which the general instinct of the Western races makes the root-concern of art. In this theory every work of art is thought of as an incarnation of the genius of rhythm manifesting the living spirit of things with a clearer beauty and intenser power than the gross impediments of complex matter allow to be transmitted to our senses in the visible world around us. A picture is conceived as a sort of apparition from a more real world of essential life."

It will, therefore, be vain to expect in Japanese designs any production that will astonish the spectator by its life-likeness, it fidelity to an actual scene. Eastern art has never attempted to compete with the work of photography. Its function is the function which the European public grants to poets but not always to painters—the seeking out of subtle and invisible relations in things, the perception of harmonies and rhythms not heard by the common ear, the interpretation of life in terms of a finer and more beautiful order than practical life has ever known.

All Asian art has recognized for centuries the fact that vision and imagination are the faculties by which the painter as well as the poet must grapple with reality. In the words of Mr. Binyon once more—" It is always the essential character and genius of the element that is sought for and insisted on : the weight and mass of water falling, the sinuous, swift curves of a stream evading obstacles in its way, the burst of foam against a rock, the toppling crest of a slowly arching billow ; and all in a rhythm of pure lines. But the same principles, the same treatment, are applied to other subjects. If it be a hermit sage in his mountain retreat, the artist's efforts will be concentrated on the expression, not only in the sage's features, but in his whole form, of the rapt intensity of contemplation ; toward this effect every line of drapery and of surrounding rock or tree will conspire, by force of repetition or of contrast. If it be a warrior in action, the artist will ensure that we feel the tension of nerve, the heat of blood in the muscles, the watchfulness of the eye, the fury of determination. That birds shall be seen to be, above all things, winged creatures rejoicing in their flight; that flowers shall be, above all things, sensitive blossoms unfolding on pliant, up-growing stems; that the tiger shall be an embodiment of force, boundless in capacity for spring and fury—this is the ceaseless aim of these artists, from which no splendour of colour, no richness of texture, no accident of shape diverts them. The more to concentrate on this seizure of the inherent life in what they draw, they will obliterate or ignore at will half or all of the surrounding objects with which the Western painter feels bound to fill his background. By isolation and the mere use of empty space they will give to a clump of narcissus by a rock, or a solitary quail, or a mallow plant quivering in the wind, a sense of grandeur and a hint of the infinity of life."

This almost symbolic quality is the chief element of the pleasure to be derived from Japanese art. Japanese designs are metaphors; they depict not any object, but remote and greater powers to which the object is related. Often the artist produces his effect by the exaggeration of certain aspects, or by expressing particular qualities in the terms of some kindred thing. If his subject happens to be an actor in some great and tragic rôle, he will not hesitate to prolong the lines of the drapery unconscionably, to give the effect of solemn dignity, slow movement, and monumental isolation. Westerners may smile at the distortion of such a figure; but they must acknowledge that an atmosphere of lofty and special destiny surrounds the form, precisely because the artist has dared to use these devices. The Japanese artist will draw a woman as if she were a lily, a man as if he were a tempest, a tree as if it were a writhing snake, a mountain as if it were a towering giant. This is the very essence of poetical imagination ; and the result of it is to endow a picture with obscure suggestions and overtones of infinite power. Symbols of existence beyond themselves, these designs are charged with an almost mystical command upon the emotions of the spectator. Western art has employed such a method comparatively little in painting. In poetry it appears frequently. The poet, when he wishes to convey the impression of a beautiful woman, does not set out her features and her stature and all the details of her aspect. He tries to awaken some realization of her by a bold and fantastic leap of the imagination straight to the heart of the matter—he makes her a perfume, a light, a music, a memory of goddesses.

The prosaic mind will never greatly care for work produced in accordance with this principle ; the conventions will seem distortions, the imaginative generalizations will seem inaccuracies, and the transcending of reality to shape a more universal and significant statement will appear nothing more than ineptitude in grappling with fact. But to the poetical mind, all these things will come with a unique and irresistible fascination ; and far more delightful than the novelty and interest of the scenes represented will be the manner of their representation.

As one enters into the spirit of these paintings and prints, it is as if one saw the world from a new angle, or had acquired the power to assemble into new intellectual combinations those sensory impressions which our own art has taught us to combine in a manner now grown a little dull and stereotyped.

Japanese art has certain conventions that are highly individual. Some of these may trouble and repel the Western eye. For example, the Japanese artist draws his figures without shadows, and makes no attempt to represent the play of light and shade over them. The scene is painted as if in a clear, cold vacuum, where the diffusion of illumination is almost perfectly uniform. In the Japanese view, a shadow is something ephemeral and transitory—a mere accident and illusion, and as such unworthy of perpetuation in art. The pattern of the object itself, freed from this momentary tyranny, should be the sole theme of the artist. Similarly, high-lights or chiaroscuro are not attempted; nor is modelling by means of these employed. A universal flatness is the result—a result deliberately aimed at.

Most of the European ideas of perspective are ignored in these works. In accordance with the ancient Chinese canon—based upon an imaginative and not upon a visual perception—the linear perspective of the Japanese exactly reverses that of Western painting. In their system, parallel lines converge as they approach the spectator. Different planes of distance may be suggested merely by placing the remote plane higher up in the picture; and sometimes no attempt is made to diminish the size of the figures in the upper plane. These devices may seem very naïve to the European. But in aerial perspective—the power to give to objects a colouring appropriate to their relative distance from the eye—the Japanese indisputably employ the utmost subtlety. When these artists differ from European custom, it is not because of ignorance, but because their way seems to them the more expressive—the better adapted to the creation of those peculiar impressions of beauty which are their aim. The longer one examines the products of these alien theories of drawing, the less certain one is likely to be of the superiority of our more scientific Western conventions.

In all Japanese art, the element of pure brushwork is of greater importance than in the art of Europe. The people, trained from childhood in the handling of the brush as a pencil for the drawing of the complex forms of written characters, acquire a facility and accuracy unknown in other lands. Fine caligraphy is esteemed an art in itself. And the Japanese painter, whose life is devoted to further exercises with the brush, may achieve a unique degree of skill. His power to sweep, guide, and modulate the width and intensity of his line is developed into a sixth sense. He can make his brush-stroke smooth-flowing as a violin-note, or splintered as a broken branch, or wavering like the flow of a river, or coldly hard and sharp as flint ; sometimes it has the edge of a knife ; at other times it dies away into imperceptible gradations ; its blacks are dazzling in their intensity, its greys are like veils of mist. The mystery of the expression of pure personality in art is nowhere more strikingly exemplified than here. To the accustomed eye the line-work of the Japanese artist is vibrant with intimate connection between hand and spirit. This command of the brush, so perfect that the passion of the artist's soul flows out through it, is one of the vital characteristics of Japanese painting.

The colour-print is one small and peculiar division of the larger field of Japanese pictorial design ; besides being subject to the general laws of Japanese æsthetics, it is distinguished by certain special characteristics that grow out of the nature of the technique employed. Of this technique, Mr. F. W. Gookin gives an illuminating exposition :—

"None but the most primitive methods—or what from our point of view may seem such—were employed. The most wonderful among all the prints is but a 'rubbing' or impression taken by hand from wood blocks. The artist having drawn the design with the point of a brush in outline upon thin paper, it was handed over to the engraver, who began his part of the work by pasting the design face downward upon a flat block of wood, usually cherry, sawn plank-wise as in the case of the blocks used by European wood-engravers in the time of Dürer. The paper was then carefully scraped at the back until the design showed through distinctly in every part. Next, the wood was carefully cut away, leaving the lines in relief, care being taken to preserve faithfully every feature of the brush strokes with which the drawing was executed. A number of impressions were then taken in Chinese ink from this 'key block' and handed to the artist to fill in with colour. This ingenious plan, which is manifestly an outgrowth of the early custom of colouring the ink-prints (sumi-ē) by hand, and which perhaps would never have been thought of had not the colour itself been an afterthought, enabled the artist to try many experiments in colour arrangement with a minimum amount of labour. The colour scheme and orna-mentation of the surfaces having been determined, the engraver made as many subsidiary blocks as were required, the parts meant to take the colour being left raised and the rest cut away. Accurate register was secured by the simplest of devices. A right-angled mark engraved at the lower right-hand corner of the original block, and a straight mark in exact line with its lower arm at the left, were repeated upon each subsequent block, and in printing, the sheets were laid down so that their lower and right-hand edges corresponded with the marks so made. The defective register which may be observed in many prints was caused by unequal shrinking or swelling of the blocks. In consequence of this, late impressions are often inferior to the early ones, even though printed with the same care, and from blocks that had worn very little. The alignment will usually be found to be exact upon one side of the print, but to get further out of register as the other side is approached.

"The printing was done on moist paper with Chinese ink and colour applied to the blocks with flat brushes. A little rice paste was usually mixed with the pigments to keep them from running, and to increase their brightness. Sometimes dry rice flour was dusted over the blocks after they were charged. To this method of charging the blocks much of the beauty of the result may be attributed. The colour could be modified, graded, or changed at will, the blocks covered entirely or partially. Hard, mechanical accuracy was avoided. Impressions differed even when the printer's aim was uniformity. Sometimes in inking the 'key block,' which was usually the last one impressed, some of the lines would fail to receive the pigment, or would be overcharged. This was especially liable to happen when the blocks were worn and the edges of the lines became rounded. A little more or a little less pigment sometimes made a decided difference in the tone of the print, and, it may be noted, has not infrequently determined the nature and extent of the discoloration wrought by time.

"In printing, a sheet of paper was laid upon the block and the printer rubbed off the impression, using for the purpose a kind of pad called a baren. This was applied to the back of the paper and manipulated with a circular movement of the hand. By varying the degree of pressure the colour could be forced deep into the paper, or left upon the outer fibres only, so that the whiteness of those below the surface would shine through, giving the peculiar effect of light which is seen at its best in some of the surimono (prints designed for distribution at New Year's or other particular occasion) by Hokusai. Uninked blocks were used for embossing portions of the designs. The skill of the printer was a large

factor in producing the best results. Even the
brilliancy of the colour resulted largely from his
manipulations of the pigments and various little
tricks in their application. The first impressions
were not the best, some forty or fifty having to be
pulled before the biocks would take the colour
properly. Many kinds of paper were used. For the
best of the old prints it was thick, spongy in texture,
and of an almost ivory tone. The finest specimens
were printed under the direct personal supervision of
the artists who designed them. Every detail was
looked after with the utmost care. No pains were
spared in mixing the tints, in charging the blocks, in
laying on the paper so as to secure perfect register,
in regulating the pressure so as to get the best
possible impressions. Experiments were often tried
by varying the colour schemes. Prints of important
series, as for example Hokusai's famous ' Thirty-six
Views of Fuji,' are met with in widely divergent
colourings."

The results produced by this technique, as it was
employed in the great period of the art, have no
parallel. When Dürer, in the fifteenth century,
brought wood and steel engraving to such brilliant
perfection, he determined the future history of
European engraving, fixing the line of greatest
development in the region of black-and-white, where,
except for sporadic excursions of debatable merit, it
has continued ever since. Fortunately, in Japan,
colour and line did not part company, but in combination progressed toward a unique triumph.

A print produced by this technique is simply a

sheet of paper upon which are impressed, by means
of hand-charged wood blocks, a series of patches of
colour that combine into a design. In general, each
of these patches is flat and unshaded ; its edges are
sharp, definite, bounded by a line as distinct as the
line of the lead used in stained glass. In the print,
as in the stained-glass window, only major lines and
important colour-masses can be shown ; thus elimina-
tion of the incidental and selection of what is vital
are imperatively demanded of the designer. Salient
curves and expressive outlines are the essential
requisite. One reason why these prints seem classic
is that they are purged of the thousand unimportant
and meaningless gradations of tone that are easy to
use in a painting and impossible here. Singular
purity and loftiness of effect is the result, together
with a certain abstract aloofness from reality that has
a high æsthetic value.

Into the drawing of these few lines, and into the
construction of these few flat colour-spaces, went all
the artist's sense of proportion and rhythm, grace
and dignity, movement and tone. On the flat wall
of his printed sheet he devised a pattern that should
weave, out of figures and objects, a decorative design
upon whose harmonious mosaic the eye would
willingly linger. There he played his music to
allure and beguile and absorb the spectator.

Like his fellow-painters of all Asia, the print-
designer did not feel that literal accuracy greatly
concerned him. If the figures moved with a stately
godlike grace in rhythmic procession, what matter
if they were taller or shorter than real beings ? If

their faces were expressive of a noble calm or a
sublime fury, why ask for a detailed mirroring of
a real face? If the landscape was beautiful, was
it important that the real scene could never look
exactly thus?

As an example of the curious conventions that
dominate this art, the observer will note the way
in which heads are drawn by these artists. With
very rare exceptions, the angle from which all the
heads are seen is the same. In the print, as in
the Egyptian wall-carvings, the head is held in a
poise dictated by a traditional formula. The face
is turned half-way between profile and full-face; the
nose approaches but does not intersect the line of
the cheek; the outline of the nose is shown, and
also the broad sweep of the brow, while at the same
time both eyes are visible. For two centuries, with
only occasional variations, this formula for drawing
the face persisted; and in the submission to this
wisely chosen type—admirably adapted as it was
to exhibit most expressively the whole map of the
features—is revealed something of that willingness
to accept discipline, style, and conventionalization
which in these artists went side by side with so much
originality.

A magic world—a pure creation of the imagination
in its search for beauty! This convention in the
drawing of the faces has much to do with the unreal
quality we find there. Something in the repetition
and uniformity of the heads produces a delicate
visionary impression, a trance-like mood—as does
the rhythm of poetry or music. Under its spell

the emotion of the spectator comes forth free from its daily bonds and preoccupations, in the liberation that only art can give.

To these regions of pure æsthetic experience the amateur turns with delight—not only as an escape from practical life, but as an escape from much that is known to the Western world as art. The childish mind loves pictures that tell a story; but the more sophisticated intelligence goes to a work of art for those elements which lie far beyond the region of episodic narration—elements that are allied to the principles of geometry, the laws of motion, the excursions of pure music, the visions of religious faith. Though these manifestations are difficult to correlate, they all arise from one fountainhead; and the best of the Japanese prints lie very close to the source of the stream.

II

CONDITIONS
PRECEDING THE RISE
OF PRINT-DESIGNING :

THE BIRTH OF
THE UKIOYE SCHOOL

# CHAPTER II

AT the outset of the seventeenth century was inaugurated the Tokugawa Dynasty of Shoguns or
military dictators, by the victories of the great
warrior and statesman Iyeyasu over rival factions.
Upon acquiring the Shogunate—a position which
had for long eclipsed the power of the Emperor—
Iyeyasu laid a wise but iron hand upon Japan
forcing all departments of industry, society, and
even art into rigid forms whose pattern was laid
down by his far-seeing mind. The same policy
guided his successors of the Tokugawa Dynasty;
so that during the whole period of print production
Japan was a land of gorgeous feudal splendour,
regulated by inflexible rules of conduct and manners
that amounted almost to caste regulations.

That subtle interpreter of the ideals of the East,
the late Kakuzo Okakura, thus analyses the state of
society at that time : " The Tokugawas," he writes,
" in their eagerness for consolidation and discipline,
crushed out the vital spark from art and life. . . .

49

In their prime of power, the whole of society—and
art was not exempt—was cast in a single mould.
The spirit which secluded Japan from all foreign
intercourse, and regulated every daily routine, from
that of the daimyo to that of the lowest peasant,
narrowed and cramped artistic creativeness also.
The Kano academies of painting—filled with the
disciplinary instincts of Iyeyasu—of which four
were under the direct patronage of the Shogun and
sixteen under the Tokugawa Government, were constituted on the plan of regular feudal tenures.   Each
academy had its hereditary lord, who followed his
profession, and, whether or not he was an indifferent
artist, had under him students who flocked from
various parts of the country, and who were, in their
turn, official painters to different daimyos in the
provinces.   After graduating at Yedo (Tokyo), it
was *de rigueur* for these students, returning to the
country, to conduct their work there on the methods,
and according to the models given them during their
instruction.   The students who were not vassals
of daimyos were, in a sense, hereditary fiefs of the
Kano lords.   Each had to pursue the course of
studies laid down by Tannyu and Tsunenobu, and
each painted and drew certain subjects in a certain
manner.   From this routine, departure meant ostracism, which would reduce the artist to the position
of a common craftsman."

Yet it would convey a wrong impression of the
Tokugawa period to suggest that bureaucratic tight-
ness of regime was its sole or most vital characteristic.   The age was marked as strongly by its

expansive powers as by the restraints that attempted to direct them. For in this epoch, the common people, set apart in a class distinct from the warriors and aristocracy, rose to a vigour and cultivation that was almost a new thing in Japanese history. " It was," writes Fenollosa, "like the rise of the industrial classes in the free cities of Europe in those middle centuries when the old feudal system was breaking up. There, too, could be seen armoured lords of castles flourishing side by side with burghers and guilders. It is the same duality which forms the keynote of Tokugawa culture taken as a whole. . . . The keynote of Tokugawa life and art is their broad division into two main streams—the aristocratic and the plebeian. These two flowed on side by side with comparatively little intermingling. On the one side select companies of gentlemen and ladies congregated in gorgeous castles and yashikis, daimyos and samurai, exercising, studying their own and China's past, weaving martial codes of honour, surrounding themselves with wonderful utensils of lacquer, porcelain, embroidery, and cunningly wrought bronze ; and on the other side great cities like Osaka, Nagoya, Kyoto, and Yedo, swarming with manufacturers, artizans, and merchants, sharing little in the castle privileges, but devising for themselves methods of self-expression in local government, schools, science, literature, and art."

Examining into the history of Japanese colour-prints, one must leave entirely aside the interesting and sometimes sublime art of the cultivated and aristocratic classes and their tradition-hallowed

schools of painting. The prints were solely the
product of the popular school; they were in a way
allied to those delicate Japanese handicrafts, such as
bronze and lacquer, which are characteristically the
output of the common people.

The Tokugawa regime was one of national peace.
The country, long disturbed by both internal and
external wars, settled down at last under the strong
Tokugawa banner to two centuries and a half of
tranquillity. The vital activity of this time was not
diffused and scattered over the whole country, but
was chiefly centred upon one spot, the ancient
"Capital of the East," Yedo, now called Tokyo.
Here, under the dominance of the great Iyeyasu, the
life of the empire was brought to a focus. Iyeyasu
forced all the great nobles, living customarily on their
estates scattered throughout the empire, to come to
Yedo and remain there in residence for at least half
of each year, in order that he might keep his hand
upon them and prevent them from springing up to
rival power. The natural effect of this regulation
was to give Yedo a supreme importance in the realm,
and to cultivate in Yedo the growth of every form of
popular activity. There, in the metropolitan centre,
all the agencies of pleasure burst into luxurious
bloom; the tea-houses, the theatres, the riverside
gardens, and the Yoshiwara or courtesans' quarter,
all took on a new and alluring splendour; and Yedo
became the great city and the great art centre of
Japan.

At this time, aristocratic art, in the hands of the
later generations of the Kano School of painters,

was not only largely inaccessible to the common people, but was also no longer in its prime. The giants of the Kano School were long since dead. In the place of their vigorous inspiration only superficiality and formalism remained. Long since dead was that lofty idealistic art, best known to us in the work of Sesshu, which had distinguished the preceding Ashikaga Period—an art which, to quote Mr. Laurence Binyon, " deals little in human figures and has no concern with the physical beauty of men and women, contenting itself mainly with the contemplation of wide prospects over lake and mountain, mist and torrent, or a spray of sensitive blossoms trembling in the air." Yet even though the earlier greatness of the aristocratic schools of painting was passing or had passed in this seventeenth and eighteenth century epoch, still the authority derived by the Kano painters from their connection with the court of the Shogun gave them dictatorship over matters of art ; and their academy imposed its technique upon all aspirants for the favour of the aristocracy. The rival school of the Tosas, associated closely with the court of the Emperor in Kyoto, was no less careful of tradition and discipline. Thus the moribund art of the upper classes stood alone like a little island, shut out from the art of the people, unable to influence it or to be influenced by it.

Therefore Japan, at the time when the popular school came into existence, was in a curious state : subject to a strict disciplinary system that kept the common people and the aristocracy apart ; enjoying

a period of peace and a centralization of resources
that gave the common people in their isolation a
favourable opportunity to develop a culture of their
own ; and suffering from a growing degeneracy in
the classical schools of painting that might be counted
on to drive at least an occasional aristocratic artist
out into the ranks of the people were any interesting
opportunity offered there.

At this juncture, early in the seventeenth century,
there arose in Yedo a new movement which later was
to produce the colour-print.

This new movement was called the Ukioye School.
The real gap between it and the older classical
schools has been by many writers grossly exaggerated.   One might well gather from them that the
Ukioye artists were the first in all Japanese art to
draw subjects selected from real life and to paint
with vivid humanism.   This is by no means the
fact.   All the subjects treated by the Ukioye
painters had been at some time used by the painters
of the older schools ; and certainly the usual subject of the Kano or Tosa painter was as real and
vivid to him as were any of the themes of the
popular artists to these creators.   Each painted his
customary environment—what was closest to his
experience and dearest to his æsthetic perceptions :
on the one hand, traditionary and religious figures,
scenes from poetry, reflections of Chinese or old
Japanese art ; and on the other hand, the pulsing
life of Yedo streets, the tea-gardens of the Sumida
River, the theatres, and the brilliant houses of
pleasure.   Yet having suggested that the gap between

the two was not immeasurable, we may grant that it was nevertheless real. Ukioye concerned itself with contemporary plebeian life, its shows and festivals and favourites of the hour, to an extent alien to the more restrained and almost monastic tradition of the older art. Ukioye means "Passing-world Picture"; there is implied in the word a reproach and an accusation of triviality. It suggests values not recognized by that orthodox Buddhistic attitude of contemplation which regards life as a show of shadows, a region of temporal desire and illusion and misery, a vigil to be endured only by keeping fixedly before the vision pictures of the desireless calm of Nirvana. But no such profound philosophy of despair and abnegation as this could find real root in the hearts of a lively populace like that of Japan; in that nation, the lonely minds of sequestered aristocrats alone could give it more than nominal habitation. The Ukioye School, since it was a popular school, remained as unshadowed by Buddhism as modern French poster-art is by Christianity; and the distance between the spiritual attitudes of Giotto and Aubrey Beardsley is no greater than that between the attitudes of Kanaoka and Utamaro. All that aureole of moral idealism which hallowed the classical Japanese art was abandoned by the popular school for a frank acceptance of the joy of the world and its enthralling lures.

The style adopted by the new school in portraying the life of the multitude allowed itself a certain keen realism, often tinged with humour and sometimes with mild obscenity. This realism appears only

occasionally, and it is generally so completely sub-
ordinated to the decorative impulse that realism is
the last word by which a Western observer would
describe it.  Only by way of contrasting it with
the idealism of the older schools can one thus classify
the arbitrary attitudes, mask-life faces, and fanciful
colour schemes of Ukioye.  This arbitrariness indicates another characteristic of the new manner.  It
was a flippant style which took nothing seriously
except itself.  Its technique departed from the sacred
traditions of Kano and Tosa brushwork and the
inheritance of Chinese painting canons.  It developed
a novel use of clear, hard outline, unrestrained sweep,
brilliantly fresh colour, and strong contrast, that
relied on no precedent for their appeal and awakened
no sanctioning echo from the classic masters.

Not unnaturally the aristocracy were repelled by
the plebeian and vulgar nature of the subjects of
the new school.  Their sensibilities were injured
by the throwing overboard of traditions of style
that stretched back through many centuries to the
founders of the art in China, and by the genuine
lack of distinction in the spiritual attitude and out-
look of many of these new painters.  The modern
European, bred of a different artistic lineage, may
regard these objections as negligible ; but he must
remember that it is perhaps his own ignorance of
Japanese classics that makes him so tolerant ; and
he may properly hesitate to condemn hastily the
aristocratic Japanese opinion.

The aristocratic opinion is readily comprehensible.
The Ukioye School without doubt lacks that almost

religious idealism by which the earlier Japanese schools of painting attained a subtlety perhaps excessively rarefied, an allusiveness almost too remote, a sublimation of intangible spiritual values that very nearly reaches the vanishing-point. No such serene cultivation of feeling is to be found in the Ukioye painters. "Great art is that before which we long to die," says Okakura ; and the overstrained intensity of his words conveys to the Westerner some conception of the passionate spirituality which the cultivated Japanese desires and finds in the works of the older painters. The Japanese connoisseur misses in Ukioye that exaltation which, in the creations of Sesshu or Yeitoku or Kanaoka, leads him up to heights whence he surveys mountain and lake lying like a visionary incantation before him, or feels the giant loneliness of pines upon a snowy crest, or enters into the ineffable spirit of the white goddess Kwannon meditating in a measureless void of clouds and streams.

These things are not to be found in Ukioye—these ultimate reaches of the Oriental spirit ; but there is here a more human and lovable beauty, and a power of design no less notable than that of the aristocratic masters.

It must be granted that the colour-prints of this school constitute the fullest and most characteristic expression ever given to the temper of the Japanese people. Asia—the region of measureless, overwhelming spaces, innumerable lives, and immemorial antiquity—Asia speaks in the older paintings ; but in the amiable prints, the one voice is the defined, circumscribed, and beguiling voice of Japan. The colour-print constitutes almost the only purely Japanese art, and the only graphic record of popular Japanese life. Therefore it may be regarded as the most definitely national of all the forms of expression used by the Japanese—an art which they alone in the history of the world have brought to perfection.

The beginnings of the Ukioye School antedated by many years the beginnings of colour-printing. Iwasa Matabei, the founder of the school, was born in 1578 and died in 1650. At first it was the aristocracy that applauded this pioneer, who was not yet alienated from them ; then some vital element in Matabei's manner kindled enthusiasm outside this circumscribed region and set in motion the forces which eventually resulted in a popular school of art.

After Matabei, the Ukioye School did not take any immediate turn toward notable development. In fact, it is doubtful whether its importance could have been far-reaching had its activity been always, as in its earliest days, confined to painting. It was, however, the destiny of the school to come into a relation with the hitherto undeveloped art of wood-engraving ; and its alliance with this popular medium increased a thousand-fold the breadth of its appeal and the force of its sway.

The art of wood-engraving in Japan originated some time between the twelfth and fourteenth centuries. Legend associates the first use of it with the great priest Nichiren, who lived from 1222 to 1282. Ryokin, also a priest, produced a woodcut which is dated 1325. No date earlier than this last can be fixed upon with any confidence. The few specimens of early woodcuts that have survived are pious Buddhistic representations of religious paintings or statues, which were probably sold to pilgrims as mementoes of their visit to some famous shrine. In artistic merit these earliest woodcuts have no interest; their importance is entirely historical.

By the end of the sixteenth century the process of wood-engraving had come into use as a means of illustrating books. From this time on, mythological, romantic, and legendary works, such as the "Ise Monogatari," were frequently so embellished. Most of the designs were very crude, and the cutting of the wood blocks displayed only elementary skill. These early books were in no way connected with the Ukioye School, which they in fact antedated; they were wholly the product of the old classical tradition. Contemporaneously with them were produced fairly vigorous but clumsy broadsides, representing historical scenes. Occasionally a few spots of coarse colour were applied by hand to these designs.

By the middle of the seventeenth century there began to appear illustrated books in which the rudimentary elements of artistic pictorial feeling are visible. A few have a slight Ukioye cast. Not until the last quarter of the century, however, did wood-engraving achieve the dignity of a fine art and the scope of a popular method of expression. That it then did so was due to the genius of Moronobu, an Ukioye painter, the first of the great print-designers.

# III

# THE FIRST
# PERIOD:
# THE PRIMITIVES

FROM MORONOBU
TO THE INVENTION
OF POLYCHROME PRINTING
(1660-1764)

# CHAPTER III

## THE FIRST PERIOD: THE PRIMITIVES

### FROM MORONOBU TO THE INVENTION OF POLYCHROME PRINTING (1660–1764).

### GENERAL CHARACTERISTICS.

THE Primitive Period, first of those epochs into which the history of Japanese prints may be roughly divided, begins about 1660 with the appearance of the work of Moronobu. The period ends a century later when, after many experiments, the technique of the art had been developed from the black-and-white print to the full complexity of multi-colour printing.

The commonly accepted name of " the Primitives " requires some explanation when applied to these artists lest it create the impression that we are dealing with designers in whose works are to be found the naïve efforts of unsophisticated and groping minds. Nothing could be farther from the truth. Thousands of years of artistic experience and tradition lay back of these productions; and the level of æsthetic sophistication implied in them was high. The word Primitive applies to these men only in so far as they were workers in the technique of wood-engraving. As producers of prints they were indeed pioneers and experimenters ; but as designers they were part of a long succession that had reached full maturity centuries earlier.

Whether it be that a new technical form, like an unexplored country, tends to exclude from entrance all but bold and vigorous spirits, or whether it be that the stimulus of difficulty and discovery inspirits the adventurer with keener powers, these Primitives were as a group surpassed by none of their successors in force and lofty feeling. They seized the freshly available medium with an exuberance of vitality that had not yet lost itself in the deserts of a fully mastered technique.

" These Primitives," says Von Seidlitz, " are now held in far higher esteem than formerly. We recognize in them not only forerunners, but men of heroic race, who, without being able to claim the highest honours paid to the gods, still exhibit a power, a freshness, and a grace that are hardly met with in the same degree in later times. Despite the imperfections that necessarily attach to their works, despite their lack of external correctness, their limitations to few and generally crude materials, and their conventionalism, there clings to their work a charm such as belongs to the works neither of the most brilliant nor of the pronouncedly naturalistic periods. For, in the singleness of their efforts to make their drawing as expressive as possible, without regard to any special kind of beauty or truth, these Primitives discover a power of idealization and a stylistic skill which, at a later period and with increased knowledge, are quite unthinkable."

To the new Ukioye School these Primitives gave the first great opening for popularity. Their broadsides and albums disseminated among the millions of Yedo the product of the new and vigorous art-impulse. They were the river-streams through which the lake reservoirs of Ukioye art returned to the sea of popular life whence the waters had come.

Fenollosa's picture of the popular life during a portion of this Primitive Period, the Genroku Era (1688–1703), is not without its significance in this connection. "This was the day when population and arts had largely been transferred to Yedo, and both people and samurai were becoming conscious of themselves. The populace of the new great city, already interested in the gay pleasures of the tea-houses and the dancing-girls' quarter, were just elaborating a new organ for expression, namely the vulgar theatre, with plays and acting adapted to their intelligence. They had just caught hold, too, of the device of the sensational novel. Now here was an army of young samurai growing up in the neighbouring squares, who were just on the *qui vive* to slip out into these nests of popular fun. For the time being, freedom for both sides was in the air. Anybody could say or do what he pleased. Fashions and costumes were extravagant. Everybody joined good-naturedly in the street dances. It was like a world of college boys out on a lark; to speak more exactly, it had much resemblance to the gay, roistering, unconscious mingling of lords and people in the

Elizabethan days of Shakespeare, before the duality
of puritan and cavalier divided them."

The subjects depicted by the Primitive artists for
the pleasure of this populace are drawn from the
flourishing life thus described. First and foremost,
the stage is represented ; and the greatest prints of
this period are, as a rule, the single figures of actors
portrayed in their rôles. But social and domestic
scenes also find place here ; and all the play of
fashion and recreation, the occupations and amuse-
ments of the ladies, the boating-parties and tea-house
scenes, the street and the festival, appear in brilliant
succession.

In the general style of their designs the Primitives
were all controlled by one fundamental aim—that of
decoration. This dominating quality appears most
clearly in the large actor-prints which we associate
with the names of Kwaigetsudō, Kiyonobu, Masanobu,
and Toyonobu. To an extent greater than the
artists of any succeeding period they eschewed
minuteness of detail and accuracy of representation,
sacrificing these things for the sake of achieving
broad decorative effects combined with vigorous
movement. A certain unique simplicity and
grandeur in the spacial and linear conceptions of
these men gives to the whole Primitive Period a
Titanic character that distinguishes it. In the best
works of this time the stylistic finish of the drawing
is masterful. It translates motion into sweeping
caligraphic lines, and creates imposing calm by the
poise and balance of severe black-and-white masses.
Just as in opera the flow of music induces in the

auditor a state of semi-trance that makes him oblivious to the patent absurdities and unrealities of the action, so in these pictures the rhythmic flow of the composition lifts the consciousness of the spectator to a plane where it ceases to take note of the incorrect report of Nature and loses itself in the enjoyment of the noble decorative conceptions that actuate the creating hand.

A profound formalism dominates these works. The figures are purely one-dimensional; the picture is a flat pattern of lights and darks bounded by the sharp outline of great curves. In the actor-pieces no real portraiture of the actor as an individual is essayed; the artist's aim is rather to convey some sense of the dynamic power of the rôle in which the actor appears. He succeeds so well that his pictures, though not representations of individuals, stand as abstract symbols of grace or of power.

Historically, one of the chief interests in this period centres upon the notable developments in technique. Wood-engraving was, as we have seen, already known when the period opened; but it had not yet been subjected to the purposes of the artist. Confined almost exclusively to crude book illustrations, it had as little artistic significance as the cheap hand-painted sketches called *otsu-ye*, which, produced by hundreds, were sold for the amusement of the populace.

With the advent of the gifted Moronobu, the book-illustration was transformed into an important and beautiful creation. Going further, Moronobu and his successors produced single-sheet prints of large size,

in black and white only, that served all the purposes
of paintings and were capable of being reproduced
without limit. These black-and-white prints were
called *sumi-ye* (Plate 1). Books and albums by
him appeared at various earlier dates, but the
first of his single-sheet prints was issued about
1670.

The second step in development came with the
realization that the brilliant colour of the older
*otsu-ye* could easily be imparted to the new prints.
So some of the sheets of Moronobu and his contemporaries were coloured by hand with orange, yellow,
green, brown, and blue, somewhat after the manner
used by the painters of the classical Kano School.
In the actor-prints there began to appear, shortly
after 1700, solid masses of orange-red pigment.
These sheets were called *tan-ye*, from the *tan* or
red lead used in them. About 1710 citrine and
yellow were used in connection with the *tan* (Plate 2).
By 1715 or a little later, *beni*, a delicate red colour of
vegetable origin, was discovered, and almost entirely
replaced the cruder *tan*. Prints thus coloured were
called *kurenai-ye*.

About 1720 it was found that the intensity of
the colouring could be enhanced by the addition
of lacquer. Red, yellow, blue, green, brown, and
violet were used in brilliant combination ; and their
tone was heightened by painting glossy black lacquer
on the black portions of the picture, and sprinkling
some of the colours with sparkling powdered gold or
mother-of-pearl. Such prints were called *urushi-ye*,
or lacquer-prints (Plate 5).

These various methods of hand-colouring prevailed up to about the year 1742. At this time, a method was perfected by which two colour-blocks could be used in printing ; and the true colour-print came into existence. Masanobu is generally credited with being the inventor of the new technique. The first colours employed were green and the red known as *beni*; and from this the prints derived their common name of *beni-ye* (Plate 6). Later many varieties of colour were tried. To some print-lovers, these two-colour prints seem unequalled in beauty.

About 1755 a method was devised by which a third colour-block could be employed, and blue was the colour at first selected to accompany the original green and red, Then blue, red, and yellow were used, and other variations ; and in the hands of such men as Toyonobu and Kiyomitsu, rich decorative effects resulted (Plate 7).

To the end of the period hand-colouring was still occasionally used for large and important pieces such as pillar-prints ; but the old method lost ground steadily, and the day of the polychrome-print was at hand.

To give in more detail the history of this period, the strict chronological method must be abandoned ; and each of the important artists must be taken up in turn as an independent creator.

### MORONOBU.

Hishikawa Moronobu, born probably in 1625, was the son of a famous embroiderer and textile designer who lived in the province of Awa. Moronobu worked at the trade of his father during his youth, obtaining thus a training in decorative invention that is traceable in all his later work.  Upon the death of his father, he came to Yedo and took up the study of painting under the masters of the Tosa and Kano Schools.  Gradually, however, the Ukioye style, in-

troduced by Matabei some years before, became his chosen province; and from painting he turned to the designing of woodcuts for book illustrations and broadsheets. Later in life he became a monk; and died probably in 1695, though some authorities say 1714.

Moronobu's importance in the history of Japanese prints is twofold.  He inspirited the Ukioye School with a new vitality; and he turned wood-engraving into an art.

The Ukioye movement, when Moronobu appeared, was still indeterminate.  A great personality was needed to crystallize the vague tendencies then in solution.

HISHIKAWA
MORONOBU.

This Moronobu accomplished; and the far-reaching effect of his work was due to the fact that he did not confine his work to painting, but took up the hitherto unexplored field of woodcuts. As we have seen in the previous chapter, there had been produced up to Moronobu's time no illustrated book that could lay claim to artistic value.  The little that had been done in this field was crude

MORONOBU: A PAIR OF LOVERS.
Black and white. Size 9×13½. Unsigned.

*Plate 1*

artizan work without charm. Now Moronobu seized
this medium and transformed it. Into his woodcuts
he poured that powerful sense of design which he so
notably possessed, creating real pictures of striking
decorative beauty. These books and prints, widely
circulated, carried to the eyes of the masses a new
and delightful diversion, spreading far and near the
contagious fascination of this lively Ukioye manner
of drawing and awakening in the populace a thirst
for more of these productions. Matabei had devised
the new popular style, but it was Moronobu who
threw open the gates of this region to the people.

Moronobu's first books appeared about 1660, and
from that date to the time of his retirement he
brought out more than a hundred books and albums
and an unknown number of broadsheets. In all of
these his vigorous, genial personality and his strong
sense of decoration make themselves felt. Such a
print as the album-sheet reproduced in Plate 1
exhibits his characteristic simplicity of sweeping
line, the masterly use he makes of black and white
contrasts, and the vivid force of his rendering of
movement. The firm lines live ; the composition is
grouped to form a harmonious picture ; a dominating
sense of form has entered here to transform the
chaotic raggedness of his predecessors' attempts.
Distorted as these figures may appear to unaccus-
tomed Western eyes, they have unmistakable style,
and their bold command of expression is the first
great landmark in Japanese print history.

All of Moronobu's work was printed in black and
white only, but occasionally the sheets were roughly

coloured by hand after they had been printed. His designs have little detail; as a rule the scene surrounding his main figures is barely suggested by a few lines; and the figures themselves are hardly more than intense shorthand notations of a theme. But how much life he gives them! No wonder that the populace loved his work, and that his many pupils bore away with them to their own productions the impress of his strong personality and animated style.

Certain of Moronobu's large single-sheet compositions (such as the Lady Standing Under a Cherry Tree, in the Buckingham Collection, Chicago, or the noble Figure of a Woman in the Morse Collection, Evanston), display so fine a power of composition and so unsurpassable a mastery of rhythmic line that there can be no hesitancy in judging him, quite apart from his historical significance, to be an artist of the first order. Nothing that he ever did was undistinguished.

The collector will not find it easy to procure adequate specimens of this artist's work. Moronobu's large single sheets are unobtainable to-day; they could never have been numerous, and the few that have survived the vicissitudes of almost three centuries are now in the hands of museums or collectors who will never part with them. Even his smaller single sheets are uncommon. His work is seldom signed.

### FOLLOWERS OF MORONOBU.

The powerful impetus of Moronobu's art communicated itself to many pupils.

MOROFUSA was the eldest son of Moronobu; he collaborated with his father, and produced designs that are in exact imitation of his father's style. His work comprises book illustrations and some large single sheets, and is very rare.

Additional pupils or contemporaries were: Moromasa, Moronaga, Morikuni, Masanojo, Moroshige, Morobei, Masataka, Osawa, Morotsugi, Moromori, Hishikawa Masanobu, Tomofusa, Shimbei, Toshiyuki, Furuyama, Morotane, Ryujo, Hasegawa Toun, Ishikawa Riusen, Ishikawa Riushu, Wowo, Kawashima Shigenobu, Kichi, Yoshimura Katsumasa, and Tsukioka Tange. Many of these are obscure figures, of whose work little is known. Most of them were chiefly book-illustrators.

NISHIKAWA
SUKENOBU.

### SUKENOBU.

The name of Nishikawa Sukenobu brings to mind that long procession of charming girl figures which year by year came from his hand—figures whose sweet monotonous faces and delicately poised bodies move with a pure grace that is perpetually delighting. Lacking the powerful decorative sense of Moronobu, whose lead he in general followed, and never attempting the massive blacks of the master's dashing brush-stroke, Sukenobu yet achieved effects that are more gracious and appealing than those of his great predecessor. Nothing

could surpass the delicate harmony of line in such
a design as the one reproduced in Plate 2; the
willowyness of the young body, the naïve innocence
of the head, the movement and rhythm of the
flowing garments, are admirably depicted. This was
Sukenobu's characteristic note; he lingers in one's
memory by virtue of it and none other; he was the
least versatile of artists.

He lived between the years 1671 and 1751. During
the period of his activity his popularity must have
been enormous. The single-sheet prints which he
produced were not many, and only a small proportion of these have come down to us. His main
work was in the field of illustrated books and
albums. More than forty of these are known to-day.
They contain chiefly scenes from the lives of women
and figures of young girls. Most of them date from
1713 to 1750. They constitute Sukenobu's claim to
rank as Moronobu's most important successor in the
field of book-illustration. Generally they are printed
in black and white only; a few are embellished with
colour added by hand. It is not always possible to
tell whether this colouring was done when the books
were published or whether it was the work of some
subsequent owner of the volume.

The delicacy of Sukenobu's designs, and the
absence of those peculiar mannerisms and exaggerations which characterize much of the work of
this period, serve to make him, of all the Primitives,
perhaps the most comprehensible and pleasing to the
European taste. To the Japanese connoisseur he
recommends himself because of the refinement of

SUKENOBU: A YOUNG COURTESAN.

Black outlines, with hand-colouring of pale green, orange and white
Size 9½×6.   Unsigned.

*Plate 2*

his work both in subject and in manner, and because of a certain classic dignity that pervades it. The collector will do well to bear in mind that the books of Sukenobu were frequently reprinted long after his death; and these later impressions, lacking the original sharpness of line and intensity of tone in the blacks, are not desirable acquisitions. The original editions of his books are still to be found occasionally. His single-sheet prints are, however, of great rarity.

## KWAIGETSUDŌ.

In the period immediately succeeding Moronobu— the early years of the eighteenth century—the work which of all others stands out with a unique and colossal grandeur is that of Kwaigetsudō.

Kwaigetsudō has long been a puzzle to the student. The original idea held by Fenollosa and other authorities, that all the prints signed Kwaigetsudō were by one man, has been abandoned; and the theory now prevails that there existed a group of artists, headed by a dominant master named Kwaigetsudō, and that all of these artists produced prints signed with his name together with their own. The most perplexing problem has been to determine which of the print-makers was the original master and which were his disciples. Dr. Kurth confidently states that Kwaigetsudō Norishige, was the original master. On the other hand, Mr. Arthur Morrison has recently expressed the opinion that the original Kwaigetsudō was solely a painter, who produced no prints whatsoever. His studio name

was Kwaigetsudō Ando; his personal name was
Okazawa Genshichi; he was a late contemporary
of Moronobu, and worked in Yedo from about 1704
to 1714, when he was banished to the island of
Oshima in consequence of his participation in a
scandal involving a gay banquet party at a theatre
tea-house attended by certain Court ladies. Later
he was pardoned, but did not resume his work.
According to this theory all the prints were the
work of his followers, who signed the name
Kwaigetsudō with various additions. This view is
probably the correct one.

The names of the Kwaigetsudō group of print-
designers that have so far come to light are—

KWAIGETSUDŌ ANCHI (or YASUTOMO);
KWAIGETSUDŌ DOHAN (or NORISHIGE);
KWAIGETSUDŌ DOSHU (or NORIHIDE);
KWAIGETSUDŌ DOSHIN (or NORITATSU).

The Kwaigetsudō work is perhaps the most
powerful and imposing in the whole range of
Japanese prints. The sheets, of large size, generally
represent the single figure of a standing woman clad
in flowing robes. So much for the theme; it is
nothing. But the treatment consists of a storm of
brush-strokes whose power of movement is like that
of writhing natural forces; out of this seething whirl
of lines is built up the structure of the monumental
figure.

The Kwaigetsudō reproduced in Plate 3 exhibits
these qualities. The body is merely suggested, but
with complete effectiveness, under the great swirls of

KWAIGETSUDO: COURTESAN ARRANGING HER
COIFFURE.

Black and white.  Size 24½×12.
Signed *Nippon Kigwa Kwaigetsu Matsuyo Norishige.*
Spaulding Collection.

*Plate 3*

the robes. The dominance of the main curves, the vigour of the blacks, and the importunate life that vitalizes every touch and line, give Kwaigetsudō a place as high as the greatest contemporaries or successors.

All the Kwaigetsudō work was printed in black and white; sometimes the print was hand-coloured by the application of spots of *tan*, or red lead. Excellent full-size reproductions of several of them are obtainable. With these reproductions the ordinary collector will be obliged to content himself, for the whole number of Kwaigetsudō prints in existence can scarcely be more than a score or two. They are perhaps the rarest of all prints.

## THE FIRST KIYONOBU.

*Kiyonobu Speaks.*

The actor on his little stage
Struts with a mimic rage.
Across my page
My passion in his form shall tower from age to age.

What he so crudely dreams
In vague and fitful gleams—
The crowd esteems.
Well! let the future judge if his or mine this seems—

This calm Titanic mould
Stalking in colours bold
Fold upon fold—
This lord of dark, this dream I dreamed of old!

With Kiyonobu begins that school of painters, the Torii, which was to take the initiative during the first half of the eighteenth century in developing the actor-portrait to a very high level, and which still later was to have the honour of claiming as its head Kiyonaga, in whom the whole art culminated. It may be convenient to list here the successive leaders of the school, who were in their turn entitled to the name of *the* Torii, and whom we shall take up in their order.

| Torii I | … | … | Kiyonobu I | … | … | (1664–1729) |
| Torii II | … | … | Kiyomasu | … | … | (1679–1763) |
| Torii III | … | … | Kiyomitsu | … | … | (1735–1785) |
| Torii IV | … | … | Kiyonaga | … | … | (1742–1815) |
| Torii V | … | … | Kiyomine | … | … | (1786–1868) |
| Torii VI | … | … | Kiyofusa | … | … | (1832–1892) |

The importance of the school terminated with Kiyonaga, or at latest with Kiyomine.

TORII KIYONOBU.

Kiyonobu I, the founder of the Torii line, was born in 1664 and died in 1729. It is said that he was first a resident of Osaka, and then of Kyoto ; and that he finally came to Yedo about the beginning of the gay and brilliant Genroku Period, 1688–1703. Thus he must have been in Yedo a few years before the death of Moronobu in 1795, and it is evident that he studied the Moronobu style. Kiyonobu's father is variously reported to have been either an actor or a painter of theatrical sign-posters ; at any rate his connection with the theatre was a close one. This circumstance doubtless determined the line of the son's activity in designing. About 1700 Kiyonobu produced the first single-sheet actor-print in black and white only. From this it was only a step to the production of *tan-ye*, which he probably invented—actor-sheets simply but brilliantly coloured by the application of orange to certain portions of the picture. In this manner he issued both *hoso-ye* (that is, sheets about 12 inches high and 6 inches wide) and sheets of larger size, perhaps the most striking being actor-portraits, sometimes several feet in height, which enjoyed an immense popularity. By about 1715 he had taken up a more delicate kind of hand-colouring known as *kurenai-ye*, which some writers think he himself devised. A few years later he adopted the *urushi-ye* technique, increasing the number of colours and using lacquer to heighten the brilliancy of the effect.

Kiyonobu's subjects comprised a few landscapes of no great interest, and figures of several types. His *forte* was the representation of actors and heroes of history. His bold and gigantic style of drawing lends some probability to the story that he was, when he first came to Yedo, a painter of huge theatrical sign-boards or posters for the exteriors of theatres. The same manner that would be appropriate for these is found in his prints—arresting, forceful, highly exaggerated. His designs must be regarded as establishing for all later times the general type to be used in actor-portraits. This constitutes his greatest historical importance.

The prints which appear to be Kiyonobu's earliest are marked by an extraordinary development of line, handled in great sweeping strokes. The brushwork is indicated with much dash and *bravura*, in the manner of the painter as distinct from the print-designer. A hasty glance might lead one to mistake some of these early compositions for the work of a Kwaigetsudō, though they are, as a rule, more uncouth.

Although power of line always remains one of Kiyonobu's characteristics, there appears in his later work a certain insistence on spaces, a treatment of the surface of the print as if it were a placque into which were to be inlaid large flat masses of a different substance. The robes are broken up into definite segments with sharp boundaries like parts of a picture puzzle, instead of remaining a surface on which to display the splintering vigour of brush-strokes. This second style is admirably adapted to the technique of wood-engraving.

The geometrical quality of some of Kiyonobu's designs is striking. There are several of his large *tan-ye* in which the whole print is nothing more than a series of great circles, brought into relation with each other, as part of the decoration of the drapery, by wild and whirling brush-strokes.

The work of Kiyonobu varies greatly in attractiveness. Some of his prints have more force than beauty; and it requires little effort to understand the contempt of the aristocracy for these crude manifestations of the mob's taste. Yet even in these grosser designs Kiyonobu realizes the power and passion of the dramatic rôle which he depicts, achieving an effect of tragic rage that is no less intense and impressive because of its lack of subtlety. Most of his prints suggest the shout and roar of bombast: this is precisely what they were meant to convey. But there are a few of another type, that embody the masterful power of line of the first Torii, joined with a simplicity and refinement of design which his work frequently lacked, or which, if present, is disguised from us by the repellent violence of the figure portrayed. One must see Kiyonobu's rarest and greatest prints in order to realize why he is regarded as so great an artist.

I have written of Kiyonobu as if he presented no difficulties; but such is not the case. A stumbling-block for the student is created by the fact that there exist many two-colour prints signed Kiyonobu. It is recorded that Kiyonobu died in 1729, many years before the date fixed upon by Fenollosa and most other authorities as the date of the invention of colour-printing. If we are to believe that the numerous colour-prints signed Kiyonobu are by the first Torii, we must either put back the date of the invention of colour-printing to an extent that is improbable in view of other facts, or we must abandon the recorded date of Kiyonobu's death and regard his life as having extended well beyond the middle of the eighteenth century. Formerly this difficulty was not appreciated, and all work signed Kiyonobu was confidently attributed to the first Torii; but at present it is generally regarded as likely that there was a second Kiyonobu who produced all the two-colour prints signed with that name.  Whether he produced any hand-coloured prints is uncertain.  This Kiyonobu II theory has met with scepticism in certain quarters, and some students prefer to accept the alternative of one of the two other possible solutions of the puzzle. Certain differences in style between the hand-coloured and the two-colour work confirm the Kiyonobu II theory to such an extent that I have felt constrained to adopt it here.  It may be disproved eventually, but it is the best solution available at present.  I shall therefore take up Kiyonobu II as a separate artist, without again drawing attention to the unsettled state of the relation between him and Kiyonobu I.

TORII KIYOMASU.

KIYOMASU.

Kiyomasu, the second head of the Torii School, has been variously regarded as the brother or the son of the first Torii.  The question of this exact relationship is a matter scarcely worth all the words that have been wasted upon it.  What is important is the well-known fact that the two kinsmen worked side by side in the same studio for many years producing work of precisely the same type.  The most experienced judges would find it impossible in some cases to distinguish between their productions.

Kiyomasu was born about 1679 ; some authorities

say 1685; but if it is true, as Von Seidlitz states, that there exists a play-bill by him which is dated 1693, the earlier of the two dates is the only possible one. Since Kiyonobu was born in 1664, the theory that they were brothers is the more probable. Kiyomasu's chief work was done contemporaneously with Kiyonobu's, in black and white, *tan-ye*, and *urushi-ye*; but later he produced some prints in two colours. His subjects were chiefly women and actors; he executed a few small landscapes and some fine representations of birds. His work must have continued some years after 1743, but appears to have terminated a considerable time before his death in 1763 or 1764.

A more prolific artist than the first Torii, Kiyomasu was in some particulars an equally distinguished one. Possibly his originality was less marked in that he merely followed the actor type which had already been created by Kioyonobu; but in the power of his draughtsmanship, reminding one again and again of a tempered Kwaigetsudō, he is no secondary figure. Nothing can surpass the vigour of linework in some of his large figure prints—great curves made with a heavily charged brush, expressing with notable simplicity the beauty of flowing drapery. His masterpiece is undoubtedly that superb figure in black and white of the actor Kanto Koroku (in the Buckingham Collection, Chicago), drawn in the Moronobu-Kwaigetsudō manner, which is reproduced in Fenollosa's "Epochs of Chinese and Japanese Art" with the erroneous attribution of Kiyonobu. This print is a triumph. Nothing finer was designed by all the succeeding generations of artists.

## THE SECOND KIYONOBU.

Kiyonobu II, who signed all his work simply Kiyonobu, was a son of Kiyomasu, and probably a nephew of Kiyonobu I. His whole name was Torii Kiyonobu Shirō. He appears to have worked chiefly from about 1740 to about 1756, the period of the predominance of the two-colour print. All two-colour prints signed Kiyonobu are by this artist and not by the first Torii, who died before the process was invented. Kiyonobu II is regarded by many collectors as the best representative of the two-colour technique. His figures have a delicacy and grace that is alien to the work of his two predecessors in the Torii School ; and his handling of the green and rose designs of these prints is charming. The great insistent colour masses and monumental figures of his predecessors undergo a change in his hands to a more detailed division of colours and a slightening of the forms of the bodies and limbs. Also the old passionate vigour of brushwork disappears in the new technique—a loss that seems a grave one.

Most writers speak of Kiyonobu II as a two-colour artist only. It is, however, fairly established that at least one of the *urushi-ye* signed Kiyonobu is by Kiyonobu II. That he did a few three-colour prints is certain. His work, like that of all these early men, is rare. It is particularly difficult to find examples of his *beni-ye* that are in good condition, since the rose-colour has in most cases entirely faded.

### OTHER FOLLOWERS OF KIYONOBU.

KIYOTADA was one of the best known and one of the most brilliant of the numerous followers of the great Torii pioneers. He is said to have been a pupil of Kiyonobu I. His period of production began not far from 1715, and ended before the invention of two-colour printing. His prints are all *tan-ye* or *urushi-ye*, some of them slightly like Okumura Masanobu in style. Certain of his *hoso-ye* have fascinating curves and superb colour—red, yellow, green, pink, and black, woven together into rich combinations.

KIYOSHIGE produced very fine actor-portraits coloured by hand, which remind one distinctly of Kiyonobu I in his later period. Large masses of colour are used by him with powerful decorative effect; and the geometrical designs of his textiles are sometimes striking. Kiyoshige's work has a strong yet graceful quality that makes him worthy of more attention than he has hitherto received. He lived to produce some two-colour prints. Dr. Kurth believes him to have been the first to use the pillar-print form for actor-portraits. His working period was from about 1720 to about 1759.

HANEGAWA CHINCHŌ was an eccentric and interesting figure, who, though a pupil of Kiyonobu I, appears to have been more closely related to the Kwaigetsudō School than to the Torii. Born about 1680 he, by birth a Samurai, became a Ronin, and entered the studio of Kiyonobu. He was erratic, proud, and isolated. In spite of his pressing poverty, he worked at print-designing only when it pleased him to do so, which was seldom ; and though he lived until 1754, his output was small. He was a poet and an aristocrat. His single-sheet prints have a curious esoteric quality—strange, stiff, beautiful curves that are not quite like the work of any other designer. Chinchō's work is of extraordinary rarity ; there can scarcely be more than a score of his prints in existence.

HANEKAWA-WAGEN is represented by two prints in the Buckingham Collection. Nothing is known of him.

KIYOTOMO, whose work appears to fall entirely within the period of hand-coloured prints, produced excellent actor designs, in some of which the line-work reminds one slightly of Kwaigetsudō. The influence of Kiyomasu appears in some of his *urushi-ye*. His prints are distinguished by their vigour and are found but seldom.

SANSEIDO TANAKA MASUNOBU produced hand-coloured and two-colour prints in the Torii manner. A print by him dated 1746 is known, but most of his work precedes 1740. He is not to be confused with the Masunobu who was Harunobu's pupil.

KIYOSOMO is said to have been a distinguished pupil of Kiyonobu I, influenced also by Okumura Masanobu.

Other men of this period, closely connected with the Torii School, were : Kiyoake, Kondo Sukegoro Kiyoharu, Katsukawa Terushige, Nishikawa Teru-nobu, Nishikawa Omume, Fujikawa Yoshinobu, Tamura Yoshinobu, Tamura Sadanobu, Kichikawa

OKUMURA MASANOBU: COURTESANS AT TOILET.

Black and white.  Size 10×15.  Unsigned.

*Plate 4*

93

Katsumasa, Kiyomizu Mazunobu, Shimizu Mitsu-
nobu, Kondo Kiyonobu, Kondo Katsunobu, Kiyorō,
Tadaharu, and Nakaji Sadatoshi.

*A Figure.*

### OKUMURA MASANOBU.

Garbed in flowing folds of light,
Azure, emerald, rose, and white,
Watchest thou across the night.

Crowned with splendour is thine head ;
All the princes great and dead
Round thy limbs their state have shed—

Calm, immutable to stand,
Gracious head and poisèd hand,
O'er the years that flow like sand.

Okumura Masanobu may be termed the central
figure of this period: not only
does he tower among the greatest
men of the time, but around him
revolve the changes in technique,
full of far-reaching consequences,
which came into being with his
invention of two-colour printing.

Furthermore, he takes on an
additional historical importance as
the founder of the Okumura
School, which continued parallel
with the Torii School, and whose
productions are characterized by
a finer development of grace and
elegance than is to be found in
the output of the rival line.

OKUMURA MASANOBU.

Masanobu was born about 1685,
and lived until about 1764—a life of very nearly

eighty years, full of varied achievements. During
the course of his career he used many names, among
which Genpachi, Hōgetsudō, Tanchōsai, Bunkaku,
and Kammyō are the most frequent. Little is known
of his life except that he began as a bookseller in
Yedo. He is reputed to have been a pupil of
Kiyonobu, but Mr. Arthur Morrison believes this
to be an error, and thinks that
Masanobu was an independent
artist educated in no one of the
Yedo schools. Whichever account
may be correct, it is at least
certain that Masanobu shows in
his work few traces of resemblance
to the first of the Torii masters.
It is equally clear that he was
early and strongly influenced by
the work of Moronobu, who died
when Masanobu was only ten years
old, but whose designs were of
course still widely known. It is
said that soon after 1707 Masanobu
founded a publishing establishment
in connection with his book-shop,
issuing prints as well as books. This must have
afforded him great opportunities for experiments in
technique, and may have been no small factor in
making possible the remarkable advances for which
he was responsible.

HŌGETSUDŌ.

Masanobu's earliest works were book-illustrations
and albums, which closely follow the manner
of Moronobu. Plate 4 reproduces one of these.

OKUMURA MASANOBU: STANDING WOMAN.

Black outlines, with hand-colouring of black lacquer,
orange, yellow, and gold powder. Size 13½×6.
Signed *Yamato no Gwako, Okumura Masanobu, hitsu.*

*Plate 5*

Parallel with them he produced a number of *tan-ye*, the large single-sheet prints in black and white, which, after printing, were coloured by hand with orange pigment. These probably date from before 1720, although exactness cannot be hoped for. About 1720 he began to do work in a medium which he is said to have invented—the *urushi-ye*, or lacquer-prints, in which the lacquer gives a new richness and luminosity to the various colours. An example of these appears in Plate 5. The device of heightening the effect by applying gold powder to certain portions of the design was also employed by him. A play of light that is extraordinarily fascinating often marks his combinations of colours. By about 1742 a new technical advance, the most vital in the whole history of the art, came into existence; and Masanobu is generally credited with its invention. This was the employment of two blocks beside the black key-block to print two other colours upon the paper. The importance of this step was immeasurable: when it was taken the doom of the hand-coloured print was sealed, and the way to still further development lay open. At first the colours used by Masanobu in his two-colour works were a delicate apple-green and the equally delicate rose called *beni*, from which the name *beni-ye* came to be applied to all the two-colour prints of this period. A print of this type appears in Plate 6. The combination of these two colours is singularly lovely, and the fresh charm of these sheets has led some collectors to prize them as the most beautiful products of the art.

Certainly Masanobu's mastery of the problem of
producing a rich and vivacious colour-composition
by the use of only two colours is noteworthy. By
varying the size and shape of his colour masses, and
by a judicious use of the white of the paper and
the black of the key-block, he produces an effect
of such colour-fullness that it requires a distinct
effort of the mind to convince oneself that these
prints are designs in two tones only, and not full-
colour prints. Masanobu lived long enough to
produce some three-colour prints, when these were
devised about 1755, but the effects he obtained in
them were possibly less fascinating than those of
his earlier process.

It can probably never be proven that Masanobu
was, in fact, the inventor of all the devices that
were attributed to him—the lacquer-print, the *beni*
print, the use of gold powder, and the first actual
prints in colour. Certainly some of them may be
credited to him ; but any one familiar with the
growth of hero-legends knows how a great name
attracts to itself in popular report achievements that
were really the fruit of scattered lesser men. To
the list of Masanobu's probable inventions must be
added the pillar-print, that remarkable type, about
4 to 6 inches wide and 25 to 40 inches high,
which was to be an important form of design from
this date on. It is possible that we must also
attribute to him the invention of the mica background—that silver surface of powdered mica which
give a curious and beautiful tone to the figures
outlined against it.

OKUMURA MASANOBU: YOUNG NOBLEMAN
PLAYING THE DRUM.

Printed in black, green, and rose.  Size 12×6.
Signed *Hogetsudo Okumura Masanobu, hitsu.*
Chandler Collection.

*Plate 6*

Of Masanobu as a designer it is difficult to speak with moderation. Through his work runs that sweeping power of line which he derived from his study of Moronobu, and, in addition, an elegance and suave grace that is the expression of his innate grace of spirit. The grandeur of certain others of the Primitives is austere and harsh, but Masanobu is always mellow and harmonious. His figures, more finely proportioned than most of the figures of the period, sway in easy motion—a mixture of sweetness and distinction characterizes the poised heads, superb bodies, and ample draperies of his women, while every resource of compact and dignified design is expended upon the impressive figures of his men. A certain large geniality, a wide, sunlighted warmth of conception, runs through his work. The dramatic distortions of his Torii predecessors and contemporaries are melted in him, as towering but uncouth icebergs melt in the sun of kindlier latitudes. At times his line-work has a force that seems derived from the Kwaigetsudō tradition; more often it is imbued with a gentler rhythm no less expressive of strength. In his finest designs he achieves notable balance of line, and a massing of colour beside which, as Fenollosa remarks, "even the façades of Greek temples were possibly cold and half-charged in comparison."

Women, out-of-door scenes, and a few actors, constitute the main subjects of Masanobu's work. As a portraitist, his few productions, such as the well-known humorous pillar-print of the story-teller Koshi Shikoden, give him rank as the greatest of his time. The landscape backgrounds in some of his smaller prints are a delightful innovation, executed with delicate power of suggesting by a few strokes the whole circle of a natural setting. The quiet charm of these landscapes surrounds with an atmosphere of felicity the beautiful figures that move through them.

A full and brilliant life stirs in all Masanobu's work. At no other period in the history of Ukioye was such effective use made of the patterns of draperies. The elaborate fashions of the brocades worn in this day lent themselves to the decorative needs of the larger prints; and frequently we find the figures clothed in a riot of striking textiles—flowers, trees, birds, ships, geometrical shapes—all mingled in the weave of the cloth, and arranged by the print-designer into a combination that is tumultuous without confusion and glowing without garishness. Masanobu's pictures seem the overflow of his spirit's wealth; they never have the ascetic and rarefied quality that sometimes appears in the work of even great artists.

Masanobu's work is scarce. His larger and more important prints very rarely appear outside of the great collections.

### PUPILS OF OKUMURA MASANOBU.

OKUMURA TOSHINOBU, a son of Masanobu who died young, was the best as well as the most famous of Masanobu's pupils. He gave promise of becoming one of the notable print-designers, and even in his short career produced work of high quality. Born about 1709, his period of production covered the years of the lacquer-prints, and ended before 1743. His *urushi-ye*, lithe in design and powerful in colouring, constitute almost his whole known work.

Okumurà Masafusa, Shuseido, Hanekawa Chiucho Motonobu, and Mangetsudō may be mentioned as other and less important pupils of Masanobu.

## NISHIMURA SHIGENOBU.

Nishimura Shigenobu is an artist about whom there is great confusion. He is variously called the father, the son, or the pupil of the better-known artist Shigenaga: the first of these alternatives is the most probable. Nothing is known of Shigenobu's life, and very little of his work is extant. Kurth says that Shigenobu founded the Nishimura School, and worked in the manner of the earliest Torii. Von Seidlitz believes that he did some work in the Kwaigetsudō manner. Fenollosa dates his work 1720–40, and thinks that he worked first like the Torii, then like Masanobu. At present it seems impossible to gather further information about this interesting artist.

## SHIGENAGA.

Nishimura Shigenaga was at one time regarded as the inventor of the two-colour process; but now that the weight of opinion attributes this invention to Masanobu, Shigenaga remains a figure whose importance is hardly diminished. He must still be regarded as perhaps the most notable master of the Nishimura School, both as a designer and as the

teacher of a group of pupils whose brilliancy is
equalled by the disciples of no other artist.

Shigenaga was born in 1697 and lived until 1756.
He used the names Senkwadō and Magosaburō as
well as his own.　Little is known of him personally,
except that he was probably the son of Shigenobu.

His work began with black-and-white prints in
the manner of Kiyonobu ; these were already
something of an anachronism at
the date when he commenced
his designing.　He then turned
to *urushi-ye*, and produced some
beautiful examples.　About 1742,
when the two-colour process was
invented, he made himself one of
the most successful masters of
it.　Dr. Anderson reproduces, as
the frontispiece of his " Japanese
Wood-Engraving," a fine example
of Shigenaga's work in this technique, but erroneously dates it as
1725—more than fifteen years too
early.　Shigenaga also did fine
work in the three-colour process,
of which he may possibly have been the inventor.
His designs comprise not only women and actors,
but also landscapes, flowers, animals, and birds.　His
versatility is one of his most striking characteristics.

NISHIMURA
SHIGENAGA.

It was from the style of Masanobu that Shigenaga
drew his most lasting stimulus ; and among his
sheets we shall find many a figure worthy to stand
beside his master's serene creations.　Dr. Kurth calls

him a "faded or weakened Masanobu"; but this
term can be applied with justice to only a portion of
Shigenaga's work. His productions are uneven;
part are indeed somewhat tame; but certain of his
designs rise to a high level. His finest works, which
are rare, are his figures of graceful women in the
Masanobu manner. But he was no mere imitator.
The Masanobu poise, the Masanobu flow and pattern-
ing of garments he did, it is true, adopt; but with
how fresh and sensitive a life does he infuse them!

Shigenaga's pupils comprise most of the great men
of the succeeding generation. Toyonobu, Harunobu,
Koriusai, Shigemasa, Toyoharu, and many others
learned from him the elements of their art. Thus
Shigenaga may be regarded as the most important
bridge between the Primitives and the later men,
passing over to them the traditions of the older
schools together with the stimulus of that fresh,
inventive, and assimilative spirit which was peculiarly
his own.

### PUPILS OF SHIGENAGA.

Among the less important pupils or associates of
Shigenaga may be named the following artists :—

TSUNEGAWA SHIGENOBU produced work much
like Shigenaga's ; in the few prints of his which I
have seen there is grace and ease, but not great
strength. His work appears to have been mainly
in *urushi-ye*. Mr. Gookin believes this name to be
merely the early name of Nishimura Shigenobu.

YŌSENDŌ YASUNOBU or ANSHIN, by whom a
fine lacquer-print with strong blacks is in the

Spaulding Collection, may, with some hesitancy, be classed here. Mr. Gookin thinks this signature may be merely one of the studio names of some more famous artist.

NAGAHIDE, dated by Strange about 1760, appears to belong to this group. The Harmsworth Collection, London, contains a print by him representing famous theatrical characters depicted by geisha, the colours partly printed and partly applied by hand.

HARUTOSHI is known to me only by one pillar-print, in the manner of Shigenaga's actors. It is doubtful where he should be classified.

AKIYAMA SADAHARU, HIROSE SHIGENOBU, and RYŪKWADO ICHIICHIDO SHIGENOBU were obscure pupils of Shigenaga.

YAMAMOTO YOSHINOBU is said by Fenollosa to have been a pupil of Shigenaga, and possibly the same as KOMAI YOSHINOBU, who is treated later under Harunobu. Dr. Kurth thinks him a member of a Yamamoto School, which comprised also YAMAMOTO DENROKU, YAMAMOTO SHIGENOBU, YAMAMOTO SHIGEFUSA, YAMAMOTO FUJINOBU, YAMAMOTO SHIGEHARU, TOMIKAWA GINSETSU also known as FUSANOBU, YAMAMOTO MARUYA KYŪYEIMON, YAMAMOTO KUZAYEIMON, and YAMA-MOTO RIHEI.

## TOYONOBU.

*A Pillar Print.*

O lady of the long robes, the slow folds flowing—
Lady of the white breast, the dark and lofty head—
Dwells there any wonder, the way that thou art going—
Or goest thou toward the dead?

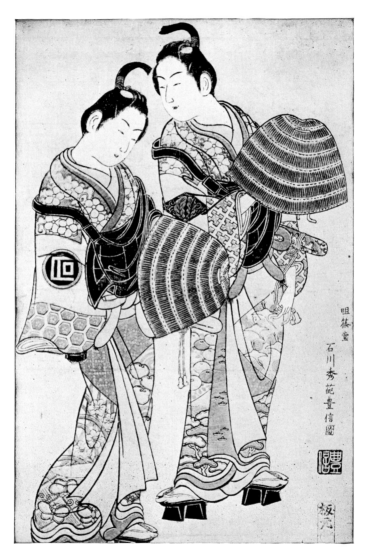

TOYONOBU: TWO KOMUSO, REPRESENTED BY THE ACTORS
SANOKAWA ICHIMATSU AND ONOYE KIKUGORO.
Printed in black and three colours.  Size 15×10.
Signed *Tanjodo, Ishikawa Shuha Toyonobu ga*.  Chandler Collection.

*Plate 7*

So calm thy solemn steps, so slow the long lines sweeping
Of garments pale and ghostly, of limbs as grave as sleep—
I know not if thou, spectre, hast love or death in keeping,
Or goest toward which deep.

Thou layest thy robes aside with gesture large and flowing.
Is it for love or sleep—is it for life or death?
I would my feet might follow the path that thou art going,
And thy breath be my breath.

Ishikawa Toyonobu, who not many years ago was regarded as an artist of secondary importance, has of late, thanks to fresh discoveries, come to be esteemed by competent observers as one of the giants of the line—one of those masters among the Primitives whose dignity of composition makes all but a handful of his successors appear petty beside him.

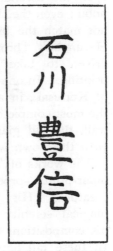

ISHIKAWA TOYONOBU.

This important artist, who sometimes signed himself Shuha, was, like so many other of the better men of his time, a pupil of Shigenaga. In his early work we find him influenced by the suave and noble figures of Okumura Masanobu more than by the figures of his direct master. Born in 1711, Toyonobu lived until 1785; and the long space of his life thus extended beyond the period of the Primitives and into the period of polychrome printing. Nevertheless his real activity terminated with the end of the Primitive Period. His earliest work was in black-

and-white or hand-coloured; from this he passed on to two-colour prints, a manner in which he produced many *hoso-ye* of flawless grace; and then into three-colour prints, in which his most important work was accomplished, and "whose classic master," as Kurth says, "he may be called." Between 1755 and 1764, the great period of the three-colour print, Toyonobu stood almost unmatched in the field. A fine example of his work appears in Plate 7. After 1764 the ascendancy of Harunobu eclipsed Toyonobu; even the classic style of the older master could not match the brilliant and popular innovations of Harunobu's "brocade pictures." He was therefore driven to take up the technique of full-colour printing. In one print he gives us figures like those of Koriusai; in another he follows Harunobu with the most complete exactness. Though forced to the wall, the old giant could still fight his rivals, and with their own weapons.

The works of Toyonobu's prime—particularly his pillar-prints—produce a singular impression of lofty greatness. His line-arrangements have always a magical serenity and balance, and the repose of his compositions is equalled only by their strength. In these tall figures, where hauntingly lovely lines never degenerate into mere sweetness, there is a combination of rigour with suavity, of force with grace, that makes him forever memorable. His masterful precision, and the curiously " towering " effect which his figures produce, as in the Girl with the Umbrella reproduced in Plate 8, serve to mark him as one of the important representatives of the grand style in design.

TOYONOBU: GIRL OPENING
AN UMBRELLA.

Black outlines, with hand-
colouring.
Signed *Tanjodo, Ishikawa Shuha
Toyonobu zu.*
Metzgar Collection.

*Plate 8*

TOYONOBU: WOMAN
DRESSING.

Printed in black and three
colours.
Size 27×4.
Signed *Ishikawa Toyonobu.
hitsu.*

113

Perhaps more than any other artist of the Ukioye School, Toyonobu devoted himself to the drawing of the nude. These rare works are among the finest of his productions, and are so distinctly an exception to the general practice of Japanese artists that they call for special remark. Certain other painters also produced a few such pictures, but they must all be regarded as sporadic phenomena running counter to the characteristic Japanese feeling. The national temper recognizes feminine beauty in art only when clothed; and it is due solely to the profounder perception of a few great artists that any such designs have come down to us. One is moved to speculation over this curious fact, particularly when one considers that the sight of the body, at least among the lower classes, must have been almost as common in Japan at this time as it was in Greece during the great period of Athenian art. But very different was the reaction produced upon the two races by this familiarity. In the Greeks, it encouraged an art whose prime aim was to give expression to those harmonies and hints of perfection that lie hidden in the imperfections of each individual body; so that we have from the Greeks those syntheses and idealizations of the human form which still haunt us like faint memories of the gods. But in the Japanese mind, the sense of the individual defects seems to have overpowered the impulse to creative idealism; and the people, as a race, turned from the nude figure to the more easily manipulated beauties of flowing robes and gorgeous patterns, translating Nature into images

of an alien richness, and love into hyperboles of
public splendour.  That part of Nature which lay
outside themselves they could indeed cope with,
as the lofty visions of landscape which they have
transcribed testify ; but with a few exceptions,
such as Toyonobu and Kiyomitsu and Kiyonaga,
they dared not attempt the final venture of
rationalizing the uses and aspects of the body.
And it is because of an inadequacy whose source
and root spring from this attitude that posterity
will perhaps rank this art below the art of Greece,
adjudging even the matchless subtlety and refinement of these designs to be no adequate
compensation for the absence of that frank Greek
courage which attempted to clarify and ennoble
the fundamental conditions of the existence of
man.

Toyonobu, great artist that he was, overstepped
the national barrier and came very near to surpassing
the finest achievements of Greek art.

## KIYOMITSU.

*Pillar Print of a Woman.*

A place for giant heads to take their rest
Seems her pale breast.

Her sweeping robe trails like the cloud and wind
Storms leave behind.

The ice of the year, and its Aprilian part,
Sleep in her heart.

Therefore small marvel that her footsteps be
Like strides of Destiny !

KIYOMITSU: ACTOR SEGAWA KIKUNOJO AS A
WOMAN SMOKING.

Printed in black and three colours.  Size 11½×5½.
Signed *Torii Kiyomitsu ga*.

*Plate 9*

*Pillar Print of a Man.*

Out of spaces hazed with greyness, out of years whose veils
    are grey,
With the slow majestic footsteps of a lord of far-away,
Comes a form that out of glooming
Rises from some old entombing
To confront once more the day.

And with splendid gesture dwarfing the confusion of our hands,
With his ancient calm rebuking the unrest of vain demands,
He with solemn footsteps slowly
Passes: and his garments holy
Leave the scent of holy lands.

Kiyomitsu took his place as the third great head of the Torii line, succeeding his father Kiyomasu. In subject and in manner, it is the Torii tradition that he carries on. We know nothing of his life, save that he was born in 1735 and died in 1785. His work falls almost entirely within the class of two- and three-colour prints. I know of only one hand-coloured print by him ; but as his dates denote, he lived far into the period of polychrome printing, and was a partaker in Harunobu's experiments in colour. Von Seidlitz is wrong in saying that no polychrome prints by Kiyomitsu are known ; a few exist and are very beautiful. He did little work after

TORII KIYOMITSU.

1765, and is to be regarded as most characteristically an artist of the Primitive Period—in fact one of the greatest. Certainly between 1755 and 1764, no one but Toyonobu could rival him ; and these two may be ranked the supreme designers of the three-colour epoch.

The outstanding feature of Kiyomitsu's work is its formalism. Whatever he touches is compressed to a pattern, and rendered into bold hieroglyphics of sweeping curves. His line is simple, powerfully dominated by a circular movement that is singularly and inexplicably delightful. His colours, even while they remain only two or three in number, never lack variety and strong decorative effect. The slightness of the use which he makes of black is noteworthy ; he compensates for its absence by choosing heavy opaque colours of rich tone. Some authorities regard him as the first to employ a third colour-block.

Kiyomitsu's work is markedly stylistic—even dominated by a certain mannerism ; one comes to recognize almost infallibly the formula he uses, and to regard as an old friend that peculiar swirl of drapery, swing of body, and artificial poise of head which appear, as in Plate 9, like an accepted convention throughout the larger number of his designs. The convention is an agreeable and highly æsthetic one, based on fundamental curves of great beauty. But the invariability with which he employs this formula gives Dr. Kurth some excuse for regarding him as a monotonous and over-estimated artist. Had we only Kiyomitsu's *hoso-ye* prints, it might be possible to agree with Dr. Kurth ; for these figures, enchanting and full of elegance as they are, certainly are dominated by a sameness of manner such as one finds in no other series of *hoso-ye*. But

KIYOMITSU: WOMAN WITH
BASKET HAT.

Black and three colours.
Size 28×4.
Signed *Torii Kiyomitsu ga.*

*Plate 10*

KIYOMITSU: WOMAN COMING
FROM BATH.

Black and three colours.
Size 27×4.
Signed *Torii Kiyomitsu ga.*

the truth of Dr. Kurth's depreciations must be questioned if one turns to the pillar-prints, which constitute the real glory of Kiyomitsu's career. The two reproduced in Plate 10 exhibit his power. Kiyomitsu may be regarded as one of the half-dozen greatest masters of the pillar-print shape of composition. Much of his finest work is in this form. Here his somewhat tight curves lengthen out into flowing beauty; and the dignity always inherent in his drawing appears at its best.

Kiyomitsu's rare nudes take a place close beside those of Toyonobu. They have a keen poetic charm; and though their vigour is less marked than that of Toyonobu's, their grace and elegance of movement is at least as striking.

The collector may find it useful to remember that long after Kiyomitsu's death, Kiyomine and Kiyofusa sometimes used the great name of Kiyomitsu as a signature to their own works. Only an inexperienced observer could mistake these late and decadent productions for the work of the original master.

### Kiyohiro.

Torii Kiyohiro has been rated by some writers as more highly gifted than Kiyomitsu. This praise appears absurdly extravagant; yet in disputing such a claim, one must admit the great charm of Kiyohiro's work. He is said to have been a pupil of Kiyonobu II; his career runs parallel with that of Kiyomitsu, and he seems frequently to imitate that artist. The period of his greatest prominence was between 1745 and 1758; his work is all in two or three colours.

A delicate draughtsman, his figures have marked grace of poise and firmness of design. His mannerism is less stereotyped than Kiyomitsu's ; some of his prints have great beauty, but he never reaches certain heights which Kiyomitsu attained. Prints by him are uncommon.

鳥
居
清
廣

TORII KIYOHIRO.

KIYOTSUNE.

Torii Kiyotsune produced delicate and distinguished prints in two or three colours, much like those of Kiyomitsu. Most of his figures are characterized by a curious slenderness and exquisiteness ; but they are somewhat lacking in vigour. After 1764 he fell under the influence of Harunobu and adopted full-colour printing, still retaining, however, that very individual type of face—a little scornful, a little fastidious in expression—which marks his designs. His work is rare.

PUPILS OF KIYOMITSU AND TOYONOBU.

Among the pupils of Kiyomitsu may be noted Torii Kiyosato, Torii Kiyoharu, Morotada, Kiyotoshi, Torii Kiyomoto, and Torii Kiyohide. Their work was almost contemporaneous with that of the master.

Amano Toyonaga, Ishikawa Toyomasu, and Ishikawa Toyokuma were probably pupils of Toyonobu.

# IV

# THE SECOND
# PERIOD :
# THE EARLY
# POLYCHROME
# MASTERS

FROM THE INVENTION
OF POLYCHROME PRINTING
TO THE RETIREMENT
OF SHUNSHO
(1764–80)

# CHAPTER IV

THE SECOND PERIOD : THE EARLY POLYCHROME
MASTERS

FROM THE INVENTION OF POLYCHROME PRINTING TO THE
RETIREMENT OF SHUNSHO (1764–80)

THE transition from primitive to sophisticated art is
very like the progression of a race from its heroic
youth to its elaborately gifted maturity. Life
grows more complex, the material riches and the
machinery of living become more diversified; but it
is still to the early days that one looks for the
strongest development of personality and the most
daring achievement in the face of great difficulties.
Sophistication, in the history of an art as of a race,
brings refinements and nuances unknown to the
pioneers ; but it cannot intensify and may often
encumber the spiritual force and essential genius of
the creators. The great individuals of the earlier
time developed all that was essential as far as it
could be developed ; the later enlargement of scope
is in the direction of the material and the accidental.
In the Primitives we find the full stature of the
spirit ; in the art of later days, with all its parade of
processes, we shall hardly find more.

In the First Period the initial impulse of print-designing manifested itself in work that was powerful and beautiful, but of simple technique. In the Second Period the barriers that confined the Primitives were swept away by new possibilities of expression. The three-colour prints gave place to prints in which an unlimited number of blocks could be employed; and this enlargement of the artist's resources produced a new and splendid blossoming. In this Second Period the art seemed to hesitate midway between the forces of the primitive inspiration, which was one of pure and stately decoration, and the more naturalistic forces that were making ready for the Third Period, with its fuller rendering of the lights and spaces of life. The presence of both groups of forces makes this Second Period possibly the most interesting of all.

The specific characteristics of the period are sharply marked. They consist, first of all, in technical advances — the mastery of full-colour printing and the realization through this process of the marvellous colour-dreams of the great masters. But beyond the technical advances there is a change in spiritual attitude; the artist, heretofore content to create a pure decoration, a masterful mosaic that expressed his æsthetic ideals, now begins to adopt a more personal attitude in his treatment of the forces and spectacles of daily existence. True, he disposes these elements arbitrarily; the picture he creates is a world of imagination; but as compared with the Primitives, he tells us more of his experience and is closer to our own. Even his most fanciful designs bring to us some remote and abstract echo of known voices. Lyric joy speaks through Harunobu, dramatic terror through Shunsho, splendour through Koriusai, mystery through Buncho ; and though the medium be a symbol, and its connection with reality as remote as that of music, yet by the vividness of the emotion evoked in us we may judge of the definiteness of the artist's motive, and realize through colour and line an intangible human voice.

The stream of art history here flowed in two main channels. One was the Katsukawa School, headed by Shunsho, which like the older Torii School devoted itself chiefly to the representation of actors. The other was the school of Harunobu, whose gracious designs of women were the most novel productions of the period. A third school was founded by Toyoharu and a fourth by Shigemasa ; but the real importance of these two schools developed only in a later epoch. During this period the great Torii School may be said to have remained dormant ; it was to awaken in the Third Period to a new splendour in Kiyonaga.

There is a passage from a contemporary record that throws light on the temper of the people and the artists at this time. I have freely translated it, with the courteous permission of Dr. Julius Kurth (Kurth's " Harunobu," R. Piper & Co., Munich), from his German rendering of a unique manuscript book in his possession, which appears to have been written by the poet Yukura Sanjin, and illustrated by

Harunobu in 1769. The book is a whimsical, devil-
may-care production of the lightest sort; but from
its pages the glitter and surge and laughter of Yedo
holiday life rise with a far-away yet curiously
distinct echo.

### AN EXTRACT FROM "THE STORY OF THE HONEY-SWEETMEAT VENDOR, DOHEI"

" Dohei hails from Oshu.   Upon his head he wears
a cap; and his mouth sends up a song when in the
Capital of the East he vends his honey-sweetmeats.
His cape is of tiger-skin, and bears a suspicious
resemblance to the loin-apron of the Devil.   His
umbrella is of scarlet crêpe, and recalls the plumed
spears of the festival-guards.   As his coat of arms
he chose a Devil's head and a skeleton; upon his
outer robe he wrote the sign, ' Dohei, Dohei.'   While
you buy his honey-sweetmeats, he sings a song of
a new style, and ends it with the refrain, ' Dohei,
Dohei ! '   Therefore the name of Dohei has become
known everywhere.   Even the smallest children all
sing this song in chorus over and over a thousand
times.   If he sells his honey-sweetmeats in the
Eastern part of the city, the people in the Western
streets are furious; if he sells them in the Southern
quarter, the people in the Northern streets are
furious.   For then they want to know why he came
to them so late.

" If on the three hundred and sixty days of the
year one goes, day in and day out, through all the
eight hundred and eight streets, one finds a tavern
at every five paces ; and it is as if this city had been

changed into a pond of rice-wine. One cannot take
ten steps without coming upon a shop in which whole
mountains of rice-cakes and other confections are
offered. If one hears in the distance an almost
heavenly music, it is the song of a lady to the strum
of a guitar. If there is a rattling like peals of
thunder, it is the ox-carts on the side streets.
People with coiffures shaped like the leaf of the
ginko-tree roll up their outer robes and jostle
shoulder to shoulder. Ladies with girdles of spun
gold and long-sleeved girlish dresses sway their hips;
and their garments, coloured like the graining of
wood, flow as do torrents of Spring. Their hats of
green paper resemble a clump of trees in Summer.
And as they wander along, the hems of their robes
flutter open, and the blood-red silk linings gleam like
maple foliage—though it is not yet Autumn! The
festive white material of their inner robes shines like
snow—though it is not yet Winter! If it were, they
would be muffled to their very noses with crêpe veils.
They have arranged their hair as if surmounted by a
cap, like tiers of little chrysanthemums. At their
thighs sparkle tobacco-wallets ornamented with silver
and gold.

"The black-and-white prints of earlier days are
antiquated now, and the only thing people care for
is the newly-devised gorgeousness of the Eastern
Brocade Pictures. Musical plays are no longer to be
seen; instead, you go to the music-girls and the
dancing-girls in the taverns. The young people want
lively entertainment, and visit the wine-shops. Out
of a vase in which, according to the ancient custom,

flowers were formerly placed, lots are now drawn to
fix upon the day for a party ; while according to the
fashionable arrangement of flowers in the hanging
jars, the flowers look like arrows from a bow.  The
vendors of fritters call out, 'Celebrated Pasties!
Celebrated Pasties!' and boast upon the brilliant
paper signs of the just-opened booths, 'Headquarters!
Headquarters!' Handkerchiefs at four coppers apiece
hang at the loins of the servants of Samurais.  The
song of the New Year's dancers rings out among
people who hitherto had sung only folk-songs.  The
caligraphist studies the Nagao style ; the poet learns
by heart the poems of the Chinese epoch, and the
minstrel the style of the Manyo anthology.  To
obtain new remedies for his stock the doctor draws
upon the old school for all kinds of herbs, and cures
eyes and noses with them—just as pumpkins are
perfected into melons.  Often the priest of Buddha
wanders, an object of derision, through the streets in
the darkness of night in search of a girl.  To be sure,
he is a very learned man; but what leads more easily
to dangerous labyrinths than love?

    " The theatres in the Sakai Street give perform-
ances continuously.  The reconstruction of the
Yoshiwara is to be finished in a few days, and people
come and go there only to drink and to sing.  They
draw water from the floods of the Sumida River, but
it will not be drained dry!  They view again and
again the flowers of the Asuka River, but these also
are without end!  The Shenshuraku Theatre enlivens
the public, and upon the Banzairaku stage man's life
is idealized.  So all are happy—like green firs that

become thicker and thicker and put forth new needles."

Into this crowded world of exuberant life came Harunobu and his contemporaries—into this underworld, if you will, but an underworld more beautiful and sun-drenched than any known to our great Western cities. Instead of the bar in the slum they had the tea-house on the river-bank ; instead of the prize-fight they had the cherry festival ; for them, vice put on robes of a certain stately beauty ; their stage was marked by the same ennobling absence of realism that distinguished the stage of the Greeks. The holiday spirit of the hour seems more spontaneous than ours ; their hearts seem less troubled by spiritual confusions. And manifestly their underworld knew beauty and brought forth an art that is now a universal human treasure ; while our underworld has been, with the rarest of exceptions, wholly sterile.

One of the most important of the underworld institutions which the prints of this period depict is the theatre. Though Harunobu turned aside from it, his great contemporary Shunsho and the whole body of Shunsho's followers found most of their material there.

The popular theatre had sprung into importance in the days of Moronobu. Previous to that time, the classic lyric drama of the aristocracy, called the Nō, had flourished in the secluded palaces of great nobles; but the mob was obliged to divert itself with nothing more interesting than jugglers and street performers.

Therefore when the theatre first came into being, in the river-bed of Kyoto, it achieved great popularity ; and when later it was transferred to Yedo, it rose during the Genroku Period (1688–1703) to a position of passionate favour. It appears never to have had a very savoury moral odour ; and before long it became associated with so much corruptness that it presented a serious problem for the Tokugawa rulers. In 1643, as a corrective measure, they had decreed the exclusion of female actors from the stage. From this time on, only men trod the Japanese boards ; the female rôles were taken by male actors whose skill in this impersonation is said to have been extraordinary.

The status of a great actor in the hearts of the people was not very different from that of a successful prize-fighter among us to-day. He was a popular idol ; his movements were the subject of the eager curiosity of the gaping multitude ; but his social rank was of the lowest. The prints of a later date show us pictures of actors with their gay companions on boating-parties or tea-house picnics, surrounded by inquisitive throngs of spectators. Famous and greatly sought after as these actors were, they occupied positions of even less esteem than the English players in the days of Queen Elizabeth. Nothing so well illustrates their ostracism from any kind of society as the words used by one of the greatest of actor-painters, Shunsho, in the preface to a book of drawings representing actors : " To be sure, I love the theatre, and greatly enjoy being a spectator, *but I have no connection with the actors*

*themselves, and do not know them in private life."*
Even Shunsho, who had created the heroic designs of
these men in their great rôles, dared not acknowledge
himself as their familiar.

When they appeared on the stage, the faces of the
actors were frequently painted with startling streaks
of red and white, an effect reproduced in some of the
prints. The elaborate robes worn when they represented heroic figures of bygone ages formed superb
material for the designs of the artists. The Japanese
stage of to-day probably does not differ very much
from what it was in Shunsho's time ; and we still see
on it that florid elaboration of gesture, bombastic
delivery, and intensification of facial expression which
the prints have perpetuated.

The actors were divided into clans or schools ; the
name of a famous head of a clan would be handed
down for generations from master to pupil. Thus
there were many of the name of Danjuro, Hanshiro,
and Kikunojo in succession, who were not related to
each other by blood. Certain clans such as the
Kikunojo specialized exclusively in women's rôles.
Each clan had its *mon* or crest, worn on the sleeve,
and each actor had a personal *mon* ; in the prints
these generally appear. In Plate 20, for example, the
circle with eight crossed arrow-buts indicates the *mon*
of Nakamura Matsuye ; in other prints, the three
great concentric squares of Danjuro, the trisected
concentric circles of Hanshiro, or the iris within a
circle of Kikunojo (Plate 9), are easily identified.

In the hands of Shunsho and his followers the
figures of these actors were used as the material for

brilliant designs.    For the moment, however, we
must return to the foremost artist of this period—one
who never loved the actors—Harunobu.


## HARUNOBU.

*Figure of a Girl.*

Ye winds that somewhere in the West—
In gulfs of sunset, isles of rest—
Rise dewy from prenatal sleep
To strew with little waves the deep—
Surely it is your breath that stirs
These fluttering gauzy robes of hers !

Come whence ye may, I marvel not
That ye are lured to seek this spot ;
Your tenuous scarcely breathèd powers
Sway not the sturdier garden flowers,
And had unmanifest gone by
Save that she feels them visibly.

O little winds, her little hands
In time with tunes from fairy-lands
Are moving ; and her bended head
Knows nothing of the long years sped
Since heaven more near to earth was hung,
And gods lived, and the world was young.

Her inner robe of tenderest fawn
In cool, faint fountains of the dawn
Was dyed ; and her long outer dress
Borrows its luminous loveliness
From some clear bowl with water filled
In which one drop of wine was spilled.

Peace folds her in its deeps profound ;
Her shy glance lifts not from the ground ;
And through this garden's still retreat
She moves with tripping silver feet
Whose trancèd grace, where'er she strays,
Turns all the days to holy days.

HARUNOBU: YOUNG GIRL IN WIND.

Polychrome, from eight blocks. Size 11×8. Signed *Suzuki Harunobu ga.*
Gookin Collection.

*Plate 11*

Come ! let us softly steal away.
For what can we, whose hearts are grey,
Bring to her dreaming paradise ?
A chill shall mock her from our eyes ;
A cloud shall dim this radiant air ;
Come ! for our world is otherwhere.

But O ye little winds that blow
From golden islands long ago
Lost to our searching in the deep
Of dreams between the shores of sleep —
Ye shall her happy playmates be,
Fluttering her robes invisibly.

The few available fragments of information about the life of Susuki Harunobu can be briefly stated. Born between 1725 and 1730, he lived in Yedo all his life in a house near the river. In 1764 he perfected a new and epoch-making treatment of colour-print technique, and died in 1770, not much more than forty years of age. We may, where so little is known, willingly follow Dr. Kurth in his ingenious tracing of a romantic link between Harunobu and the hamlet of Kasamori, whose pine-trees, red temple-torii, and beautiful tea-house waitress O-Sen haunt his work recurrently ; but we must be content to regard this as at least half fancy. Harunobu's direct teacher was Shigenaga, and he was influenced early by Toyonobu ; but it was to Sukenobu and Kiyomitsu that he turned for the inspiration of those characteristic figures which he

SUSUKI HARUNOBU.

created during the six great years of his real
activity.

Harunobu's work before the year 1764 is relatively
unimportant.    It consists of prints of actors and
legendary subjects, printed in two or three colours ; a
few of his *hoso-ye* prints of this period have charming
delicacy of line and colour, and at least one of his
actor pillar-prints is a work of notable dignity ; but
upon the whole his work is not very individual.    Any
one of a dozen of Shigenaga's pupils might have
done almost as well.    Before 1764 these men were
all his equals ; after 1764 he took a step which few
could keep pace with and which none could outstrip.

In 1764 he brought forth that synthesis of the
resources of his art which was to shake the Ukioye
world.    Whether he was the actual inventor of polychrome printing is not certain ; some authorities
attribute the invention to an engraver named
Kinroku ; but it is very clear that Harunobu was
the first to seize upon and realize the possibilities
of the discovery.    Some technical hindrance, such
as the difficulty of securing perfect register from
many blocks on the wet stretching sheets, had
prevented the earlier completion of the process ;
and it is possible that it was a printer who discovered
the simple device needed to overcome the difficulty.
This, however, is a matter of mere mechanics and
has no bearing upon the question of the real glory
of. Harunobu.    What is important is that he seized
the new technique and made out of it an instrument
responsive to every subtlest breath of his beauty-
haunted spirit.

HARUNOBU: LADY TALKING WITH FAN-VENDOR.
Polychrome. Size 11×7½. Signed *Harunobu ga*. Chandler Collection.

*Plate 12*

The old three-colour prints had achieved fine effects by means of powerfully conceived but essentially simple mosaics of colour. Now Harunobu turned the three-stringed lute into the violin, capable of expressing the most delicate modulations of tone. Beginning with combinations of only four or five colours, he gradually increased the number of blocks used. It is certain that he used eight blocks on at least one 1765 calendar print. In the end he had at his command a palette which, by the use of no less than twelve or fifteen blocks, and with the limitless number of shades obtainable by superimposing one colour upon another, made the whole rainbow his. Constant experiment marked his further progress. We have, for example, one print which he originally printed from eight blocks, and later varied by increasing the blocks to ten, and still later to thirteen. From year to year an ever fresh succession of complex colour-harmonies emanated from his fertile brain.

Until the invention of polychrome printing, Harunobu had not adequately expressed himself; now, having found his true instrument, he played divinely. The year 1765 was a Jubilee year, celebrating the nine-hundredth anniversary of the entrance of Sugawara Michigane, the great statesman, painter, and humanist, to the Court of the Emperor. This circumstance, in connection with the desire of literary men to present to their friends specimens of the new prints as New Year cards, led Harunobu to produce a number of dated calendar-prints of this year—a fortunate occurrence which has been of great aid

to students of his work. The theory that these
dated prints are the expression of Harunobu's naïve
exultation over the new discovery is now generally
discredited. Since the calendars are dated 1765,
Mr. Gookin's suggestion that they were probably
made in the last months of 1764 seems reasonable ; and this date must therefore be regarded as
marking the beginning of polychrome printing.

The brilliant new prints fittingly ushered in the
festal year. And the public was not too busy with
its celebrations to take note of the change. The
new manner with its wealth of colour-beauty won
instant popularity ; and under the name of " Brocade
Pictures of the Eastern Capital " grew to such fame
that by 1767 prints in the old style were almost
driven out of the market, and Harunobu was
unquestioned lord of Ukioye.

It is not strange that in the glow of success and
ambition he should have put behind him his old
actor-pictures. " I am a Japanese painter," he wrote
proudly ; "why should I paint the portraits of this
vulgar herd ? " And at this moment feeling himself
akin to the great classical tradition whose refined
beauties had been handed down from ancient China
mingled with the beauties of poets and sages, he
determined that he would lift from the Ukioye
School the stigma of vulgarity which the theatre
had given it, and invest it with some of that gentle
cultivation which fills like light the old Chinese paintings of Ming gardens. Therefore he turned his
energies to the depiction of another world than
the theatre—the life of aristocratic ladies, of young

HARUNOBU: GIRL VIEWING MOON AND BLOSSOMS.
Size 11×8.  Signed *Harunobu ga*.  Chandler Collection.

*Plate 13*

145

lovers, of those famed beauties who in humbler station were the flowers and sunshine of the tea-house and the festival. Plate 14 portrays one of these. His method of handling the figures—a peculiar mingling of naïveté and sophistication, like that of a minstrel singing incredible enchanted legends with complete seriousness—was a new and never-recovered note in the history of Ukioye.

From this time on, during six years, Harunobu produced a series of prints whose grace is unsurpassable. The firm and refined strokes of his brush endowed with a fresh charm all that was lovely in the flowing draperies and serene faces of the young girls of Japan. He was the painter of youth. The type which he introduced was the slender and gracious embodiment of youthful girlhood. And an indescribable delicacy and purity of manner clothes as with clear light these girl-figures of his. His draperies, as in Plate 11, are never drawn naturalistically, but always with a certain conventionalization that produces folds and swirls more abstractly beautiful than a literal rendering. He for the first time in colour-printing made a practice of giving to his figures a background that exhibited fully the scene of their daily lives. Instead of the heroic figures of the Primitives, stalking through space in colossal grandeur, he drew the familiar forms of everyday existence nestling among their natural surroundings. The world he pictures is, however, one of mortals who hardly know the burdens of mortality. Like the women of Botticelli, they seem to poise in an atmosphere of more rarefied loveliness

than anything we know in reality. Rich as may
have been the beauty of the tea-house girl, O-Sen,
whom Harunobu loved and painted, and of the little
seller of cosmetics, O-Fuji, who appears many
times in his pictures, they were but the starting-
point, the exciting agency, from which Harunobu
passed on into a secret fanciful world of his own
to evoke his dream-maidens. Half of the charm of
these figures, such as the one in Plate 12, lies in this
unreal and unhuman impression they make; they
are not Japanese women or any women, but living
fairy-tales, butterfly creatures out of nowhere. All
that is joyous and playful in the Japanese spirit lifts
them on wings of fantasy into regions of universal
delight. They are the most fragrant flowers of
Japanese art.

It follows that Harunobu's subjects are almost
always light and trivial scenes—a girl playing with
a cat, a young man and a maiden walking amiably
together, young girls engaged in some delicate occu-
pation, or, as in Plate 13, pausing in pensive reverie.
A gentle joy pervades most of them, or at least a
gravity so light that it is nearer joy than melancholy.
Harunobu does not handle these scenes with any
especial insight into life; they are not windows
through which we may look and see the human souls
of the people he portrays. They are nothing more
than gay, pleasing moments—records of fortunate
hours—froth and foam over the real deeps of life.

Yet as the spectator allows the pure and delicate
atmosphere of one of these creations to enter his
spirit, he gradually becomes aware that not this

HARUNOBU: COURTESAN DETAINING A PASSING SAMURAI.
Size 11×8.  Signed *Harunobu ga.*

*Plate 14*

149

trivial scene, not this light episode, was Harunobu's real theme; his real theme was the great harmonics of colour and line.   Out of colour and line his immeasurable genius evoked lofty improvisations.   He dedicated the fervour of his passion and his vision to the creation of these orchestrations of tone, these modulated arabesques of contour.   Beyond his cheerful groups, beyond his felicitous arrangements, lies the history of his prodigious essay to impose his sense of beauty upon one section of chaos. Kurth is quite right when he calls him "the great virtuoso of colour."

Most of Harunobu's prints are of small size, almost square.   In this form his refinement found its most perfect expression.   If we would see an aspect of Harunobu that is of more impressive proportions, and realize that scope as well as daintiness was in him, we must turn to certain rare pillar-prints which were done chiefly in the years immediately preceding his untimely death.   Here dignity combines with grace, and an exalted sweep of composition adds nobility to that exquisite colour which here no less than in his small prints finds place.   Two of these pillar-prints, reproduced in Plate 15, may serve to illustrate this last phase of Harunobu's greatest triumph.

The first print is a soft grey and lavender study of a girl.   Within the long, narrow space, against a background of cool unbroken grey, rises the figure, whose bent, pensive head looks down at the ball she is dangling before a cat at her feet.   Her hair, a mass of strong black against the clear grey background, is drawn in a conventionalized manner that

is perhaps the noblest formula ever devised for the
painting of hair—as pure of line as a Greek helmet.
Drooping from her slender shoulders fall robes whose
slow curves seem moulded by the touch of faint and
gentle airs that breathe around her.  The long drapery
is interwoven with hints of mauve melting into rose—
more like ghosts of the palette than colours—and
touches of translucent salmon and amber and grey
are repeated like an arabesque of lights down the
folds.  The folds sweep in great restful curves like
those of vines hanging in festoons from summer
branches.  At the girl's girdle a strong note of dull
green strikes like a bass chord across the composition;
and smaller spots of the same colour carry this motive
diminishingly down to the bottom of the picture.

It is a sentiment, an emotion, a dream—as much
an abstraction as a musical composition.  In the lines
of the dress, in the poise of the head, in the limpid
tones of the whole picture, is secreted the dwell-
ing-place of a peace, a solemnity, an awe never
to be forgotten.  It is reminiscent of the grandeur
of the Primitives, but more etherialized; and there
lingers about it still, persisting from earlier times,
the penumbra of that hierarchal purity and spirituality
peculiar to archaic art.  Like those strange and
memorable archaic statues of the Priestesses in the
Museum of the Akropolis at Athens, like the fres-
coes of Giotto at Assisi, it holds the secret of an
untainted beauty that is lost to later artists.

The second pillar-print is one which, following the
opinion of Professor Fenollosa and Mr. Gookin, may
be regarded as one of the supreme triumphs of

HARUNOBU: SHIRAI GOM-
PACHI DISGUISED AS A
KOMUSO.

Size 27×4½.
Signed *Suzuki Harunobu ga.*

*Plate 15*

HARUNOBU: GIRL
PLAYING WITH
KITTEN.

Size 26×4½.
Signed *Suzuki Harunobu ga.*

Harunobu's career, and one of the greatest prints we know. It represents Shirai Gompachi, the white-robed lover of the beautiful Komurasaki, wandering in disguise with the basket-hat and flute of a *komuso* or dishonoured Samurai. There is no background; against the clear white paper the long lines of the tall figure flow in curves of jet black and purple-grey, with here and there lights of orange and white. By a simplicity of selection that is more than Greek, Harunobu has woven from these few curves an effect that is like an incantation. It has in it the power to reach into the secret storehouses of the spectator's emotion and awaken echoes from those intimations of eternal perfection which haunt every heart. Fenollosa writes: " There is something unearthly about its line themes, orchestrated in black and ghost-tints, which lifts one to the infinities of Beethoven's purest melodies. The dreamy clarinet-player seems to droop and melt away into regions of sublimity where no earthly ear shall follow his dying chords. Thus indeed we are glad at last to have Harunobu pass, transfigured, from our vision."

*Pillar Print by Harunobu.*

    From an infinite distance, the ghostly music !
Few and slender the tones, of delicate silver,
As stars are broidered on the veil of evening. . . .

    He passes. by, the flute and the dreaming player—
Slow are his steps, his eyes are gravely downcast ;
His pale robes sway in long folds with his passing.

    Out of the infinite distance, a ghostly music
Returns—in slender tones of delicate silver,
As stars are broidered on the veil of evening.

Certain puzzles for the collector and student arise in connection with Harunobu.

This is the first knotty point. Shiba Kokan, a contemporary artist who outlived Harunobu by forty-eight years, is obscurely connected with Harunobu's work. " Look out when you buy Harunobu prints! " he writes in his memoirs, published long after his death. " A great portion of the most popular ones are skilfully forged, and the forger was I, Shiba Kokan ! " This warning holds good to-day, and in many cases no one can say with confidence whether certain sheets are by Shiba Kokan or Harunobu. Kokan claims, in particular, to have been the author of those with transparent draperies, those done in the Chinese manner, and those in which snow on bamboos is rendered by embossing without outline blocks. All these and other characteristic beauties of Harunobu's work he would annex, and it is doubtful if we shall ever know whether he is the greatest liar or the greatest forger in history. Probably his statements must be regarded as partly true. Until we know, however, every print signed Harunobu is suspect; for if Shiba Kokan could deceive the public of that day, we shall not be likely to detect his forgeries. There is only one consolation for the collector : if the prints of Shiba Kokan, signed Harunobu, are as beautiful as those of Harunobu, then not the collector is the sufferer, but only the unfortunate person who tries to write an accurate account of this hopeless entanglement.

Other forgers, contemporaneous or slightly later, probably took advantage of Harunobu's popularity :

coarse reprints from recut blocks turn up frequently in the market; and, worst of all, very fine modern forgeries and imitations of his work abound. These last two classes are the only ones that need cause the collector anxiety; they should of course be guarded against with the utmost care, for they are quite worthless. Their impure and muddy colours generally betray them to the practised eye. No means of detecting them is safe for the inexperienced amateur except a minute comparison with an unquestioned original impression of the same print. On the other hand, the contemporaneous forgeries, if beautiful, are no inconsiderable treasures.

The name Kyosen furnishes another puzzle. It is signed to prints unmistakably by Harunobu, to prints unmistakably not by him, and to prints which he also signs. The solution seems to be that Kyosen is simply the name of the printer or engraver who did work for Harunobu and for other designers. Kyosen himself sometimes designed prints, but in such cases he signed distinctly as artist. The signature Kyosen does not, therefore, indicate a separate artist, and its presence on Harunobu's prints need not cause doubts as to Harunobu's authorship. Senga, a printer, and Takahashi Gyokushi and Takahashi Rosen, engravers, also signed certain of Harunobu's prints.

KYOSEN.

A further difficulty arises in the relation of Harunobu to Koriusai, an artist whom we shall

soon treat by himself. At times his work comes
so close to Harunobu's style that earlier authorities
believed his name to be merely a later signature of
Harunobu. This position is now entirely discredited,
and it is agreed that Koriusai was a distinct person,
a friend and successor of Harunobu. But it is not so
sure that Koriusai may not have signed certain of his
own designs with Harunobu's name after Harunobu's
death ; the striking resemblances of some such sheets
to Koriusai's work makes one unwilling to regard
the relation between the two as settled. In the case
of certain unsigned prints, it is impossible to determine with assurance which of the two was the
creator. As a rule, however, the colour-schemes of
the two are totally different, Koriusai running
characteristically to schemes in which blue and
orange are dominant. Dr. Kurth seems to think
it barely possible that prints signed " Koriu " may
be by Harunobu ; but this theory is untenable,
both because the internal evidence of the prints is
against it, several of Koriusai's most characteristic
prints being thus signed, and because of the difficulty
of believing that Harunobu, the greatest of living
Ukioye artists, should at the height of his fame have
signed to his work the name of a younger and less
noted contemporary.

Those prints in the Harunobu manner which are
unsigned and unsealed also offer perplexities, since
we must look entirely to internal evidence to discover
whether they are by Harunobu.

Harunobu's work is among the most highly prized
in the whole list. The great collections have many

of his prints, but in the market one finds the fine
ones to be limited in number.   In his case, even
more than in the case of other artists, perfect condition is a vital requirement.   For, in the process of
fading, his prints lose that delicate colour-orchestra-
tion which is their supreme glory.   The same changes
in tone that would hardly detract from the beauty
of a fine Kiyomitsu might easily rob a fine Harunobu
of most of its significance.   If one has once seen the
copies in such collections as that of Mr. Frederick
W. Gookin, of Chicago, Mr. Charles H. Chandler, of
Evanston, Messrs. William S. Spaulding and John
T. Spaulding, of Boston, or Mr. Howard Mansfield
of New York, one loses all interest in the battered
riff-raff of the dealers' counters.

### KORIUSAI.

*Koriusai speaks.*

Let whoso will take sheets as wide
As some great wrestler's mountain-back
    Space cannot hide
        His lack.

Take thou the panel, being strong.
'Tis as a girl's arm fashioned right—
    As slender and divinely long
        And white.

That tall and narrow icy space
Gives scope for all the brush beseems.
    And who shall ask a wider place
        For dreams?

It is an isle amid the tide—
A chink wherethrough shines one lone star—
    A cell where calms of heaven hide
        Afar.

One chosen curve of beauty wooed
From out the harsh chaotic world
Shall there in solitude
Be furled.

The narrow door shall be so strait
Life cannot vex, with troubled din,
Beauty, beyond that secret gate
Shut in.

Lo! I will draw two lovers there,
Alone amid their April hours,
With lines as drooping and as fair
As flowers.

I will make Spring to circle them
Like a faint aureole of delight.
Their luminous youth and joy shall stem
The night.

And men shall say : Behold ! he chose,
From Time's wild welter round him strown,
This hour ; and paid for its repose
His own.

Koriusai's life is shrouded in those mists prevalent
in the cases of most Ukioye artists. It is known that
he was a Samurai, or feudal retainer of knightly rank;
upon the death of his master, Tsuchiya, he became,
as was the custom, a ronin—that is, a retainer without a lord—and established himself near the picturesque Ryogoku Bridge in Yedo as a painter.  He
originally used the name Haruhiro.  Shigenaga was
his first teacher, Harunobu his second ; his work can
safely be dated between 1770 and 1781.  By the end
of this period Kiyonaga was beginning to advance
achievements that eclipsed Koriusai's.  As Fenollosa
points out, it was Koriusai's misfortune to collide
with Harunobu at the beginning and with Kiyonaga

KORIUSAI: MOTHER AND
BOY.
Size 28×4½. Signed *Koriusai ga.*

KORIUSAI: TWO LOVERS IN
THE FIELDS—SPRING
CUCKOO.
Size 27×4½. Signed *Koriusai ga.*

*Plate 16*

161

at the end of his career; could we obliterate those two, we might think of Koriusai as "the most beautiful Ukioye designer."

Koriusai was already working in Harunobu's manner at the time of the master's death; and afterward he continued Harunobu's experiments. His characteristic device in colour is the predominance of a strong orange pigment, based on lead, which when originally applied had the utmost brilliance, but which now is frequently changed by chemical decomposition into a rich mottled black. Combining this orange with a blue of his own devising, he obtained novel and striking effects.

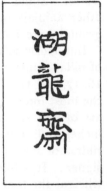

KORIUSAI.

Koriusai's small prints have often a beauty almost equal to Harunobu's, but they lack individuality of invention. They never surpass the triumphs of the older master in this form. Koriusai seldom can catch Harunobu's perfect grace and repose, his luminous atmosphere and subtle colour. But in his large sheets he produced a few compositions whose elaborate magnificence is a new and individual achievement. The styles in hair-dressing which came into vogue at this time were no small element in enabling him to create his stately figures; the wide lines of the coiffure, more solid and massive than in Harunobu's day, lent itself admirably to strong decorative treatment. In a series of large sheets called "Designs of Spring

Greenery," each picture representing an Oiran and her two or more young attendants, some of the prints are disfigured by the heaviness of the faces ; but others, from which this exaggeration is absent, are of almost unparalleled splendour in colour, even though somewhat monotonous in their repetitions. One of this type, in the Morse Collection, Evanston (described at No. 155 of Fenollosa's Ketcham Catalogue) is surely one of the greatest prints in the world. Some of Koriusai's designs of birds and other animals, occasionally printed with mica backgrounds, are admirable compositions.

But Koriusai's distinctive glory lies in the sphere of pillar-prints, of which five are reproduced in Plates 16, 17, and 18. This form of composition is one of the most interesting and exacting to be found in the art of any race ; the tall sheet, generally about 28 inches high and only 5 inches wide, furnishes a mere ribbon of space that taxes all the resources of a designer. It is like a Greek frieze placed on end ; but whereas the frieze gives space for a multitude of processional figures, and is essentially a stage for the depiction of a social pageant, this slim panel demands the exclusion of all but a few significant lines. In this particular it is the finest of art-forms. It exacts the quintessence of selection—one narrow glimpse of some cross-section of life. Its limitations are like those of the lyric, requiring a concentrated and finely chosen vision.

The shape was first devised by Okumura Masanobu as a modification of the wider and shorter sheets commonly used by the Primitives for their large pictures.

KORIUSAI: TWO LADIES.　　KORIUSAI: A GAME OF TAG.

Size 29×5.　Signed *Koriusai ga.*　Size 26×5.　Signed *Koriusai ga.*

Plate 17

As is often the case in the evolution of a fine art-form, it was not Masanobu's mere whim, but structural exigencies, that prompted the invention, the need being to provide long narrow pictures that could be hung upon the square wooden pillar of the Japanese house. Kiyomitsu and Toyonobu used this shape admirably ; and the final and most perfect form for its dimensions was fixed and brought into general use by Harunobu. It became a favourite shape among the greatest of the later artists ; and no small number of their supreme achievements are in this form. To the modern European eye, no other seems so distinctively characteristic of the special Japanese genius.

Pillar-prints are almost invariably works of the first importance—*pièces de résistance,* deliberate and studied productions, representing the best effort and highest powers of the artist. For they were intended to be mounted and rolled, like *kakemono* ; and the artist could therefore foresee for them a degree of attention that he could hardly expect in the case of the loose square sheets. The peculiar shape is in itself so interesting and beautiful, and so ringing a challenge to the powers of the designer, that in many cases the best work of the artist is to be found only in this form.

Pillar-prints are to-day far rarer than prints of the square variety. They were probably produced in editions of smaller numbers than the square prints ; and, further, the use to which they were put as hanging pictures exposed them to hazardous vicissitudes and generally resulted in eventual destruction.

Koriusai's variations on the limited themes whose treatment is possible in this narrow space display daring, originality, and power of concentrated selection. He is the supreme master of the pillar-print; no one else has produced so many fine ones, and practically all his finest work is in this form. The infinite variety of his designs and the fertility of his invention make a series of his pillar-prints one of the most absorbing features of a fine collection. In one print (Plate 17), he dashes the intense black line of a screen down through the middle of his picture and sets the delicate eddies of a child's and a young girl's garments playing around its base. In a second (Plate 18), a girl in robes of gorgeous colour stands like a calm peacock, with glowing orange combs alight in her hair; while in a third (Plate 16), the whole space waves and sings with the forms of grasses, a flying cuckoo, and a maiden carried in the arms of her lover through fields of spring. And in a fourth (Plate 17), he draws the figures of two women, one behind and a little above the other, the one in the background luminous with soft neutral tints, the one in the foreground robed in a black whose intensity cuts sharply through the otherwise monotonous sweetness of the picture. To the grace of Harunobu, Koriusai has here added a vigour all his own, and a richness surpassing that of his teacher.

To-day Koriusai's small prints are rather rare, as are also the birds and the large-size sheets. His pillar-prints, which are his greatest works, were produced in such numbers that, contrary to the rule that applies to the pillar-prints of all other designers,

SHIGEMASA: TWO LADIES.

Size 28½×5.
Unsigned.

KORIUSAI: A COURTESAN.

Size 27×4½.
Signed *Koriusai ga.*

*Plate 18*

a good many of them have survived. It is still possible to secure examples that are among the foremost of all print treasures.

### OTHER FOLLOWERS OF HARUNOBU.

SUSUKI HARUSHIGE is reported to have been the son and pupil of Harunobu. The few prints of his that are known have a grace of line that might well be a son's heritage, if such things were inheritable. The unholy rascal Shiba Kokan alleges that this name was one which he himself used, as well as Harunobu's; it is reported, on the other hand, that it is merely Koriusai's early name. It is probable that Kokan's statement must be believed.

HARUSHIGE.

SHIBA KOKAN has already been mentioned as the forger of Harunobu's work. His ability needs no further recommendation when we admit that we cannot with certainty tell his prints from Harunobu's. This is his chief title to fame. He was born in 1747 and died in 1818. During his life he signed many names to his work and attempted many manners. From the Dutch at Nagasaki he learned something of the rules of European perspective, and tried, in the eighties, with success but without much beauty, to carry them over into Japanese art. In addition, he introduced shadows into some of his compositions— a device alien to the whole spirit of Chinese and Japanese painting. He was the first Japanese artist

to attempt copper-plate engraving.    Queer renderings
of European scenes by him remain to us.    In a hundred different spheres of art, invention, and speculation
he tried his hand.    His intellectual curiosity in every
field reminds one of Leonardo da Vinci.    He remains
one of the most interesting and puzzling figures of his
time—an adventurer, a restless experimenter, a forger
and a man of extraordinary though chaotic genius.

A poem written when he was dying has a curious
vibrancy : "Kokan now dies, for he is very old ; to
the passing world he leaves a picture of the world
that passes."

KOMAI YOSHINOBU did work in the style of
Harunobu during the seventies.    He furnishes
another example of the obscurity that covers so
much of Japanese print history ; for it is not known
whether he was an independent artist. or identical
with Yamamoto Yoshinobu, who produced two-colour
prints in the fifties, or worse yet, an early signature
of Koriusai.    The first theory is the most probable.

MASUNOBU.

His work is rare, beautiful in
colour, and well worthy of further
research.

MASUNOBU, the second of that
name, whose work, in clear, delicate colour and charming arrangement, generally follows Harunobu's
closely, is also not definitely
located.    He appears to have been
originally a pupil of Shigenobu
and Shigenaga.    Most writers erroneously regard him
as the same man who, under the name of Sanseido

Tanaka Masunobu, produced two-colour prints in the forties, and hand coloured prints still earlier.

One of the Second Masunobu's pillar-prints, representing a girl with an open umbrella jumping from a balcony to meet a waiting lover, has a unique and most charming individuality of poise and colouring. His pillar-prints, of which about ten are known, are particularly fine.

UJIMASA, KAMEGAKI HŌRIU, MURANOBU, TACHIBANA MINKO, BANTO, CHIRYU, RYUSHI, KISEN, and SUIYO are rare men who worked contemporaneously with Harunobu. The Hayashi Catalogue also names SHOHA, SOAN, SOGIKU, KOGAN and SEIKO.

KUNINOBU is an artist of extreme rarity, whose few surviving prints show distinction of line, based on the Harunobu manner. His work, done about 1775, stands out from the work of Harunobu's horde of followers; he was evidently a noteworthy artist, of whom one wishes we knew more.

FUJINOBU worked in the manner of Harunobu in the early seventies. His output was small, and little of his work survives. It may be that he was the same individual as Yamamoto Fujinobu, who has already been mentioned as Shigenaga's pupil.

KOMATSUKEN is a name signed to certain calendar-prints for the year 1765. The style is greatly like Harunobu's. His name may also be read *Shoshoken*. Mr. Gookin thinks him to be identical with Fusanobu, who has been previously mentioned.

HARUTSUGU and SUSUKI HARUJI, said by some to be the same person, produced a few pleasing prints about 1770.

## SHUNSHO.

*Portrait of an Actor in Tragic Rôle.*

His soul is a sword;
His sword with the spirit's breath
Is bathed of its terrible lord,
In whose eyes is death.

And the massive control,
And the lighted implacable eye
Leash a fierce and exalted soul
Of dark destiny.

.     .     .     .     .

With the strength of the hills—
Kiso's iron mountains of snow—
He waits : time brings and fulfills
The hour for the blow.

He waits ; and the white
Full robes round his shoulders sway,
With woof of pale orange alight,
Pale green, pale grey.

Like a falcon, flown
To bleak mid-regions of sky,
He poises.   One image alone
Holds his sinister eye—

A vision, a prey
Towards which he shall soon be hurled—
And his fury shall darken the day,
And his joy, the world.

.     .     .     .     .

A music enfolds him
Like the thunders that are poured
Across heaven ; it holds him
With the song of the sword.

It enthrals, it inspires,
And its zenith shall be
Lightning of unleashed desires
Crashing along the sea.

SHUNSHO: AN ACTOR OF THE ICHIKAWA SCHOOL
IN TRAGIC ROLE.

Size 12×6.  Signed *Shunsho ga.*

*Plate 19*

Those actor-types which Harunobu and his school so scornfully cast aside became the chosen speciality of the greatest of his rivals and contemporaries, Katsukawa Shunsho. As one examines sheet after sheet of Shunsho's theatrical prints, Harunobu's contemptuous words concerning "this vulgar herd," the actors, lose their significance ; for here pass in gorgeous procession a series of lofty, intense, and unforgettable figures charged with the quintessence of heroic force.

The designer of these prints was born in 1726 and died about 1792 —some authorities say 1790. His period of greatest activity covered the years 1765 to 1780, thus including the working periods of both Harunobu and Koriusai, and ending as Koriusai's did when in the eighties Kiyonaga's star rose blindingly. He lived for a while at the house of his publisher, Hayashi ; sometimes in his early work he used in place of a signature a seal shaped like a small covered jar with handles, on which Hayashi's name is inscribed.

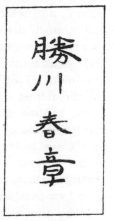

KATSUKAWA
SHUNSHO.

The legend is that he was too poor to own a seal in the early days of his struggle and so borrowed that of his landlord!

Shunsho had no antecedent teachers among the print-designers. He sprang instead from a school of painters who did not design for prints. These, headed by Choshun and his son Katsukawa Shunsui,

had since 1700 been producing rich paintings of
women in elaborate drapery. The Buckinghain.
Collection contains one print by Shunsui, but it is
an almost unique rarity. Shunsho, by a curious
shift in the stream of art history, not only took up
prints, but even took up the department of prints
least in line with the tendencies of his own school,
the department of actor-representation, which was
the speciality of Kiyomitsu and the old Torii
School, and which Harunobu's popular innovations
had almost driven out of fashion. To this work
Shunsho brought the new technique of Harunobu
and great native individuality; and with the fresh
armament of full colour he defended magnificently
the threatened stronghold of actor-prints. His popularity became enormous. He grew quickly to the
stature of one of the great and far-reaching powers
in Ukioye history. Side by side with Harunobu, he
in his separate field executed year by year actor-
portraits which by their vigour of line and brilliancy
of colour-combination take a place as high as that
held by the works of his rival.

No contrast could be more striking than that
between them. The one is all grace, the other all
force ; the one loves to linger in quiet gardens, the
other drags us up to the icy heights of tragic crisis.
Shunsho's sense of dramatic composition was keen ;
and, as we see in Plate 19, his ferocious actor-faces
peer out with a vivid menace, his tense actor-limbs
shake with a concentrated and imprisoned fury not
the less impressive because of its intentional exaggeration. They have not Harunobu's unreality of

SHUNSHO: THE ACTOR NAKAMURA MATSUYE AS
A WOMAN IN WHITE.

Size 11×5½.  Unsigned.

*Plate 20*

179

perfect grace, but the utterly different super-reality of magnified passion. In repose they are like statues; in action they have the vigour of those natural forces—waves, river currents, storms of thunder—which, as in the Shunsho print reproduced on the cover of this volume, so often form their backgrounds.

Shunsho's figures of women—or rather his figures of men acting the parts of women, according to the invariable custom of the Japanese stage at this time —are less violent, but often as tense. Two of these appear in Plates 20 and 21. In long sweeping robes of brilliant dye they move with the step of a Clytemnestra, or poise in strange attitudes of arrested motion not unworthy of an Antigone. All his figures are dynamic—the storehouses of volcanic forces whose existence he suggests by restless line-conflicts.

Shunsho's predecessors in actor representation had never equalled the intensity of these figures and faces. Shunsho tears the heart out of a rôle and holds it up for us to see. He gives the passion of the actor such expression as would have been impossible to Kiyonobu, twisting the face into a distorted and grandiose mask beside which the faces of the Primitives seem wooden and meaningless.

The spectator whose æsthetic sense embraces only a love of tranquillity will find no beauty in these disturbing faces and forms—unless perhaps the beauty of pure colour is enough to beguile him. It may well do this; few things have power to bring a richer sense of æsthetic satisfaction than a succession of fine Shunshos, in each one of which a new colour-arrangement unfolds new harmonies.

Shunsho's work includes a very great number of actor-prints in the narrow upright *hoso-ye* form and a few large square prints. He also issued a series of small illustrations for the " Ise Monogatari," an old romantic chronicle which furnished many favourite subjects to the artists. These are quiet in design and soft in colour ; to them the eye may turn for rest if wearied by the straining actors. In collaboration with Shigemasa he produced a set of ten small prints representing sericulture, which have considerable charm. In 1776 the same pair of artists brought out a series of book-illustrations called " Mirror of the Beauties of the Green Houses," representing groups of courtesans occupied with the various activities of daily life—in the street, the house, the garden, and the temple. This book has been called the most beautiful ever produced in Japan ; when one examines its chief rival, " The Mirror of the Beautiful Women of the Yoshiwara," by Kitao Masanobu, one need have no hesitancy in giving Shunsho's and Shigemasa's the first place. This means, very probably, the first place among the illustrated books of the world. Its pages, printed in rose, purple, brown, yellow, and grey, are rich and delicate. Sheets from all these books are often found mounted as separate prints. Shunsho's few known pillar-prints are generally magnificent.

Because of his enormous productiveness, Shunsho's work in *hoso-ye* form is common, frequently in fine condition. Most of the *hoso-ye* prints were originally

SHUNSHO: THE ACTOR NAKAMURA NOSHIO IN
FEMALE ROLE.

Size 12½×6. Signed *Shunsho ga*. Gookin Collection.

*Plate 21*

issued in joined groups of three; the groups are seldom found intact now. The grace of his women has made them more generally popular than his impressive men, and they are consequently harder to obtain. It must be noted that Shunsho's work is uneven, and that the majority of the pieces offered are either tame and uninteresting examples of potboiling or caricatures that lack the intensity which lifts certain of the artist's most grotesque figures to tragic heights. The matchless Shunsho collection of Mr. Frederick W. Gookin is full of such prints as rarely come into the market to-day. Occasionally the more distinguished ones are met with ; and they are treasures which the practised collector eagerly seizes. Fortunately print dealers are not, as a rule, conscious of the greatness of the difference, and they will frequently offer side by side a print that is merely one of Shunsho's commonest pieces of hack-work and a print that is one of the glories of the Ukioye School. On such occasions the collector has the pleasure of profiting by his own discrimination.

Shunsho's large square prints and pillar-prints are of extreme rarity.

### BUNCHO.

Connected by association with the school of Shunsho, yet lifted by his originality to a place quite apart from it, is the artist Ippitsusai Buncho. His master, a certain Ishikawa Kogen (or Yuki-moto) of the classical Kano School, seems to have meant little to him ; from the beginning of his production, about 1765, Shunsho's and Harunobu's influence chiefly guided him. He and Shunsho jointly published in 1770 three volumes of actor-portraits enclosed in fans. Little is known of his life except that he was originally a Samurai; he is said to have turned from his original master to the Ukioye School and to have led a life of dissipation until eventually his friends persuaded him to abandon such things and procured for him the honorary title of Hokyo. After this, we hear nothing of him. He died in 1796.

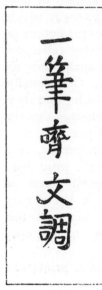

IPPITSUSAI BUNCHO.

Buncho's work attracts the observer with a charm different from that of any other Ukioye artist. A curious mannerism in his way of drawing faces and a fascinating perverse grace in the attitudes of his figures mark his prints. Practically all his work is in the *hoso-ye* form. His subjects are chiefly young male actors in the rôles of women. Harunobu's influence, manifest in Plate 22, brought him grace but not sweetness. There is an astringent quality in his work that prevents it from ever being serene. His figures, whose line-work is the apotheosis of suavity and studied refinement, are arched into slightly strained and tortured attitudes; complex forces seem to dominate them like unseen winds; consuming or delicate passions move obscurely

BUNCHO: COURTESAN AND HER ATTENDANT IN
SNOWSTORM.

Size 13×5½. Signed *Ippitsusai Buncho ga*.
Mansfield Collection.

*Plate 22*

through their limbs and faces. Their heads poise at unnatural angles as if consciously turning their indifferent eyes from the spectacle of common things toward a secret and hypnotizing world of their own. These alien beings haunt one; it seems as if they had some mystery to reveal, some disturbing wonder to communicate could one but make them speak.

Part of Buncho's strangeness lies in the fact that he seeks for his figures not a human but an abstract and geometrical grace. His famous print, often reproduced, of the actor Segawa Kikunojo as a lady in white carrying an orange umbrella beneath a willow-tree, is a study in the harmonics of pure line; to this end every other element of representation has been sacrificed. Line exists here not merely to bound a form but for its own inherent beauty. Buncho is the greatest of all masters of the geometry of lines and spaces; these have, as he arranges them, the inevitability and clarity of a mathematical demonstration.

His use of colour is equally notable and strange. By employing tints that are almost discords he produces arresting and fascinating effects. His combinations of orange and slaty grey, or dull red and slaty blue and pale yellow, or pink and purple, have an uncanny vibrancy that makes them stand out in one's memory.

Buncho's strangeness has a further aspect. There is in him an intangible spiritual abnormality. I am led to localize this in his portraits of the actor Segawa Kikunojo, and to imagine a curious relation between the two. Some of his portraits of this actor are the

flower of his work. In them appears a passionately
rarefied beauty ; they have an unusual pitch, like the
overstrained vibration of violin strings stirred by
some heavy blow. Segawa Kikunojo was the foremost woman-impersonator of his time. His grace in
such rôles is attested by prints from the hands of
many artists ; but none rise to the unearthly beauty
of Buncho's. Even if we knew nothing of the life of
the Japanese stage at this time, or of the custom of
actors like Segawa Kikunojo to dress and live like
women when off the stage, we might still be put on
inquiry by the peculiar ethereal quality of some of
these portraits. For art whose initial impulse lies
in morbid regions often flies into regions of the most
disembodied spirituality for expression. Flowers of
the morass frequently have a pale delicacy that is
alien to the flowers of the field.

It is, however, with a confession of fancifulness
that I reconstruct the following story to account for
Buncho. He, a Samurai, was driven by keen artistic
sensibility to the study of painting under a classical
master. From this studio he was lured by the glitter
and glamour of Ukioye into the world of prints and
actors, and sank into a slough of dissipation above
which gleamed the balefully beautiful star of Segawa
Kikunojo. Haunted by a perverse susceptibility,
his tense-strung nerves vibrated at that morbid
touch into notes of such disembodied sweetness as
the world has scarcely known elsewhere ; and at last
he passed into retirement and death, still the puppet
of a disturbing illusion. He was an unbalanced
temperament, a dreamer of keen and attenuated

SHUNYEI: AN ACTOR.
Grey background. Size 14×9½. Signed *Shunyei ga.*

Plate 23

beauty that has nothing in common with the normal wholesome life of earth.

His prints are exceedingly rare ; many a good collection possesses not a single fine specimen of his work.  I had never seen or heard of a pillar-print by him until very recently ; but lately an interesting one has been found in Japan.

## SHUNYEI.

Shunsho's vigorous style had many followers, among whom Shunyei is commonly regarded as the most important.  He was born in 1767, and lived until 1819.  His teacher Shunsho's manner dominated his work from his earliest years, though some late sheets exist in which he followed Kiyonaga.  It is believed that originally he used the name Shunjo ; fine work is extant with that signature.  He had many pupils, and was himself an able painter ; but his ordinary work is largely derivative.  At times, however, his *hoso-ye* actor-prints achieve an effect of great power by the use of large masses of colour. He had a certain sharpness of observation—a certain knack of catching in his portraits the peculiarities of his models, that produces an effect less dignified but more vivid than Shunsho's.  A sense of humour glimmers through his rendering of some of these keenly drawn and intimately characterized actor-faces.  Unmistakable as may be

SHUNYEI.

the features of a Danjuro or a Hanshiro drawn
by Shunsho, one nevertheless feels that the personality of the actor has been largely dominated
by Shunsho's supreme interest in the passion or
terror of the rôle ; and though he pictured the face
of the actor, the spirit which he sought was
wholly the spirit of the part.  Shunyei, on the
other hand, often managed to retain the idiosyncrasies of the sitter and his peculiar spiritual
flavour ; and though his works are not often as
beautiful as Shunsho's, they are frequently more
human.  On the whole, we may say that Shunsho created generalized types, Shunyei reproduced
observed individuals.

Shunyei produced, besides the actors in *hoso-ye*
form by which he is best known, a few large
heads and full-length portraits of actors marked
by a strength of drawing and a breadth of characterization different from his usual work.  One
of these is reproduced in Plate 23.  On a grey
background, this powerfully designed figure stands
out with gigantic simplicity in masses of dull
colour.  The prints of this rare type are perhaps
Shunyei's best.  Beside them must rank the large
actor-heads, interesting to the collector because of
their relation to the work of another great artist,
Sharaku.  It is still uncertain whether Sharaku
or Shunyei was the inventor of this type of
large bust-portrait.  Dr. Kurth assumes, for the
greater glory of Sharaku, that he was the precursor ; but the question cannot be regarded as
settled.

SHUNKO: THE ACTOR ISHIKAWA MONNOSUKE
IN CHARACTER.

Size 13×9.   Unsigned, but stamped with Jar Seal.

*Plate 24*

## SHUNKO.

The equal of Shunyei among Shunsho's other
pupils is to be found in Katsukawa Shunko. He
was the spiritual image of his master, except that
he had not his master's full command of terror. His
figures, as in Plate 24, poise or sway with gentler
emotions; as a rule, they are agreeable rather than
impressive. One comes to recognize him frequently
by the peculiar suavity of his designs. It is true
that he sometimes approaches very near to Shunsho's
power; but this is less charac-
teristic and less interesting than
his quieter manner. It is un-
necessary to treat of him at
great length, for most of his work
is of a type whose main qualities
have been treated fully under
Shunsho. It is not known when
Shunko was born; he died in
1827.

SHUNKO.

It may be noted that he some-
times sealed his prints instead of signing them, using
a jar-shaped seal much like that which Shunsho had
made famous.

In the Spaulding Collection, Boston, is a remarkable full-size triptych by Shunko, representing
a party of actors picnicking in the country.
The style shows it to be greatly influenced by
Kiyonaga; and the whole composition of this
beautiful piece is different from most of Shunsho's
work.

OTHER FOLLOWERS OF SHUNSHO AND HIS
SCHOOL.

SHUNRI was another pupil of Shunsho; he appears
to have been a competent designer, but no great figure.
SHUNTOKU, SHUNKI, SHUNKAKU, SHOYU, SHUNYEN,
SHUNKEN, and SHUNKYOKU may be described in
the same words. Each has perhaps produced a few
beautiful works, but their originality is not marked.

RANTOKUSAI SHUNDO, a gifted pupil of Shunsho,
has left work so rare that one cannot make any very
definite statement about him. His few known prints
are admirable. One suspects that this signature is
merely the early name cf some well-known artist.

SHUNSEI, SHUNRIN, SOBAI, and SHUNKIO are
later artists ; their importance is small.

SHUNTEI, "owing partly to illness and partly to
systematic indulgence in drink" (Strange), and
partly to complete lack of natural distinction, produced nothing of interest ; and his coarse battle-
scenes may be classed with the crude work characteristic of a later period. He worked chiefly
between 1800 and 1820.

KINCHO SEKIGA is said to have been a pupil of
Buncho.

SHUNKO II was a pupil of Shunyei. His name is
written in different characters from that of the first
Shunko. KICHOSAI SHUNKO also produced actor-
prints.

YUMISHO was a very rare pupil who adopted
Kiyonaga's style in line-work. The same may be
said of YENSHI, some of whose work is very beautiful ;

he appears to have come much under the influence of Yeishi. Several of his triptychs are fine.

### TOYOHARU.

Utagawa Toyoharu is a strangely equivocal figure in print history; his fame is great, but no surviving print of his, so far as I have been able to ascertain, is of a quality to justify fully his reputation. Born in 1733, he studied with Shigenaga and probably with Toyonobu, produced a limited number of prints in the sixties and seventies, withdrew from prints to painting when Kiyonaga's new style grew to splendour, and died in 1814. He is said to have been a sensitive and delicately strung individual who shrank from competition and worked obscurely. His best-known work is a series of twelve designs for the various months done in collaboration with Shunsho and Shigemasa; each print is divided diagonally into two scenes—a device of unfortunate and ingenious ugliness. The figures, however, have a certain delicate grace. His pillar-prints, which are rare, have considerable beauty.

UTAGAWA
TOYOHARU.

Toyoharu has been called a greater artist than Shunsho. It may be true, yet I am inclined to regard this view either as the result of his painting

and not his print-designing, or as part of a great
Toyoharu myth, for which the later success of his
pupils is responsible    Certain it is that of his surviving prints few are noteworthy, and that he was
greater as a painter and teacher than as a print-
designer.   We shall remember him more as the
instructor of Toyokuni and Toyohiro and as the
·precursor of Hiroshige than for any of his own
prints that remain to us.

As a figure-painter, he is known as the founder of
the Utagawa School.   As a landscape-painter, he
made successful use of European perspective, which
he probably learned from Dutch engravings, and
was perhaps the first Ukioye print-artist to return to
the habit of the older schools and treat landscape
not as a mere setting but as a thing by itself.   His
scenes are too stiff and too crowded with petty
details to lay any real claim to beauty.   He used
as the dominant note in many of them the orange
colour so dear to Koriusai ; but no pigment can well
be imagined that is less fitted for landscape-render-
ing.   Yet the historical importance of these prints
is great ; for they are, so to speak, the grandparents
of the marvellous landscapes of Hiroshige.

UTAGAWA TOYONOBU is believed by some authorities to have been merely Toyoharu's early name ;
others think him identical with Ishikawa Toyonobu ;
and still others regard him as an independent artist
who was a pupil of Ishikawa Toyonobu, his greater
namesake.   The few prints we have by him—I know
of less than half a dozen—are not sufficient to enable
one to form an opinion as to this.

TOYOMARU and TOYOHISA were among Toyoharu's pupils.

## SHIGEMASA.

Kitao Shigemasa may be called the great chameleon of the Ukioye School: a discriminating chameleon, who chose only the greatest artists of each decade from whom to take his changing hue. As M. Raymond Koechlin expresses it, "it was his destiny to reflect in his art the art of the most original of his contemporaries." Born about 1740, he lived until 1819. His teacher was Shigenaga; this master died not long after Shigemasa commenced work with him. Thus Shigemasa began painting early enough to be influenced by the last of the Primitives; and his first prints, dating from about 1764, are graceful three-colour renderings of actor-themes in the manner of Kiyomitsu, and more brutal ones in the manner of Kiyo-masu. With the rise of Harunobu and the perfection of polychrome printing, Shigemasa turned to that style; later he followed Koriusai, in whose manner he produced some wonderfully beautiful large sheets of women and some fine pillar-prints. Still later he followed the style of Shunsho. Together with this artist he produced in 1786 a set of ten small sheets representing the various stages of sericulture, in which he surpasses his collaborator. The same two artists had

KITAO SHIGEMASA.

earlier collaborated, in 1776, to produce the famous
illustrated book "Mirror of the Beauties of the
Green Houses." These illustrations are not signed ;
but comparing them with Shigemasa's portion of the
sericulture series, which are signed separately by the
two artists, we may well believe that a large part of
the peculiar grace of the "Green Houses" is
Shigemasa's and not Shunsho's contribution. With
Shunsho and Toyoharu, he collaborated in a series of
designs for the twelve months, of which I have
already spoken under Toyoharu. Like so many
other artists of this period, Shigemasa gradually
withdrew from work in the eighties before the blaze
of Kiyonaga's glory. Kiyonaga himself was perhaps
influenced by the older artist.

Shigemasa's draughtsmanship is the one quality
that marks him through all his changes ; from first to
last, it is superb. With a fine firmness and ease he
produces, as in Plate 18, designs in which restraint
combines with great expressiveness. His faces have
repose and distinction ; his draperies are drawn with
notable simplicity and dignity ; his cool and quiet
colour is admirable. Through all his styles runs a
fastidious delicacy of feeling, and what Fenollosa
terms "an even mastery." He never attempted the
impossible or strained towards the unattainable ; all
his work has the stamp of a calmly working, reserved,
confident artist. The deliberate, flawless craftsman-
ship of his works places him beside the greatest.

Considering the length of his career, he produced
surprisingly little work ; important prints by him are
now rarer than those of any other artist of this

period. His pillar-prints, which are particularly fine, have been for many years proverbially few. As a rule only his earlier prints are signed. His surimono are, however, generally signed with the brush-name Kosuisai. Sheets from his numerous books are often mounted as separate prints. Collectors differ in their opinions as to whether it is advisable thus to take to pieces the sheets of a bound volume, such as the " Green Houses." Any such act, in dealing with art treasures, should be approached only after careful consideration ; but it seems in this case a desirable method of preserving and exhibiting what are, after all, wholly separate pictures.

# V

# THE THIRD
PERIOD:
KIYONAGA
AND HIS
FOLLOWERS

FROM THE
MATURITY OF KIYONAGA
TO HIS RETIREMENT
(1780 1790)

# CHAPTER V

## THE THIRD PERIOD: KIYONAGA AND HIS FOLLOWERS

### From the Maturity of Kiyonaga to his Retirement (1780-1790).

WITH the fully developed and complex technique which had been brought to perfection by the time of Harunobu's death, the colour-print took on a new richness of expression and reached its culmination in the Third Period.

Generalizations attempting to define the difference between the work of this and the preceding periods are perilous ; but we shall perhaps not be venturing too dangerously if we summarize the change of attitude as a step toward naturalism combined with a deepening of ideal significance.

In the period of the Primitives the artistic impulse was almost wholly one of decoration—an attempt to express in line and colour the great themes of design that stirred within the brain of the artist. The Primitives were inspired by what Von Seidlitz calls the desire of " presenting single characteristic motives of movement." Their creations had no relation to observed fact or to an exact rendering of

Nature ; they were the shadows of lofty dreams of form projected by the luminous spirit of the artist against the wall of space.

The designs of the Second Period, though hardly more realistic than those of the First, were nevertheless nearer life. The delights and passions of real men, even though fancifully regarded, coloured the conception of the artist as he approached his work ; so that we find in Harunobu the exquisite joys, in Shunsho the terrific revolts, and in Buncho the supersensible longings of the heart. Yet it is all symbolistic, all fictional, and nothing real is portrayed ; the sharply limited world of these prints is a world of imagination from which no paths of communication open to regions of everyday. The perception of these artists did not enter into and interpret the seen earth ; absorbed in the creation of a personal dream, it imposed its arbitrary categories upon objects from without, and had little respect for their intrinsic beauty. With magic incantations, the designer shattered the forms of the real world to bits and whimsically remoulded them nearer to the heart's desire. This attitude—a mixture of adolescence, playfulness, and vision—may be described by the phrase " naïvely imaginative."

The decorative impulse of the Primitives and the naïvely imaginative impulse of the Early Polychrome masters changed in the Third Period to a different variety of inspiration—the naturalistic and interpretive. By naturalistic and interpretive, I mean the attempt to seize a number of detached elements of observed life and weave them into a design that reports not only the idiosyncrasies of the artist, but also some sense of the deep nature of the elements themselves. The artists of this period, while mastering the decorative impulse of the Primitives and the imaginative freedom of the Early Polychrome masters, found reality more interesting and more worthy of faithful attention than did their pre decessors. Buncho flew off at a tangent to life on the wings of geometrical design, but Shuncho lingers observant among beautiful women in quiet gardens: Harunobu abandoned the real world for his harmonious dreams of colour, but Kiyonaga weaves into harmonies the perfect forms which his creative imagination evokes from the imperfect forms of actual men.

The earlier artists had hinted at landscape backgrounds; this period was the first to go farther and relate the landscape pictorially and spacially to the figures. The world of these designs is no longer the world of a lovely but private dream; we seem to enter a region as wide and free as life itself, inhabited by groups of superb and gracious figures that are as unforgettable as the Greek gods.

This period may be regarded as one of those few moments of equilibrium in the history of art when the spiritual dominance of the artist and the claims of real fact meet in a perfect balance. Toward one extreme lies fancifulness; toward the other extreme, realism; and in the centre, this narrow isle of quiet where the two forces join in harmony. Since man lives neither by bread alone nor by dreams alone, the moments when he reconciles the claims of his visions

with the facts he must face are the high peaks in his
history.  Mind and matter, hope and experience,
longing and limitation, for an instant combine in
a reconciliation that interprets and ennobles his
environment.  This is art's maturity, its fine and
perfect flower.

All these things are implicit in the prints of
Kiyonaga prime.  He who can take pleasure in the
Hermes of Praxiteles or the Fête Champêtre of
Giorgione will not find the meaning of Kiyonaga's
noble figures hard to read.

In examining the work of Kiyonaga and his contemporaries, it will be impossible to ignore the fact
that during this and the succeeding period the foremost artists found the chief themes for their designs
among the Oiran, or courtesans of the Yoshiwara.
Nor can we omit some consideration of the curious
position of these women.  Such an inquiry has not
the unpleasant features that a similar inquiry would
have were the scene Europe.  In the Japan of the
late eighteenth century the typical Oiran was no
creature of the mire, but a cultivated and splendid
figure whose mental charm was as great as her
physical attractiveness.  The poet and the painter,
the student and the young aristocrat, found in her no
unworthy companion ; and as she strides glowing
through the designs of Kiyonaga or Shuncho she
seems rather a beloved of the gods than a mistress
of men.

The Yoshiwara or licensed quarter of Yedo was
established in 1614 as part of the general Tokugawa
regime of orderliness and control : even by that date

**KIYONAGA: THE COURTESAN HANA-OJI WITH ATTENDANTS.**

One of a Series "Designs of Spring Greenery."
Size 15×10. Signed *Kiyonaga ga.*

*Plate 25*

the authorities had tired of the cruel and ugly chaos that prevails in these matters to-day in our cities. The name of the quarter was derived from the fact that it was located in the midst of an ancient "yoshiwara" or rush-moor. In 1657, after a fire that demolished all the buildings, the quarter was moved to a site half a mile north of the great Asakusa temple in the north-east outskirts of the city, where it remains to this day. Within this moated and walled enclosure about a quarter of a mile square, to which access was obtained through one great gate, stood orderly rows of large houses crowded close together. The front of each house was latticed; behind the bars appeared the splendidly clad inmates. These were of many grades and ranks; it is, as a rule, the highest class only that are represented in the prints.

The high-class Oiran was a notable personage. Her state was like that of a princess. Attendant upon her were customarily two small girls, called Kamuro, who acted as lady's-maids; and one or two older girls, called Shinzo, whose duties were those of a kind of maid-of-honour. Her attire, of a gorgeousness wholly different from the costume of the ordinary woman, bedecks her in many of the prints with truly royal splendour. Poets sang of her; artists painted her; the common people talked of her with the same frank and admiring interest that our populace bestows upon theatrical favourites. Moralless though her life was, it was not in any external sense degraded; she stood in the position in which have stood all the great courtesans of history.

The names of the more famous among the Oiran
have come down to us wrapped in glowing tradition.
Hana-ōgi of the House of Ōgi-ya, the most beautiful
and deeply loved courtesan of her time, moves immortal through the designs of Kiyonaga, Shuncho,
Yeishi, Utamaro, and their contemporaries. She was
a pupil of the poet Tōkō Genrin, and ranked as a
distinguished artist in both Chinese and Japanese
verse. At one time, obeying the dictates of a profound attachment, she dared all perils and fled from
the Yoshiwara with her lover. These facts, together
with the filial piety for which she was renowned,
doubtless augmented her romantic fame. Of her
beauty and lordly carriage the prints leave us no
doubt. Again and again we find lavished upon her
well-beloved figure all the resources of the greatest
artists. In Plate 25 she is the leading figure, with
her attendants grouped around her ; in Plate 32 she
stands beside a latticed window opening on to the
Sumida River, alone and meditative.

It is necessary for any one who would understand
the art of the period to put aside preconceived
notions and realize that these courtesan-portraits are
not representations of low gutter creatures, but that
they portray women of the highest degree of intellectual refinement who were in real life much like the
cultivated *hetairæ* of ancient Athens, the companions,
friends, and beloveds of Pericles and Plato.

And as one examines the few records which
Japanese writers have given to the Western world,
the conviction grows ever stronger that at this time,
when the free and romantic love of men and women

KIYONAGA: LADY WITH TWO ATTENDANTS.

One of a Series "Brocades of the East." Size 15×10. Signed *Kiyonaga ga.*
Gookin Collection.

*Plate 26*

was a thing alien to the businesslike Japanese marriage system, the one region where love as we understand it might flourish—the one region where might arise·those desperate attachments of heart for heart which we regard as heroic—was the isolated enclosure of the Yoshiwara. There no shrewd parents arranged the unwilling, blind match; there the hampered spirits of that day found freedom, however perilous; and there alone men and women, though surrounded by an atmosphere of sordid corruption, faced death as did the Tristram and Iseult of our legends, in the service of a passion more precious than life itself. . . . For the Oiran could turn lover.

## KIYONAGA.

*Festival Scene.*

What gods are these, reborn from gracious days
To fill our gardens with diviner mould
Than therein dwelling? What bright race of old
Revisits here one hour our mortal ways?
Serene, dispassionate, with lordly gaze
They move through this clear afternoon of gold,
Equal to life and all its deeps may hold,
Calm, spacious masters of the glimmering maze.

What gods are these? or godlike men? whom earth
Suffices, in a wisdom just and high
That not repines the boundaries of its birth
But fills its destined measure utterly—
Finding in mortal sweetness perfect worth,
Not yet grown homesick for the wastes of sky.

The reader will perhaps have noted how many artists of the preceding period withdrew toward the close of their careers from the field to which a new conqueror had come. This universal victor was

Kiyonaga. No other Ukioye artist ever so dominated his period. All earlier print-designers were
gradually driven into retirement by his colossal
success, and the majority of his contemporaries
adopted his style. In him all previously developed
resources met; after him began that long decline
which led through intermediate stages of such hauntingly lovely decadence to the final death of the art.
The Torii School now awoke from its quiescence,
and for the second and final time
assumed the dominance it had in
the days of Kiyonobu.

KIYONAGA.

Little is known of Kiyonaga's
life. Born in 1742, he worked as
a young man for a bookseller in
Yedo. He studied painting under
Kiyomitsu, became the fourth head
of the Torii School, produced the
most important portion of his work
between 1777 and 1790, and not long
after 1790 retired from any large
amount of further print-designing.
His death occurred in 1815.

Though Kiyonaga was a pupil of Kiyomitsu, little
of that artist's influence is visible in his work. It is
true that his earliest sheets, actors in *hoso-ye* form,
are precisely like Kiyomitsu's; but he appears to
have abandoned this style very quickly, and most
of his early actor-prints resemble Shunsho's more
than his master's. In certain of his early works
Harunobu's influence is evident; and the long-dead
Moronobu's manner of line-work sometimes appears.

KIYONAGA: THE COURTESAN SHIZUKA WITH ATTENDANTS IN
THE PEONY GARDEN AT ASAKUSA.

Left-hand sheet of a triptych.  Size 15×10.  Signed *Kiyonaga ga.*

*Plate 27*

From Masanobu he perhaps inherited the grand carriage of his women. Later, Shigemasa's style influenced him, and Koriusai had a marked effect upon his development. He absorbed inspiration from all these artists, gathering to himself the best in the heritage of the past, and then struck out with a boldness that is never bizarre, an originality that is never affected, into his own natural and masterful manner.

By about 1777 he had developed his distinctive style. Its most obvious characteristic lies in the new quality of the figures he depicts. His types perhaps grew out of those of Koriusai; but he combined with Koriusai's richness a monumental quality to find the equal of which we must go back to the Primitives. It is his union of the pre-Harunobu dignity with the Harunobu grace and colour, in a superb and easy synthesis of his own—a truly grand style—that has made him by common consent the foremost Ukioye artist.

The type of figure which Kiyonaga created is expressive of a more stable equilibrium of spiritual forces than any seen before. It embodies a normality of attitude characteristic of the great culminating periods of art. The primitive artist expresses himself in figures whose mannerisms and constraint suggest the limitations of his technique; the decadent artist, as we shall see later, pours his visions into figures of a slender langour and relaxation that parallel his own weariness and satiety; but the artist of the prime draws large-limbed, wholesome, magnificently normal figures as the symbols of his magnificently normal mind.

These figures of Kiyonaga's mature period are unforgettable creations. Tall and strong, moving with the unconscious and stately grace of superb animals, they carry the suggestion of a spiritual structure even more glorious than the structure of their bodies; and one looks upon them with a sentiment not unlike awe, as upon princesses of some land of the gods. Kiyonaga's perfect drawing, operating through a naturalistic yet highly imaginative convention, ennobles the forms he portrays as did the convention of the Greek sculptors; and he comes nearer to the Greek sentiment toward the nude than does any other Japanese artist except Toyonobu. His nudes themselves are not what I now refer to, but rather to that sense of bodily presence, that consciousness of the limbs beneath the draperies, which, as in Plate 28, one finds recurrently in his pictures. He keeps his draperies simple, denying himself the gorgeous brocades of birds and flowers which Koriusai used so richly. The garments he draws are beautiful; but he does not lose in their ornamentation the lines of the splendidly proportioned body beneath; muscles contract and limbs move under the fine folds; and our sense of the textiles is dominated by our sense of the organism within.

The movements, gestures, and attitudes of these figures are tranquil and strong; their forms are never melting or seductive, but always touched with a fine rigour. In one notable diptych, where a group of women and a seated man are gathered on the terrace of a tea-house overlooking the seashore,

KIYONAGA: TWO WOMEN AND A TEA-HOUSE WAITRESS BESIDE
THE SUMIDA RIVER.

One sheet of a triptych.  Size 15×10.  Signed *Kiyonaga ga*.
Gookin Collection.

*Plate 28*

vigour of spiritual sanity and refinement of pictorial composition touch the highest point reached in the whole course of the art. The harmonies of this particular design, "The Terrace by the Sea," embody the best and most characteristic powers of Kiyonaga.

We have never seen in bodily presence such people as Kiyonaga's. Yet, as Turner is reported to have said of his sunset, "don't you wish you had?" These figures are serene, supernatural, Olympian; fictional, just as Harunobu's are, but differing from his in that they interpret possible development and portray the human ideal, and do not lie apart from reality in a region of private vision.

Kiyonaga saw, as the greatest artists of mature epochs have always seen, that the fictions of personal fancy are not so interesting or so beautiful as imaginative renderings of reality. In so far as he respected reality he was a realist. Yet he was never the dupe of that realism which attempts to report photographically. In his renderings fact took a harmonious place alongside of those idealizations which were personal to him. Kiyonaga saw Nature with clear eyes, and on the solid foundation of observed fact he reared the noble structure of his vision of life —a vision in which the world is peopled by a race such as the human race ought to be.

This was Kiyonaga's primary contribution to Ukioye art. Consequent upon it he introduced certain important innovations.

We have seen how Harunobu, dreaming in colour and pushing to the farthest limits the refinements of technique in colour-printing, produced miniature jewelled improvisations that have never been equalled. Harunobu customarily elaborated every portion of his sheet with these inlayings of beautiful tones, enriching his figures with gauffrage and tinting his backgrounds of sky and water. He resembled a worker in enamels who must cover every inch of his surface with luminous hues.

But just as Harunobu toward the end of his life felt these effects to be only partially adequate, and turned to the larger world of pillar-prints—so from the beginning Kiyonaga found this jewelled delicacy to be incompatible with the scope that was the need of his specific genius. He discarded all those lovely tricks of the engraver and the printer which had been almost an end in themselves to Harunobu. He abstained from giving to his backgrounds Harunobu's exquisite neutral tones, feeling that they could only suffer by the addition of tint. He was no colour-dreamer, but a great harmonist of lines and spaces ; and the lofty skies and wide horizons that create distance behind his figures attest his wisdom.

Similarly he was unable to content himself with the flawless grace of line that Harunobu and Buncho had mastered. Either from the powerful and massive brush-strokes of Moronobu or from the even more expressive brushwork of Shigemasa, he derived a style that is one of his chief glories. No use of line was ever more virile than his. The brush seems to vibrate in his hand ; the strokes are instinct with life along every fraction of their length ; the line narrows, widens, swirls, breaks, and flows in perfect response

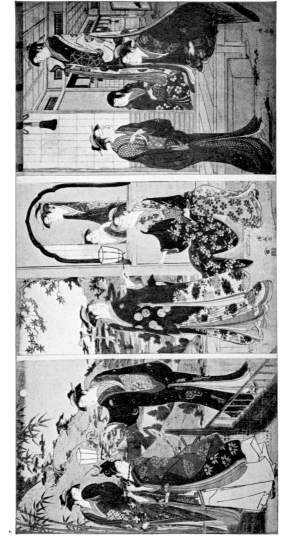

KIYONAGA: YOSHITSUNE SERENADING THE LADY JORURIHIME.

A triptych. Each sheet size 15×10. S'gned *Kiyonaga ga*. Spaulding Collection.

*Plate 29*

227

to the will of the mind behind it. So individual is Kiyonaga's touch that it would be possible for an expert to attribute to him a print of which only one square inch survived.

It is characteristic of Kiyonaga's style that he did not confine himself to the small square sheets used by Harunobu and the small oblong *hoso-ye* used by Shunsho. His most important work is in the form of the large full-size sheets which he adopted from Koriusai. In these he rose to a height unparalleled in Ukioye ; and M. Koechlin is quite right in esteeming Kiyonaga's sense of elaborate composition, here so impressively displayed, as his chief grandeur.

In the series of large sheets without backgrounds, " Designs of Spring Greenery," one of which is reproduced in Plate 25—Kiyonaga produced work not very different from that of his collaborator Koriusai. Only in certain sheets is there a harmonious grasp of the full possibilities of pictorial composition. But proceeding to other series, the gap widens. In the series " Present Day Beauties of the Yoshiwara," he advanced to his own unique field. Possibly he touched the supreme height in the great group " Brocades of the Customs of the East," which includes such well-known prints as the two salt-water carriers on the seashore, the three singers at the bath, the two ladies conversing with a flower-vendor, and the print reproduced in Plate 26.

From these prints Kiyonaga proceeded to still further combinations, devising compositions in which two, three, or even five sheets unite into one wide design. For the triptych we have Kiyonaga to thank.

The triptych was not, it is true, literally Kiyonaga's
invention; many artists in the First and Second
Periods had produced *hoso-ye* sheets in sets of three
that could be joined together to form one picture.   In
fact, each set of three was originally one sheet printed
from one set of blocks; and it was convenience and
economy rather than the idea of producing any real
three-piece composition that led to the production of
these sets.   The prints were almost always conceived
as separate pictures ; they seldom gain by juxtaposi-
tion, and frequently suffer by it.

Far other was the impulse that led Kiyonaga to
his diptych and triptych compositions.  The great
triptych of the " Disembarkment," the diptych of
the " Night Expedition," the " Serenade " triptych
reproduced in Plate 29, and the whole series of
diptychs called " Twelve Months of the South," to
which belongs the marvellous " Terrace by the Sea,"
are all dominated by an indigenous rhythm of line
and colour.  These designs have not Shunsho's
startling force, nor Harunobu's minutely detailed
grace, nor Koriusai's richness ; all these elements
Kiyonaga sacrifices for a broader sweep and a more
unified pictorial quality.  His designs co-ordinate
the elements of line, colour, figures, and landscape
into total impressions of such large harmony as we
have not seen before and shall hardly see again.  To
over-estimate the genius that produced the grouping
of his best work is impossible ; to realize it fully
requires careful analysis, so unobtrusive and inevitable are its effects.

Kiyonaga's greatest works are these triptychs and

KIYONAGA: GEISHA WITH
SERVANT CARRYING
LUTE-BOX.

Size 27×4½.
Signed *Kiyonaga ga.*

KIYONAGA. WOMAN
PAINTING HER
EYEBROWS.

Size 27×5.
Signed *Kiyonaga ga.*

*Plate 30*

diptychs in which he depicts the holiday life of his Olympian figures. Even single sheets from them are treasures; for though they combine into still greater compositions, each one, as we may see in Plate 27, or in any one of the sheets of Plate 29, is a perfect unit that can stand alone. His pillar-prints, of which two appear in Plate 30, are ranked among the foremost works in this form.

Eventually Kiyonaga's finest manner passed. Though the vigour of his brush-strokes remained, his figures began to take on an exaggerated length and slimness characteristic of the coming decadence. Therefore his retirement from print-designing, a little after 1790, was not, as in the case of Harunobu's untimely death, an irreparable loss. His greatest work was finished. Why he retired is not known; the various speculations on the subject are not very enlightening.

Though the finest Kiyonaga prints rarely come into the market nowadays, the less important examples of his work are by no means impossible to obtain. His smaller prints, and his pillar-prints in particular, are among the most attractive acquisitions remaining for the collector. The large single sheets, if fine impressions and in fine condition, are among the foremost of the collector's treasures. The great triptychs are almost unprocurable, except in poor condition.

The collector must patiently await his opportunity. There is probably not a single Kiyonaga obtainable anywhere to-day that is of the quality of that unique group of marvellously printed masterpieces which once belonged to Fenollosa, and which is now one of the glories of the Spaulding Collection in Boston. Similarly, the Mansfield Collection in New York and the Buckingham Collection in Chicago contain Kiyonagas which are the result of long years of search and which could not be duplicated in all the markets of the world combined.

### PUPILS OF KIYONAGA.

TORII KIYOMASA was the son of Kiyonaga. His work, produced between 1810 and 1825, is without special distinction.

Among the minor pupils may be named Kiyotsugi, Kiyohisa, Kiyokatsu, Kiyotei, Kiyotoki, Kiyoyuki, Kiyohide II, Kiyotsune II.

Every artist of the day was influenced by Kiyonaga ; among those difficult to classify otherwise may be named the following men :—

SANCHŌ, who worked in the neighbourhood of 1780, produced prints somewhat in the manner of Shuncho. Delicacy rather than strength distinguished him in the few examples of his work I have seen.

HARUMITSU is an artist whose work is known to me only by one pillar-print in my collection. Fenollosa, who once owned the print, noted on the margin of it : "A rare man. Name may be also read Shunkō, but not the same as the pupil of Shunsho. A follower of Kiyonaga." And this is all the information I have been able to obtain about him. It is possible that he is the same as Shunko II.

SHUNCHO: GROUP AT A TEMPLE GATE.

A diptych.  Each sheet size 15×10.  Signed *Shuncho ga*.  Mansfield Collection.

*Plate 31*

235

## SHUNCHO.

Your lovely ladies shall not fade
Though Yedo's moated walls be laid
Level with dust, and night-owls brood
Over the city's solitude.
Far be the coming of that day !
Yet that it comes not, who shall say?
Who knows how long the halls shall stand
Of your once-golden wonderland?
Perhaps shall Nikko crumble down,
Its carvings worn, its glow turned brown
Through many winters.  On that hill
Where great Ieyasu's brazen will
In brazen tomb now takes its rest,
Perhaps the eagle's young shall nest.
Kyoto's gardens cannot last.
At Kamakura, where the vast
Form of the Buddha fronts the sea,
A waste of waves may someday be. . . .
    Ah, stale and flat the warning bell
Whose melancholy accents tell
Impermanence to hearts that guess
Time's undiscovered loveliness.
A fairer Yedo shall arise ;
A richer Nikko praise the skies ;
Ieyasus mightier than of old
Shall cast the world in wiser mould ;
Fresh gardens shall be spread ; new faith
Shall spring when Buddha is a wraith—
And more puissant hands than yours
Shall paint anew life's ancient lures.
Yet when he comes who shall surpass
Your beauty that so matchless was,
A joy shall light him through your eyes,
A flame shall from your embers rise,
Your gentle art shall make him wise
In mastery of melodies.
And though your wreath in dust be laid,
Your lovely ladies shall not fade !

Nothing is known of the life or personality
of Katsukawa Shuncho.   His name and certain

peculiarities of his drawing indicate unmistakably
that he began his career as a pupil of Shunsho ; but
he soon fell under the influence of Kiyonaga and
became that artist's most notable follower.   His main
work lies between the years 1775 and 1800; it is
thought that he stopped designing prints before the
latter year, though he is said to have lived until
after 1821.   His designs, one of which appears in
Plate 31, comprise chiefly figures of women, drawn
with extraordinary grace of line
and softness of colouring.

SHUNCHO.

Except in a few early actor-
prints, Shuncho had only one
manner—that which we have come
to call the middle Kiyonaga style.
It was early in his career that he
threw off the harsh dominance of
Shunsho.   M. Raymond Koechlin
points out that had he remained
under that influence he would
without doubt have been lost
in the banal horde of designers
of actor-prints who spiritlessly followed that great
artist.   For there was nothing in common between
the rugged masterful genius of Shunsho and the
luminous grace of his pupil.   Kiyonaga's style,
however, Shuncho could adopt and utilize to express
his own peculiar and mild sense of beauty, with a
perfection that makes him stand out unique among
Kiyonaga's disciples.   Other pupils of Kiyonaga
followed the master for a longer or shorter while ;
but all the others sooner or later developed styles

SHUNCHO: TWO LADIES
UNDER UMBRELLA.

Size 27×4½.
Signed *Shuncho ga.*

SHUNCHO: THE COURTESAN
HANA-OJI—THE SUMIDA
RIVER SEEN THROUGH
THE WINDOW.

Size 27×5.
Signed *Shuncho ga.*

*Plate 32*

of their own or copied the styles of other leaders—
often eccentric and decadent leaders, far inferior to
him whom they had abandoned. But Shuncho,
having adopted the Kiyonaga manner at its noblest,
when the proportions in the drawing of the figure
were most natural and dignified, never departed from
it except to make it slightly less naturalistic, in
accordance with what he had learned from his
first master Shunsho. That this was so manifests
Shuncho's purity of feeling, and also reveals his
strange lack of desire to experiment in new manners.
No artist so great as Shuncho has ever been so little
endowed with initiative and invention. I fancy that
he marks the point in the development of the
Ukioye School where, after the progressive force of
Kiyonaga had spent itself, the art stands still for a
brief moment of perfect balance before it begins to
take its course down the long slope of the decline.

In many respects like Kiyonaga, Shuncho can
hardly be regarded as second even to his master,
except in originality. He lacked Kiyonaga's great
creative imagination—an imagination which brought
into being the Olympian style. But his gifts enabled
him to assimilate this style perfectly and turn it to
his own slightly different uses. His sense of composition is rather undistinguished when compared with
Kiyonaga's ; but the delicacy of his drawing, the
restrained harmonies of his colour, and the clean
vitality of his line have a beauty that we could ill
afford to sacrifice even for Kiyonaga's strength.
Kiyonaga brings down the gods in all their noble
dignity to walk the earth in calm magnificence ; but

Shuncho leads us into a secret heaven where the
loveliest and most flower-like of the gods have
remained behind.  His is a softer beauty, touched
with remote half-lights, vibrant with faint wistfulness ;
his superb women turn in mid-joy as though far and
grave music had suddenly drifted to their hearing ;
their perfection passes over into the region where
beauty becomes sadness.  No women in the whole
range of Japanese art so haunt one's memory as do
his ; no beauty seems at the same time so flawless
and so charged with the burden of transitoriness.
One cannot but feel that where Kiyonaga's healthy
vision saw only the happiness and brilliance and
splendour of the forms that swept by him in the
mortal procession, Shuncho saw also the ghostly fleet-
ness of their passing and the melancholy of their
radiance sunset-bound ; and around his figures this
sense throws a quiet tender light, a suggestion of
brooding and caressing sweetness.

In his finest prints the softly luminous colour and
the gently sweeping lines of his ladies move sometimes through the palely glowing rooms of palaces,
but more often through sunlit fields and gardens and
blossoming groves—regions of delight and cloud-
less skies, scenes of eternal happiness.   His colour-
schemes in these natural settings are artfully contrived to produce, through the limited agency of flat
tints, an impression of crystal-clear atmosphere
around and behind the figures.   In both his triptychs
and his pillar-prints there often stretches away this
delicate world of hills or seashore or river-bank that
plays no small part in the incantation of beauty.

SHUNCHO: TWO LADIES
IN A BOAT ON THE
SUMIDA RIVER.

Size 26×4½. Unsigned.

*Plate 33*

YEISHO: TWO COURTESANS
AFTER THE BATH.

Size 25×5. Signed *Yeisho ga.*

His pillar-prints, of which three are reproduced in Plates 32 and 33, are especially fine ; I sometimes think that here he surpasses Kiyonaga.

And yet there is about all his work a strange impersonality, an absence of any note that brings to our notice Shuncho himself, the observer and recorder. He is detached even from his own most perfect work. Compare him with Harunobu or Sharaku or Utamaro, and observe how invisible he is —how his designs have a transparency that absolutely conceals him.

In historical importance and in originality Shuncho is secondary to Kiyonaga ; in absolute beauty his work deserves a place beside that of the master. As a colourist—his most distinguished rôle—he was perhaps the greater of the two.

The collector may be interested to note that practically all Shuncho's work is printed with the utmost sharpness and refinement ; poor impressions of his prints are almost unknown. In this particular he is in striking contrast to many of his contemporaries ; and one may perhaps trace his care to the training of Shunsho, of whose work also I have seldom seen a really poor impression. Shuncho's work is unfortunately not common ; finely preserved copies are scarcer than Kiyonaga's.

## SHUNZAN.

Katsukawa Shunzan was a little-known artist who worked from about 1775 to about 1810. He was first, as his name would suggest, a pupil of Shunsho ; in his rare early prints in *hoso-ye* form he produced

actors in the manner of that school with considerable
charm of line, but without great vigour.   Even in
these early pieces Shunzan's lean-
ing towards sweetness and suavity
suggests that he was not at home
in the Shunsho manner ; and it is
not strange to find that he later
turned to Kiyonaga, under whose
powerful influence he produced his
best-known work—beautiful ladies
in robes of splendour.  He generally
copied the Kiyonaga type of figure
closely, but a little stiffly ; and he
was not often master of those
harmonies of arrangement and
grouping which distinguished his teacher.   But occasionally his colour is very rich and glowing.

SHUNZAN.

Either he produced little or else time has been
even less than normally kind to his work, for few
prints by him survive.

## SHUNMAN.

Kubo Shunman was one of those singular artists
who fascinate us almost as much by mystery as by
beauty.   Living from 1757 to 1820, or, as some
authorities say, to 1829, he was at one time a pupil
of Shigemasa ; but he later turned to Kiyonaga
as his final and most important teacher.   From
Kiyonaga he learned the rudiments of his style ;
yet on the whole his work resembles Kiyonaga
very little.   An individual touch dominates all his
compositions.   He may be called the symphonist

of greys ; for a large part of his most notable production is done in modulated shades of this colour, heightened and made luminous here and there by carefully calculated touches of green, yellow, red, or violet. His figures are drawn in a manner less solid than Kiyonaga's; as in Plate 45, the lines seem tormented and strained into arabesques of peculiar and restless beauty. The harmony of his colour is kept by this sharp intensity of line-work from sinking into mere sweetness and flatness.

KUBO SHUNMAN.

These figures of Shunman, sketched with the curious uneasiness of line of which I speak, stand before backgrounds of equal strangeness. The landscapes seem instinct with an obscure life; the Talking Oak of Dodona was never more haunted than are they. His great six-sheet composition, "The Six Tamagawa," is positively disturbing in the feeling of supernatural forces that it awakens. As Fenollosa says: "Everything he does has a strange touch. The Kiyonaga face becomes distorted with a sort of divine frenzy ; trees grope about with their branch-tips like sentient beings ; flowers seem to exhale unknown perfumes, and the waters of his streams writhe and glide with a sort of reptilian fascination." Or, as Mr. Arthur Morrison puts it : "There is a touch of fantasy in most of his published designs, as well as in some of his original pictures—an atmosphere as of some strange country where the trees, the rocks, the flowers, and the streams are alive with human senses and mysterious communion."

For reasons not wholly clear, the work of Shunman is received by the Japanese connoisseurs with more favour than that of most Ukioye artists. Some obscure quality of restraint and imagination relates him to the older classical schools in a way that makes him acceptable to their aristocratic exclusiveness of taste.

Shunman's best prints are so rare as to be beyond the dreams of the ordinary collector. His complete "Tamagawa'" is a work for which all the great collectors in the world compete. His smaller prints and book-illustrations are, however, procurable ; and his surimono are excellent and fairly numerous. His pillar-prints, of which only three or four designs are known to me, are remarkably fine.


## KITAO MASANOBU.

*Two Women.*

What floors have ye trod ? What sky-paven places have opened
    their halls to your eyes?
What light was yours, through summerward spaces watching the
    swallow that flies?
What holy silence has touched your faces—what hush of paradise?

I think that he died of a longing unspoken who dreamed you
    to walk in our ways.
The wheel at the cistern, the pitcher is broken : ye wot not that
    dust decays—
Ye, torn from the heart of the dreamer as token to dreamers of
    other days.

Kitao Masanobu was another of the pupils of Shigemasa who marched eventually beneath the banner of Kiyonaga, though he retained to the last much of his first master's manner. Born in 1761, he lived until 1816. His occupations besides painting were various: he kept a tobacco-shop, and was best known in his own day under the literary name of Kyōden, for his highly popular novels and comic poems. He produced very few prints, but those few are of distinguished quality, all of them probably the product of his early years, before he reached the age of thirty. At least one of these, reproduced in Plate 31, is an unsurpassable triumph. His resemblance to his first master is so marked that it is not always possible at first glance to distinguish his prints from those of Shigemasa. In fact there is a certain unsigned pillar-print, representing the two lovers Komurasaki and Gompachi, which is still of doubtful authorship, some authorities attributing it to Shigemasa, while others assign it to Masanobu.

MASANOBU
(KITAO).

Possibly Kitao Masanobu is most widely known for his elaborate illustrated book, " Celebrated Women of the Tea Houses and their Handwritings." This volume was published about 1780; I have already referred to it in dealing with the great illustrated book of Shunsho and Shigemasa. It consists of seven large double-page illustrations in many colours, and is a highly praised work, sheets of which are often mounted as separate prints. It appears to me, however, to have been overrated ; and my impression is that in these designs elaborateness has smothered composition and richness has obliterated beauty.

Kitao Masanobu's single-sheet prints are lamentably few, as are also his pillar-prints ; but from those that remain to us it is possible to rank Masanobu as an artist second to only the very greatest. Spirituality is a clumsy word to use in describing work so definitely embodied as this ; yet none other conveys the sense of his peculiar and grave harmony. The mature beauty of his work carries us back to the perfection of Shigemasa.

The collector will search long before he finds an important print by this artist to add to his collection.

## MASAYOSHI.

Kitao Masayoshi, who frequently signed himself Keisai or Shosin, was a curious and original designer, who lived from 1761 to 1824. Though a pupil of Shigemasa, he appears to have drawn a large part of his inspiration from a source outside the Ukioye movement—the Kano School of painting, in which the classical traditions still flourished. In his main period, contemporaneous with Kiyonaga, his work was little influenced by the great master. His designs are marked chiefly by the vividness of his observation of flowers, animals, and landscape, and by his technical skill in recording them. His books of sketches are his best-known works—drawings in a manner new to wood-engraving ; he seldom

KITAO MASANOBU: THE CUCKOO.

Size 15½×22.　Signed *Masanobu ga.*　Spaulding Collection.

*Plate 34*

251

employs any key-block, but leaves the main body of his colour in broad impressionistic sweeps of the brush without definite boundary.  He approached Nature somewhat as did Hokusai in later days, with a sharp perception and infinite interest.  His work lies aside from the main current of Ukioye history—an interesting backwater that comes more properly within the region of classical painting than within that of prints.

Single-sheet prints by Masayoshi are very rare. His book-sheets are somewhat more frequently met with.

# VI

# THE FOURTH
# PERIOD:
# THE DECADENCE

FROM THE
RETIREMENT OF KIYONAGA
TO THE
DEATH OF UTAMARO
(1790–1806)

# CHAPTER VI

## THE FOURTH PERIOD: THE DECADENCE

FROM THE RETIREMENT OF KIYONAGA TO THE DEATH OF
UTAMARO (1790–1806)

THE change that confronts us as we turn from the period of Kiyonaga to that of Utamaro, Yeishi, and Toyokuni is one whose significance is not at first sight wholly clear. We find the sound and classic figures of Kiyonaga gradually replaced by new and fascinating types—slender drooping bodies, wonderfully piled coiffures, elaborately brocaded robes; and the virile drawing of the earlier master gives way to the sinuous curves and arresting plasticity of the new designers. The favourite types of this time are almost as unreal as those of the Primitives, but they convey a totally different feeling; on the one hand, in their curious perverted way, they are far more realistic than the Primitives ever dreamed of being; and on the other hand, they seem the products of minds weary of reality, who turn to the phantasies of the not wholly normal spirit for their ideals and their consolations.

It must not be supposed, however, that the transition to this style of the Decadence was a sudden

one. The painters who had most perfectly assimi-
lated the style of Kiyonaga were the very ones who,
in this period, turned to the depiction of figures in
which every line betrays the weariness of the hour
and its craving for novelty. The apex of creative
energy in this art had been reached and the inevitable
decline was under way.

Of the forces that produced this decline we have
comparatively little knowledge. Fenollosa's account
of the social conditions of the period throws some
light upon the problem. " It was," he says, " a period
of crisis in Tokugawa affairs. The cleavage between
the aristocratic and the plebeian strata of Japanese
life, which had become placidly conscious of itself in
the days of Genroku, now threatened a moral, a
social, if not a political disruption. The new factors
of popular education—art, prints, illustrated books,
the theatre, novels, contact with the Dutch at
Nagasaki—all had stimulated the spirit of inquiry
and of unrest which had penetrated back in investigation to the facts of the Shogun's usurpation ;
which wrote new, popular histories of the national
life ; which gave plays and novels a semi-political
aim. This deeper wave of self-consciousness on the
part of the people was met by the authorities
with sterner repressions. The better elements that
might have drifted into improving the popular
standards in pleasure and art were driven out by
a strict censorship. There was thus a sort of natural,
or unnatural, selection which tended to isolate and
give prominence to the coarser side of the popular
feeling. If the issue were squarely made between

Confucius and rank demoralization, there was little resource for the commoner but to choose the latter. Thus there arose a sort of alliance between the theatre and the houses of pleasure on the one hand, and the disaffected among the literary and political agitators upon the other. Men, great men who sowed the seeds of the revolution which ripened in 1868, had to flee for asylum, not to Buddhist temples, but to the labyrinths of the Yoshiwara, where, in the care of a romantic love lavished upon them by its then highly cultivated *hetairæ*, they could print and disperse, from their hidden presses, seditious tracts which set the heart of the nation on fire. It was not the ideals of a ripe self-consciousness, such as Kiyonaga had attempted; it was a struggle of living desires against outworn conventions and hopeless tyrannies. Hence, the two phases of a new Ukioye art—its pressure outward toward fuller scientific realisms, and its frank recreations in the vulgarities of its surroundings."

In addition to the restlessness growing out of such political conditions, we should remember that it is not the nature of the human race to be satisfied even with perfection for very long. Kiyonaga, with all his placid beauty, could not forever suffice men who felt themselves to be living as passionately "modern" lives as we do to-day. Change was required to keep them interested; and since the idealization of sound vitality could hardly be pushed farther than Kiyonaga had taken it, the obvious path for the artist lay in the direction of fantastic variations on the old theme and in the idealization of the erotic phantoms evoked by uneasy weariness. New refinements had to be introduced; new emotions had to be stirred; and the unending search for novelty led in due time to strained efforts, perverted mannerisms, and distorted outlooks upon life.

So much for that part of the decadence which was due merely to the desire for change. But there was another element of even more definite operation. It is fairly clear that part of the fatal development resulted [from that slow drift toward realism which we have seen growing, period by period, since the days of the Primitives. The age of Harunobu, with its new technical resources, had abandoned pure decoration and aspired to put into its designs something of the flavour of life. The age of Kiyonaga, with its complete mastery of technique, had projected into its designs its observation of real beings—drawn with a fine idealization, but nevertheless based on a deep fidelity to concrete forms. The age of Utamaro had a choice of only two steps left to take if it were to advance to any new position—a step in the direction of still closer fidelity to nature, or a step in the direction of complete revolt from naturalism into regions of wild phantasy. Characteristically, it took both!

Particular instances will show this. Utamaro and Sharaku recorded the peculiarities of real things with a sharpness of observation and an accuracy of rendering that the earlier artists had never approached. And at the same time they used these sharply mastered details of nature as mere brick and mortar out of which to construct fantastic edifices of the most unbridled imagination. Because they were geniuses, they did this and created masterpieces; but they left to later times and lesser artists only the sterile heritage of a deadening realism which they had found it convenient to employ, but to which they themselves had never been truly subject.

At the beginning of this period Yeishi, Choki, Sharaku, and the young Utamaro produced work that ranks quite as high in beauty as that of preceding days. Yeishi's visionary figures of women, drawn with a disembodied and fragile grace, are in their way matchless things, whose only fault is their lack of virile strength. Choki's finest works are wholly beyond praise. Sharaku, the supreme master of actor-portraits and one of the great artists of the world, created designs of stupendous power; if there is any trace of decadence in him it is not weakness but brutality. Utamaro, in his earlier years at least, was as wholesome as Kiyonaga; and even when, in later times, he turned to figures that have about them an indescribable atmosphere of languor and decline, he made of them designs that are to many people the most beautiful productions of the whole school. In all of these men, technical power and sense of composition were of unimpaired vigour. Why, then it may be asked, should we speak of the decadence?

The answer lies partly in the fact that these productions, as a rule, express in their languid or overstrained figures tendencies of emotional super-refinement and nervous tension that impress every beholder with a sense of disintegration, and partly in the history of later days. For the moment, the rivalry between the great men of the period was so keen as to sustain what was, after all, the dying effort of their art. The successes of each one spurred the others on to new types and new feverish devices, feeding thus the flames of the desire for novelty among the people. But the end was at hand. By 1800, in the later work of Utamaro, in most of the work of Toyokuni, and in practically all the work of their followers, genuine artistic weakness appeared, sensationalism took the place of vigour, garishness supplanted harmony, and crude emotions, crude drawing, crude colour became the common feature. The ancient sense of style gave way to a desire to push pictorial effects beyond their legitimate boundary, and the edge of the abyss was in sight.

But before that moment came there remained sixteen years in the productions of which we shall find beauties less sane and sound than those of Kiyonaga, but nevertheless perpetually delighting.

## HOSODA YEISHI.

*Portrait of a Woman.*

> Out of the silence of dead years
> Your slender presence seems to move—
> A fragrance that no time outwears—
> A perilous messenger of love.

> From far your wistful beauty brings
> A wonder that no lips may speak—
> A music dumb save as it clings
> About your shadowy throat and cheek.

> Longing is round you like that haze
> Of luminous and tender glow
> Which memory in the later days
> Gives vanished days of long ago.

And he who sees you must retrace
All sweetness that his life has known,
And with the vision of your face
Link some lost vision of his own.

The long curves of your saffron dress—
The outline of your delicate mould—
Your strange unearthly slenderness
Seem like a wraith's that strayed of old

Out of some region where abide
Fortunate spirits without stain,
Where nothing lovely is denied,
And pain is only beauty's pain.

.    .    .    .    .

Strange ! that in life you were a thing
Common to many for delight,
Thrall to the revelries that fling
Their gleam across the fevered night—

A holy image in the grasp
Of pagans careless to adore ;
A pearl secreted in the clasp
Of oozy weeds on some lost shore.

My thought shrinks back from what I see,
And wanders dumb in poisoned air—
Then leaps, inexplicably free,
Remembering that you were fair !

.    .    .    .    .

Belovèd were you in your prime
By one, of all, who came as guest,—
A wastrel strange, whose gaze could climb
To where your beauty lit the west.

One,—in whose secret heart there moved
Some far and unforgotten stir
Of ancient, holy beauties loved,—
Here paused, a sudden worshipper.

Methinks he moved in dusks apart
Through that profound and trembling hour
When you within his doubting heart
Touched all the desert into flower.

And where you rose a world's delight,
For him the dark veils from you fell,—
As earthly clouds from star-strewn night
Withdraw, and leave a miracle.

Not Oiran then, but maid; remote
From tyrant powers of waste desire.
Who drew these hands, this slender throat,
Saw you 'mid skaken winds of fire.

You were a shape of wonder, set
To crown the seeking of his days.
For you his lonely eyes were wet;
With you his soul walked shrouded ways.

And though the burning night might keep
You servient to some lord's carouse,
For him you rose from such a deep
With maiden dawn-light on your brows.

.    .    .    .    .

Pale Autumn with ethereal glow
Hovered your delicate figure near;
And ever round you whispered low
Her voices, and the dying year.

A year—a day—and then the leaves
Purpureal, ashen, umber, red,
Wove for you both through waning eves
A gorgeous carpet gloomward spread.

And with that waning, you had gone,
Through changes that love fears to trace—
No later lover could have known
Your wistful and alluring face—

Your music, quivering in thin air,
Had fled with life that filled your veins—
But he for whom you were so fair
Dreamed; and the troubled dream remains.

.    .    .    .    .

Time, that is swift to smite and rend
The common things that spring from earth,
Dares not so surely set an end
To shapes of visionary birth.

There often his destroying touch
Lingers as with a lulled caress,
Adding, to that which has so much,
An alien ghostly loveliness.

So shall your beauty, crescent, pass
From me through many a later hand,
Each year more luminous than it was—
O April out of Sunset Land !

The career of Hosoda Yeishi as a print-designer
began about 1780 at the time when Kiyonaga was
in full sway, and lasted until
shortly after the beginning of the
nineteenth century—a date when
Kiyonaga had for some years
been in retirement. Thus in
Yeishi perhaps more fully than
in any other artist except Utamaro may be observed the crucial
transition from the period of Kiyonaga to the period of complete
decline.

YEISHI.

Yeishi was originally a noble of
high rank who studied under Kano
Yeisen, the court painter ; and not
even in the last years of his career,
when vulgarizing influences were
dominant, did he lose the refinement and aristocratic
delicacy that are his most striking characteristics.
Shortly before he became a Ukioye painter he had
been attached to the household of the Shogun
Iyeharu. It is not difficult to imagine the horror
of Yeishi's early circle of associates when he threw
over conventionality and station, and plunged into

the *vie de Bohème* of a popular painter. "This
youth," remarks Fenollosa, "doubtless shocked all
his friends in tiring of the solemn old Chinese poets
who had been gliding about in impossible landscapes
since Tanyu first labelled them, and of the semi-
serious, long-headed old gods who gave knowing
winks to their turtles and storks, and in running
off to such abominable haunts of the cow-headed
Buddhist Satan as Danjuro's theatre-pit, fragrant
with the odours of *saki* and raw fish, or the lantern-
hung balconies of merry damsels on the river-boats."

But the elegant court gentleman was not destined
to sink in the maelstrom. To this underworld he
brought his own subtlety of vision and evoked
from it figures of unfading beauty. At the outset
Kiyonaga was his guide—a guide perhaps too blindly
followed. Certainly Yeishi's first productions, superb
as they were, cannot be called his most characteristic. Plate 35 is an example. They are wholly
in the Kiyonaga manner except that they have a
touch of fragility and delicacy that is alien to
Kiyonaga. The proportions of the figures are the
same, but Yeishi's curves are less naturalistic ; they
seem the product of one whose hungry visions lapped
like waves against the shore of reality, shaping it into
contours determined by their own demands. The
" feeling of repose " which Mr. Strange notes is not
repose at all but weariness. At first the perfect poise
of these forms may deceive us ; but as we advance
along the calendar of Yeishi's work we find it pervaded by a spirit less serene, more high-strung, more
drugged with beauty than was Kiyonaga's.

YEISHI: THREE LADIES BY THE SEASHORE.
One sheet of a triptych. Size 15×10. Signed *Yeishi ga.*

*Plate 35*

In what we may call Yeishi's second style, he gives the peculiarities of his nature full expression. The tall slender figures cease to recall Kiyonaga's ; the robust vigour goes out of them ; they become impalpable, wistful creatures, hovering before us with slow grace, moving by us in grave procession. These beautiful women are like creatures seen in a dream ; they have the solemnity and aloofness of priestesses intent on the performance of secret rites. Their long robes sweep in stately pageant ; their delicate heads bend in exquisite weariness.

Fenollosa strangely speaks of the " keenness of Yeishi's characterizations," and says that, "with no idealizations to trouble him, he put down what he saw as frankly as a young reporter." This is a surprising misinterpretation. Yeishi was perhaps more notably a visionary than any other Ukioye artist ; he was haunted by supersensible intimations, perverted by a search for unearthly beauty. A fascinating painter ! He has not the brilliancy and versatility of Utamaro ; but the taste is hard to please which finds monotony in his series of perfections. In his second period—his most individual and powerful—he produced compositions that are hardly inferior to Kiyonaga's. Yeishi may be regarded as one of the few designers who perfectly mastered the triptych form. His arrangements are simpler than Kiyonaga's but no less beautiful. A notable series depicting various polite occupations from the life of Prince Genji are so harmonious in design, so lovely in colour, and so instinct with spiritual refinement as to rank among his finest works.

In some of these triptychs Yeishi introduces his interesting colour-invention—a scheme of grey, yellow,
violet, blue, and black, which he handles superbly.
Among his other triptychs, " The Treasure Ship "
is especially notable. In this print, a barge whose
prow is shaped like the head and breast of the
mythical *Hoho* bird seems adrift on a river of peace ;
its wonderful freight—nine noble ladies engaged in
the refined entertainments of paintings, games, and
poetry—express the nostalgia of Watteau's figures
and the line-beauty of Botticelli's. The repose of
heaven is upon them, and the delicate satiety of
heavenly beings.

Yeishi was one of the few painters besides Shunman who successfully managed grey as a dominant
tone. In certain of his prints he produced notable
results in this manner, using a style in which lights of
yellow and purple are arranged with beautiful effect.
Sometimes, though rarely, he omitted them altogether,
as in Plate 37, and contented himself with modulations of pure grey that are the last word in subtlety.

He produced a considerable number of notable full-
size sheets depicting single figures of women seated
or kneeling, engaged in gracious occupations such as
flower-arrangement. Some of these are without
background ; others have backgrounds of pale grey
wash ; while still others, perhaps the finest of all,
stand out against luminous yellow grounds. One
of these appears in Plate 36. In these prints is
displayed Yeishi's power to draw exquisitely the
long sweeping curves of draperies ; and the strangely
pensive, hieratic quality of his faces is at its best.

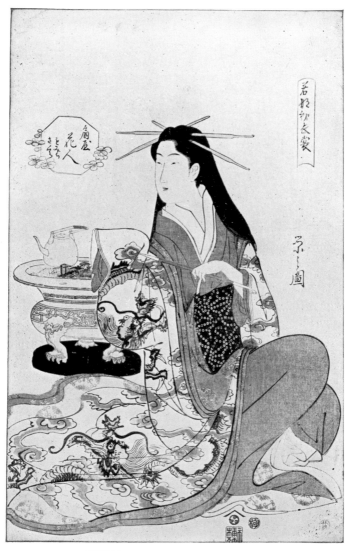

YEISHI: LADY WITH TOBACCO-PIPE.
Yellow background.  Size 15×10.  Signed *Yeishi ga*.

Plate 36

Their charm lies not in the brushwork, which is never as free and bold as Kiyonaga's, but in the sentiment of remote beauty of which these haunting curves are such pure symbols. He also produced a number of groups of courtesans on parade, with little or no background, after the fashion inaugurated by Koriusai and Kiyonaga. These appear stiff beside Kiyonaga's; but they have nevertheless great charm of line and colour. His album of the Thirty-six Poetesses, about 1800, is a series of fantastic and gorgeous colour-dreams. His series of standing women against chocolate or silver backgrounds rises in colour to the level of Sharaku.

Yeishi could not, however, escape the influence of the growing decadence. The public taste at the end of the eighteenth century was debased by a craving for gaudy eccentricities. Utamaro led in the rush to gratify this craving; and even the aristocratic Yeishi was unable to resist the general decline. Therefore toward the end of his career as a print-designer his work greatly altered. His figures grew very tall and willowy; their necks became so exaggeratedly thin that they seem unable to support the great pile of the coiffure; an attenuated snaky-ness distinguishes their lines; and the curves of their garments are distorted into the most fantastic folds and swirls. It was in this period that Yeishi produced most of his large bust-portraits on yellow or mica grounds; in these he followed the lead of Utamaro, who had influenced him considerably during his whole career. The noble and grave faces of his earlier days became wooden and distorted:

and when Yeishi at last stopped print-designing and returned to the life of society and painting from which he had been so long a renegade, the loss was not a great one; for the degradation of the age's taste had engulfed him—as, indeed, it did all his contemporaries.

Yeishi's ordinary work is not particularly rare. Even his slightest prints have so much charm that they may be highly recommended to the attention of the modest collector. Yeishi's important works are of great scarcity. His figures on yellow or mica ground, his grey prints, his large heads, and his pillar-prints are quite as difficult to obtain as any of the prints of this or the preceding period; his best triptychs are extraordinarily hard to procure.

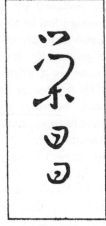

YEISHO.

YEISHO.

Of Yeishi's many pupils, Shoko-sai Yeisho stands out as the most important. Nothing is known of him except that his work was done toward the end of the eighteenth century.

Yeisho may be regarded as the veritable shadow of Yeishi. He wholly adopted his master's style; but he was not able to impart to his figures that reserved aristocratic poise which was Yeishi's distinguishing mark. Instead, Yeisho's figures not infrequently have a certain very pleasing and

YEISHI: INTERIOR OPENING ON TO THE SEASHORE.

Left-hand sheet of a triptych. Printed in several tones of grey. Size 15×10.
Signed *Yeishi ga.* Metzgar Collection.

*Plate 37*

plausible elegance, fuller and rounder than his master's. His curves sweep more assertively and less subtly ; and his decorative effects are often superb even though not particularly complex. He too passed from the manner of Kiyonaga into that of Utamaro ; but his middle period is his most characteristic. In this he produced many fascinating single sheets of seated or kneeling women, several admirable pillar-prints, as in Plate 33, some large bust-portraits that are perhaps his finest works, and a number of triptychs. These last, as a rule, lack the element that is the real glory of the triptych—a broadly grasped correlation of complex elements into one great harmonious composition. Yeisho's triptychs are merely three sheets placed side by side with only a rudimentary attempt at unification. But so completely attractive are the separate figures and the great sweeping curves of his best work that these triptychs are nevertheless delightful productions—more striking than many a subtler composition. They have, however, a stereo-typed quality that makes one unwilling to take Yeisho very seriously as an artist. His curves sweep splendidly, but they are dominated by a formula.

Yeisho's works are not common ; they are far rarer than Yeishi's. Yeisho may serve to illustrate the difficulty of appraising these artists. I had hardly written the foregoing estimate of Yeisho when I received as a gift from a friend a large bust-portrait of a woman by Yeisho which is so unexpectedly magnificent and so much finer than any work of Yeisho's I had ever seen that my previous opinion had to be modified. In subtlety of line and delicacy of colour this head is at least equal to Utamaro's finest works in the same manner ; it utterly contradicts my previous impression of Yeisho's stereotyped quality. Now, what has happened to me in the case of Yeisho is happening to students of Japanese prints every day ; and not until the last secreted treasure is brought to light and made known can we be confident that we are even approximately right in the ranks which we assign to the various designers.

### OTHER PUPILS OF YEISHI.

Yeishi's vigour, barely sufficient to create his own exquisite works, could not transmit itself to any very vital body of pupils. Though his disciples were many, no one of them achieved independent renown ; the seeds of life were not in the teacher. Out of a large number, the following pupils may be named as the most important :—

ICHIRAKUTEI YEISUI, of whom nothing is known, inherited from his master an elegance of line that is often pleasing, He cannot, however, be regarded as an important or original artist. His large bust-portraits, with charming piquant faces, are his best-known works. His prints are rare but not especially sought after.

GOKYO, an interesting artist who probably died young, worked in the same manner as Yeishi. His prints, soft and pleasing in colour, are very rare indeed ; the few known examples of his work have a distinction worthy of more attention than they have hitherto received. Had he lived he might have given the school of Yeishi a fresh fame.

YEIRI, of whom not much is known, sometimes signed himself "Yeishi's pupil Yeiri." He is to be distinguished from the almost contemporaneous Rekisenti Yeiri. The latter worked more in the style of Utamaro; his work is rare, and his finest prints are beautiful and valuable. It was Yeishi's pupil Yeiri who created that rare and astonishing portrait of Kitao Masanobu which must take a place beside the most brilliant portraiture of any time or land.

YEISHIN is known only by half a dozen prints; these, though attractive, are not as greatly prized as their scarcity might lead one to expect.

CHOTENSAI YEIJU is a slightly stiff and not very interesting disciple whose work is rare.

VEICHO also is notable chiefly for his rarity.

YEIRU followed his master with little originality.

YEIKI and SŌRAKU are later unimportant pupils who followed Utamaro also.

### UTAMARO.

*Portrait of a Woman.*

In robes like clouds of sunset rolled
About the dying sun,
In splendid vesture of purple and gold
That a thousand toiling days have spun
For thee, O imperial one !—

With the cunning pomp of the later years,
With their pride and glory and stress,
Thou risest ; and thy calm forehead bears
These like a crown; but thy frail mouth wears
All of their weariness.

Thou art one of the great who mayest stand
Where Cleopatra stood :
Aspasia, Rhodope, at each hand ;
And even the proud tempestuous mood
Of Sappho shall rule thy blood.

Thy throat, in its slender whiteness bare,
Seems powerless to sustain
The gorgeous tower of thy gold-decked hair—
Like a lily's stem which the autumn air
Maketh to shrink and wane.

More haunting music, more luring love
Round thy sinuous form hold sway
Than the daughters of earth have knowledge of ;
For thou art the daughter of fading day,
Touched with all hope's decay.

And the subtle languor, the prismic glow
Of a ripeness overpast
Burns through the wonderful curving flow
Of thy garments ; and they who love thee know
A loathing at the last.

For they are the lovers of living things—
Stars, sunlight, morning's breath ;
But thou, for all that thy beauty brings
Such songs as the summer scattereth—
Thou art of the House of Death.

.        .        .        .        .

But there was one in thy golden day
Who saw thy poppied bloom,
And loved not thee but the heart's decay
That filled thee, and clasped it to be alway
His chosen and sealèd doom.

He who this living portrait wrought,
Outlasting time's control,
A dark and bitter nectar sought
Welling from poisoned streams that roll
Through deserts of the soul.

Ah, dreamer ! come at last where dreams
Can serve no more thy need,
Who hast by such bright silver streams
Walked with thy soul that now earth seems
A waste where love must bleed—

Thou whom such matchless beauty filled
Of visions frail and lone,
For thee all passion now is stilled ;
Thy heart, denied the life it willed,
Desireth rather none.

And thee allure no verdant blooms
That with fresh joy suspire ;
But blossoms touched with coming glooms,
And weariness, and spent desire,
Draw to thy spirit nigher.

Wherefore is nothing in thy sight
Propitious save it be
Brushed with the wings of hovering night,
Worn with the shadow of delight,
Sad with satiety.

For thou hast enmity toward all
The servants of life's breath ;
One mistress holdeth thee in thrall,
And them thou lovest who her call
Answer ; and she is Death.

. . . . .

Now Death thy ruined city's streets
Walketh, a grisly queen.
And there her sacred horror greets
Him who invades these waste retreats,
Her sacrosanct demesne—

In robes like clouds at sunset rolled
About the dying sun,
In splendid vestments of purple and gold
That a thousand perished years have spun
For her, the Imperial One.

Utamaro, the central and in some ways the most fascinating figure of this period, has been from the first a great favourite in the esteem of European collectors. His graceful, sinuous women are the images that come most readily to the minds of many people at the mention of Japanese prints. In his own time and land his popularity was equalled by that of no other artist.

It was by his portraits of women that Utamaro won his great fame. Passing outside the influence of Kiyonaga, he developed in his designs of the last decade of the nineteenth century his characteristic feminine type. Her strange and languid beauty, the drooping lines of her robes, her unnatural slenderness and willowiness, are the emanations of Utamaro's feverish mind ; as her creator he ranks as the most brilliant, the most sophisticated, and the most poetical designer of his time. His life was spent in alternation between his workshop and the haunts of the Yoshiwara, whose beautiful inhabitants he immortalized in prints that are the ultimate expression of the mortal body's longing for a more than mortal perfection of happiness. Wearied of every common pleasure, he created these visions in whose disembodied, morbid loveliness his overwrought desires found consolation.

UTAMARO.

UTAMARO: OKITA OF NANIWAYA, A TEA-HOUSE WAITRESS.
Mica background.  Size 12½×9.  Signed *Utamaro, hitsu.*  Chandler Collection.

*Plate 38*

Utamaro was born in 1753 in the province of Musachi. Early in life he went to Yedo and there studied under the noted Kano painter and book-illustrator Toriyama Sekiyen, whom some authorities say was his father. Almost from the beginning of his career he lived with the famous publisher Tsutaya, who issued his prints ; and this relation continued up to the date of Tsutaya's death in 1797.

In Utamaro's early work, which began with an illustrated book in 1776, the influence of Kiyonaga was strong. Shunsho's and Kitao Masanobu's characteristics are sometimes also visible, but Kiyonaga's style is the dominating one. Some of his early work is signed Toyoaki.

In 1780 the first important product of Utamaro's career saw the light—his famous "Gifts of the Ebb-Tide"—a book of exquisitely conceived and delicately printed representations of shells and rocks on the seashore. The effort of a trained conchologist to produce accurate descriptive drawings of these objects could hardly achieve a more scrupulous fidelity than do these pages, which have in addition an æsthetic charm of a high order. The same characteristic appears in his celebrated "Insect Book" of 1788. These two works, dominated by a scientific realism that was new to Ukioye, may serve as an indication of the growth of that naturalistic spirit whose effect upon the stylistic ideals of the art was later to be so destructive.

In the decade between 1780 and 1790 Utamaro produced many additional books. Notable among them are the "Customs of New Year's Day" (1786),

" The Mad Full Moon," a series of lovely moonlight
landscapes in monochrome (1789), and "The Silver
World," a series of delicate snow scenes (1790). The
single-sheet prints which he issued during this decade
are exceedingly beautiful works of a type that the
inexperienced eye would never recognize as Utamaro's. The figures are like those of Kiyonaga's
prime, but drawn with a slenderness of line and
restlessness of poise that strikes a different and
shriller note. His work of this period may be distinguished by the fact that the signature is written
in a squarer, more compact, and more formal manner
than the sprawling, cursive signature of his later days.
The two long, tail-like lines of the later signature, by
which even the casual tourist learns to recognize
Utamaro's name, are wholly absent.

With 1790 begins the classic period of Utamaro's
work. This was the year of Kiyonaga's retirement
and, according to some authorities, of Shunsho's
death. With the two giants of the older generation
gone, Utamaro was left to compete for leadership
with Yeishi, Shuncho, Choki, Toyokuni, and the
lesser men. During the decade from 1790 to 1800
Utamaro was, except for the isolated figure of
Sharaku, outstandingly the most versatile and
brilliant among them. All were profoundly influenced by him, and he had not a few imitators
who attempted to profit by his popularity.

During this last decade of the nineteenth century
Utamaro produced the greatest of his works.
Among these must be counted the remarkable
series of half-length figures on silver backgrounds,

UTAMARO: TWO COURTESANS.

One of a Series "Beautiful Women Compared with the Fifty-three Stations of
the Tokaido Road." Size 15×10. Signed *Utamaro, hitsu.*

*Plate 39*

287

for which no admiration can be too extreme. One of them appears in Plate 38. The type of face which Utamaro drew in these prints differs from the Kiyonaga type ; it has something of the girlishness of Harunobu or Sukenobu—wholesome, rounded, with eyes that are large and not narrowed to slits as in his later years, and with coiffure of modest proportions. It resembles the type characteristic of Choki at this time. These charming figures, drawn with subtle precision, stand against their dull silver backgrounds in colours whose few and soft tones produce an effect so harmonious as to almost justify Von Seidlitz in calling Utamaro "the first colourist of his nation." The prints of this class are as rare as they are beautiful. The collector who is familiar with nothing but the later work of the artist can have only an imperfect conception of the greatness of Utamaro. They constitute the purest and most tranquil of his productions, and perhaps the high point of his genius.

This 1790 decade, when Utamaro was at the zenith of his powers, saw many triumphs besides the silver-portraits. He was incessantly busy with experiments of every kind ; pushed by the keen competition of Yeishi, Choki, and the others, he laboured incessantly for new effects and passed on to new manners. Plates 39 and 41 are examples. Discarding the type of head that had appeared in the silver-portraits, he devised that more restless, haunting type by which we best know him. The ethereal and supple bodies, the slender necks, the slightly strained poses, all indicate the nervous

hyper-æsthetic tension of the hour. Toward the
end of the decade his peculiarities grew even more
marked. The necks of his figures became incredibly
slender; the bodies took on unnatural length; a
snaky languor pervaded them. One print, his
famous "Woman Seated on the Edge of a Veranda,"
reproduced in Plate 40, may serve as representative
of them all. The drawing of the draperies and of
the figure beneath them is studied with extraordinary fidelity; in fact, so human and real a
figure is hardly to be found in the work of any
preceding artist. But on the other hand, Utamaro
has used his keen realistic power merely as a
scaffolding, and has proceeded to build up on it a
work that goes over almost into the region of
symbolism. In the slender delicacy of this figure,
the splendid black of her elaborate coiffure, the
drooping fragility of her body, the sensuous grace
and refinement, the languor and exhaustion—in all
these speak the super-sensible gropings and hungers
of Utamaro himself. Out of a living woman he
created his disturbing symbol of the impossible desires
that are no less subtle or painful because they are born
of the flesh. With nerves keyed beyond the healthy
pitch, he dreamed this melody whose strange minor
chords alone could stir the satiated spirit. He caught
and idealized the lines and colours of mortal weariness.

"Woman," says Von Seidlitz, "had always played
a prominent part in the popular art of the country,
but now Utamaro placed one type of the sex in the
absolute centre of all attention—the type, namely, of
the courtesan initiated into all the refinements of

UTAMARO: WOMAN SEATED ON VERANDA.
Size 13×8.  Signed *Utamaro, hitsu.*

Plate 40

291

mental culture as well as of bodily enchantment, and then playing in the life of Japan such a part as she must have played in Hellas during the golden age of Greek civilization. For expressing the inexpressible, the simple rendering of nature did not suffice; the figures must needs be lengthened to give the impression of supernatural beings; they must have a pliancy enabling them to express vividly the tenderest as well as the most intense emotions of the soul; lastly, they must be endowed with a wholly peculiar and therefore affected language for uttering the wholly peculiar sensations that filled them. . . . It is true that soon after he yielded to the general tendency of his age . . . and gradually insisted on these attributes to exaggeration, even to impossibility, while his fame of having been the first to give such morbid inclinations completely satisfactory and therefore unsurpassable expression is a title of somewhat doubtful value, even if in any case a high historical significance cannot be denied it. Nevertheless, we must not forget that within this domain of the hyper-æsthetic Utamaro was the creator of a most original and individual style. Nay, if we could only admit the morbid and exaggerated to be as fit subject-matter for art as the healthy and sane, we must grant that this style is one of altogether enchanting originality, and that, however dangerous might be its immediate influence upon the spectator, and particularly upon possible successors, it does none the less lift us beyond the cramping limits of reality, and is therefore not wanting in idealism of a kind."

But weary as seems the spiritual content of these end-of-the-century designs of Utamaro's, there is no lack of brilliant vigour in their composition. The great triptychs—such as the "Night Festival on the Banks of the Sumida River," or the "Firefly Catchers," or the "Persimmon Pickers"—stand among the finest prints we know. In colour, rhythm of line, and dramatic quality of composition they are triumphs. There is a startling beauty in even those extraordinary bust-portraits in which the enormous coiffure, minute neck, slips of eyes, and dot of a mouth, carry exaggeration to a bizarre and delirious extreme.

Not long after 1800 the pressure of work brought upon him by his great popularity, together with the effects of a none too well spent life in the Yoshiwara, combined to strain his powers unduly. His work no longer kept its earlier freshness ; his exaggerations became coarser ; his invention grew less fertile. He began to rely on the assistance of his pupils, as we know from his "Book of the Green Houses" (1804), in which several collaborated with him. Doubtless many an Utamaro print of this time is their work.

In the year 1804 came the final catastrophe. Consequent upon the publication of the well-known triptych representing the ancient Shogun Hidevoshi entertaining his five concubines in the eastern quarter of the capital, the ruling Shogun Iyenari took umbrage at the salacious disrespect to his ancestor and the delicately implied allusion to himself, and Utamaro was thrown into prison for his offence. There he remained, it is said, for a year ; when he emerged, it was with impaired health and a broken spirit.

UTAMARO: A YOUTHFUL PRINCE AND LADIES.

Left-hand sheet of a triptych.  Size 15×10.  Signed *Utamaro, hitsu.*

Plate 41

His productions after this time were not comparable with his earlier work. In the year 1806 he died, and with him died the great days of the Japanese print.

In this rapid survey it has been impossible to do justice to the many-sided powers of this great designer. His beautiful landscapes, his fine animal pictures, the tender and whimsical mother-and-child and domestic scenes he produced, have all had to be ignored in favour of his central achievements—his unparalleled designs of the courtesan of the Yoshiwara in her weary glory. Certainly no more varied and distinguished talent than his illumines the roll of Ukioye artists. Beside his perpetually fresh invention even the great Kiyonaga seems stereotyped and academic.

To-day the poorer examples of Utamaro's work are still readily procurable. His greatest works are rare. Certain of his triptychs, his silver half-length portraits, and his large heads on mica backgrounds, are very uncommon. But with patience and judgment the collector may still obtain now and then a fine specimen of Utamaro's work.

But some care is necessary. Even during Utamaro's life his work was forged by unscrupulous persons who hoped to reap the benefit of his popularity; and his pupils, under his direction, produced an unknown quantity of work signed with his name. After his death, from about 1808 to 1820, the Second Utamaro worked in the manner of his predecessor, issuing work that cannot with certainty be distinguished from the late work of the master. Besides these perils there is the fact that Utamaro's prints have been well reproduced in recent years ; and reproductions are sometimes put forward as originals by ignorant or dishonest dealers. Considerable familiarity with authentic examples of Utamaro's best work, or expert advice, can alone protect the would-be purchaser.

### PUPILS AND FOLLOWERS OF UTAMARO.

Though Utamaro's influence upon his contemporaries was incalculably great, he left behind him a body of pupils who were almost without exception rather insignificant artists. With cruder colour and composition, they carried still farther the vulgarities of Utamaro's declining period. Among them may be mentioned the following men :—

UTAMARO II, whose original name was Koikawa Shuncho or Harumachi, was a pupil of Sekiyen ; he married Utamaro's widow, and from about 1808 to 1820 continued to produce prints in the debased Utamaro manner. Dr. Kurth believes he must be distinguished from another Koikawa Shuncho whose family name was Kurahashi, and who died in 1789. The whole matter is by no means clear.

BANKI and SHIKIMARO were among the best of this group. Particularly the former, before Utamaro's death, produced some fine work.

TAMAGAWA SHUCHO was a rare pupil of Utamaro who worked about 1790 to 1810.

KIKUMARO I (who also called himself KITAGAWA TSUKIMARO), KIKUMARO II, TANIMOTO TSUKIMARO, TAKEMARO, TOYOMARO, YUKIMARO I, YUKIMARO II, YOSHIMARO I (also called KITAO SHIGEMASA III),

YOSHIMARO II, REKESENTI SOGAKU, GOSHICHI,
HIDEMARO, MITEMARO, MINEMARO, KITAMARO,
MICHIMARO, TOSHIMARO, HANAMARO, ISOMARO,
ASHIMARO, KANAMARO, KUNIMARO, YOSHIMUNE,
YOSHITORA, YOSHITSUYA, YOSHIKI, YOSHIMORI,
YOSHITOSHI, YOSHIKATA, YENCHO, YUMIAKI,
HOKOKUJIN FUYO, CHIKANOBU, SHINTOKU, SHUN-
KIOSAI, HISANOBU, SORAKU, SENKA, RYUKOKU,
SEKKYO, SEKICHO, SEKIHO, SEKIJO may all be classed
as late followers, fellow-pupils, or rivals of Utamaro.

BUNRO, some of whose work is fine, was a rare
imitator of Utamaro. He worked chiefly about
1800 to 1810.

### SHARAKU.

*Dramatic Portrait.*

Whence art thou come,
Tall figure clasping to thy tragic breast
Thy orange robe, a flame amid the gloom—
By what wild doom
Art thou forever onward—onward pressed?

A wreath is on thy brow,
A crown of leafage from some lonely haunt
Where might Medea's shade brood ministrant.
Thy shoulders bow
Beneath what fearful weight, what need, what vow?

A leopard fierce—
A ghost that wanders down the wandering wind—
A fury tracking toward some shaken mind—
Where shall I find
The divination that thy veil shall pierce?

How shall I wrest
From thee the secret of thy lofty doom—
From what wild gulf of midnight thou dost come
Who, with clutched breast,
Stalkest forever onward—onward pressed?

Few people approach Sharaku's work for the first time without regarding him as a repulsive charlatan, the creator of perversely and senselessly ugly portraits whose cross-eyes, impossible mouths, and snaky gestures have not the slightest claim to be called art. At first these strange

TOSHIUSAI
SHARAKU.

pictures may even seem mirth-provoking to the spectator—a view of them which he will remember in later years with almost incredulous wonder. To overcome one's original feeling of repulsion may take a long time; but to every serious student of Japanese prints there comes at last a day when he sees these portraits with different eyes; and suddenly the consciousness is born in him that Sharaku stands on the highest level of genius, in a greatness unique, sublime, and appalling.

Toshiusai Sharaku is a figure more shadowy than most, even in this region of shadows. The wilful neglect of a public that hated him has folded him in a mystery deeper than the mere accidental obscurations of time. Of his birth and death we know absolutely nothing, nor of the name of his teacher, if he had one. The resemblance between his work and that of Shunyei cannot be fully explained until we know more accurately their relative dates. Kiyonaga's

SHARAKU: THE ACTOR ARASHI RYUZO IN THE ROLE OF ONE OF
THE FORTY-SEVEN RONIN.

Silver background. Size 14×10. Signed *Toshiusaı Sharaku ga.*
Spaulding Collection.

*Plate 42*

noble drawing certainly affected his style. The influence of Shunsho upon his colour-schemes is fairly obvious; but we do not know whether this was due to personal contact, or only to familiarity with Shunsho's work. The one indisputable fact about Sharaku is that he was originally a Nō-performer in the troupe of the Daimyo of Awa. The Japanese authorities state that he worked at print-designing only one or two years, somewhere between 1790 and 1795. Dr. Kurth, in his stimulating but somewhat too imaginative volume, "Sharaku," believes that the evidence justifies us in fixing Sharaku's working period as a much longer time—1787 to 1795; but he cannot be said to have wholly proved his case. Whether or not these dates are accurate, we may at least say that Sharaku's years of activity lay chiefly within the early part of the last decade of the eighteenth century.

Sharaku's work consisted entirely of startlingly powerful and ironic portraits of actors, some in the form of large bust-portraits, some in the form of full-length figures of *hoso-ye* size, and a few large sheets each containing two full-length figures. Their savage intensity is arresting and unforgettable; it at once drives one to consider what manner of man could have created them.

Sharaku was, as we have said, professionally a member of the Nō-troupe of the Daimyo of Awa. This fact is of far-reaching significance.

The Nō was a highly developed and aristocratic form of lyrical drama, based upon ancient and classical legends; it was full of a poetry and allusiveness that made it incomprehensible to the populace, who, indeed, had no opportunity to see it; it was as much the exclusive concern of the cultured aristocracy as the private revival of a Greek tragedy is with us to-day.  In brocaded costumes, perhaps the treasured reliques of centuries ago, the Nō-dancer appeared upon his empty stage before a hushed audience of nobles—his face masked, as were the faces of the Greek actors, his voice lifted to an unnatural pitch of vibrant chaunting; and with stately motions, elaborately devised steps, and stereotyped gestures, he intoned the rolling strophes of the drama's long and hallowed strain.  A complex formalism pervaded every word and step; in no art-form with which I am familiar is an accepted convention, a totally unrealistic medium, so rigidly adhered to as in these Nō-plays.

The Nō-actors were a caste utterly apart from the actors of the common stage.  They were the protégés and associates of great nobles who would not, save incognito, appear in the presence of the common actor.  The gap between the two classes of actors was as great as that between Sir Johnston Forbes-Robertson and a juggler at a fair—one, the inheritor of a distinguished literary tradition, the interpreter of our classic dramatic heritage; the other, a crude beguiler of the populace, with station no higher than the pedlar.  Caste-feeling may very well have been rather harsh between the haughty Nō-performers and their despised and ostracized brothers of the gutter.

As we have noted, the Nō-dancer wore a mask; these masks are creations of the greatest interest.

They are carved out of wood, frequently with a skill that makes them striking works of art. It is impossible to convey in words the remarkable degree of characterization which they express. The smooth guilelessness of the young girl, the deep wrinkles of the old man, the leer of the rascal, the savagery of the villain, are all in their turn summarized in these haunting representations whose simplicity of outline is matched only by their intensity of effect. Nature seems to speak in them—but a heightened nature, stripped of all incidentals; the very essence of the character of the rôle is revealed to our eyes the instant the actor, wearing his impressive and vivid mask, steps upon the stage.

Bearing these things in mind, we may follow Dr. Kurth ("Sharaku," München, 1910) in his imaginative summary of the probable effects of the calling of a Nō-dancer upon the mind and art of Sharaku:—

"Picture a richly endowed painter—at first only dimly conscious of his powers—as in a mystery-play he treads the consecrated stage in the sacred precincts of a temple of Tokushima or in the shadow of the cryptomerias and firs of the Hachisuka castle—a fantastic mask covering his features, other masked spectres before his eyes—surrounded by the atmosphere of the occult tradition of ancient and lofty dramatic art—while, in the depths of his soul's abysses, chained Titans would storm up to the outer world, and confused pictures of his future creations hover before his spirit, . . . and we shall realize that this man, as a painter, must become a dramaturgist.

"And if we summon to our vision the gorgeous stretches of Awa—its chasmy mountains with the forests rustling around them—its picturesque sea-lapped beaches—its sun-drenched groves of oak—its glowing scarlet maples—the brilliant flowers of its Spring—the evergreens of its Winter—then we shall realize that this man, as a painter, must become a colour-dreamer.

"Brooding spirit that he was, he, an Edipus, approached venturously to the Sphinx of passion that peers forth from the faces of men. Uncanny powers lurked in the grotesque furrows and demoniac grimaces of his Nō-masks, but nothing little or shallow—nay, in spite of all grotesqueness, only the significant and symbolic. And then he looked down from his buskined height upon the popular actors— bombastic barn-stormers—greasy low-comedians— louts from nowhere, as the illustrious Harunobu had called them—performers who brought before their gaping audience not, as did he, august things in strangely wonderful guise, but often things far too human in strutting stage-pomp. He looked upon them, a guild not only despised but sometimes even outlawed—a guild that stood on the same plane as the idiotic profession of the wrestler,—a class whose vulgar faces could not hide their swaggering gutter-vanity and their cringing lust for applause behind even the red paint of the ferocious warrior-rôle or the corpse-coloured rice-powder used when aping women. And if we see him thus, we shall understand that this man, as a painter of actors, must eventually become a pitiless satirist."

It was therefore with the colossal and tragic gestures of the Nō-dance in his soul, the distorted and monumental intensity of the Nō-masks in his eyes, and the contempt and irony of the Nō-performer for the common actor in his heart, that Sharaku, coming to Yedo, took up his terrible brush to depict the Yedo actors as he saw them. The resulting series of portraits is surely one of the supreme examples of graphic characterization and devastating contempt that the world has ever seen.

In the earlier portion of Sharaku's work, among which are his large portraits on yellow backgrounds, the originality of the man is already striking enough ; but his acid qualities are hardly at their fullest development. Certain of his *hoso-ye* prints must belong to this first period ; in these, after the manner of Shunsho, he devoted his attention chiefly to the attaining of a powerful dramatic rendering of the rôle he was depicting. Strutting Daimyo, beguiling woman, ferocious warrior, shrewd peasant—he made each part move with the vigour and force of the seen stage. Shunsho was never more impressive ; and here, in addition, there is in every design a strange distortion of line, a disturbing abnormality of pose, that makes one realize that no mere copyist of Shunsho is at hand.

Then, beginning with an astounding series of twenty-four portraits with mica backgrounds (Plates 42, 43, 44) representing actors in the play of the Forty-seven Ronin, Sharaku's mood changes. He ceases to remind one at all of Shunsho; it is rather the scrutinizing individual characterization of Shunyei

that he recalls. But Shunyei never reached the point
to which Sharaku is now coming. The dramatic
force, the histrionic illusion of his pictures abates no
jot; but beyond it, disturbing lights and movements
are lurking. The mighty rôle towers like a shadow
before us in its full dramatic sweep; but from the
depths of the shadow peers with stealthy glance the
indwelling personality of the actor—like a jackal's
eyes seen suddenly in a king's tomb. This contra-
diction—this complex of two utterly antagonistic
forces—is one of the miracles of Sharaku's genius :
it is an antinomy which he resolves sufficiently to
produce an equilibrium, but not enough to take from
these portraits the insoluble mystery of two spirits,
the tangle of two meanings, the explosive and in-
scrutable life that makes them unforgettable.

Thus the sweeping rhetoric of the stately rôle and
the sudden naturalistic cry of the discovered actor's
soul meet in a discord unique, subtly calculated,
magnificent, and harrowing. Sharaku pierced deep
into the hearts of his sitters to grasp the weak, the
grotesque, the pathetic, the tragic ; he appraised the
lust, the horror, the vacuity that was there, and these
qualities he dragged out to the light through the
avenues by which he had entered—through the eyes,
the lips, the hands—tearing these gates into terrible
and distorted breaches eloquent of the booty that
had been forced through them. No portraits so
blasting as his have ever been created by another ;
no other hand has so devastatingly shattered the
conventional contours of faces to reshape them into
the awful images of their own hidden potentialities.

SHARAKU: THE ACTOR ISHIKAWA DANJURO (YEBIZO) AS THE DAIMYO
KO NO MORONAO IN THE DRAMA OF THE FORTY-SEVEN RONIN.

Size 14×10. Silver background. Signed *Toshiusai Sharaku ga*.

*Plate 43*

To call Sharaku a realist is a silly, untruthful attempt to muffle in words forces that one does not understand. He was hardly more a realist than Kiyonaga. He saw in the spectacle before him certain elements of beauty and terror; he selected and moulded them into his cunningly devised designs; and the result was as much a creation of the visionary mind—a true idealism—as the pictures of the fairy-tale-telling Harunobu. It is no mere realism, but an insidious dissection and a mordant reconstruction, that is so striking in these works. The most savage efforts of modern caricature are child's play beside Sharaku's disintegrating analysis and his satanic reassembling of features. He does to the face and its concealed passions what Michael Angelo's anatomical figure does to the nerves and muscles—revealing appallingly the secrets of structure and the machinery of power.

Yet, in spite of all the distortions and exaggerations and displacements, Sharaku's satyrical faces live. They have an unnatural and monstrous life—like the life of Gothic gargoyles and fabulous animals, whose parts are brought together into an incredible yet organic creation. Looking upon them, one realizes that for Sharaku beauty meant not sweetness or grace, but vitality—the clench and rending of the earthquake forces of life. He sought no harmonies of sentiment like those of Harunobu; he plunged wholly into a maelstrom of powers whose magnificent surge and flow was to him the sole end and the sole consolation.

He drew no courtesans, no scenes from the daily

life of the people, no festivals, no tea-house gardens
by the river ; but with a baleful concentration he, the
proud master of the esoteric Nō drama, kept his
eyes fixed unswervingly upon the pathetic mimes of
the vulgar stage—outcasts, common lumps strutting
for an hour of glory in gorgeous robes and heroic
rôles before a gaping populace. How one longs for
one more work from Sharaku's hands—a portrait of
himself, seated in the stalls, watching the play at its
height! One can almost imagine the peering eyes,
the tight lips, the hidden hands. . . .

So far I have spoken chiefly of the large heads of
Sharaku. But it must not be forgotten that he produced a number of designs in *hoso-ye* form that are
the very flower of his work. Kurth places certain of
these early in Sharaku's career ; he is, perhaps, wrong
in this, for many of those which he thus dates give
evidence of an art so mature and masterful that they
must be at least contemporaneous with the Ronin
Series. Such are the print of Arashi Ryūzō as an
aged noble in robe of black with violet girdle, and
the print of Segawa Kikusabrō in robe of olive and
purple holding an open fan. In the finest of these
*hoso-ye* the dramatic force of the composition is so
subtle that the element of caricature takes a subordinate place. A lyric mood pervades them. It is
impossible to contemplate these figures without a
sense, not merely of the irony and contempt which
they sometimes embody, but also of the tragic heights
on which they move. Lofty conflicts, desperate
destinies, immense strainings toward desired goals,
immense despairs before impassable barriers—these

SHARAKU: THE ACTOR KOSAGAWA TSUNEYO AS A WOMAN IN THE
DRAMA OF THE FORTY-SEVEN RONIN.

Silver backgrouned.  Size 14×10.  Signd *Toshiusai Sharaku ga.*
Ainsworth Collection.

*Plate 44*

are some of the emotions that confront us here. The echo of the tragedy of the Greeks is around them; their gestures seem the shadows of titanic cataclysms. Kiyonaga gave us the gods; Sharaku gives us those who fought against the gods. If it were my fortune to choose, out of the tens of thousands of prints that I have seen, one print which could alone be saved from some impending universal destruction, I am not sure whether I would take Harunobu's flawless "Flute Player," or Kiyonaga's serene "Terrace by the Sea," or that terrible print of Sharaku's, illustrated in both Kurth and the catalogue of the exhibition at the Musée des Arts Décoratifs, in which the orange-robed figure of Nakayama Tomisabrō stalks by with an intensity of passion that makes one's flesh creep—a vibrancy of line, colour, and emotion that seems the apogee of beauty and terror.

The *hoso-ye* prints have, upon the whole, more poise and serenity than the busts; and they will perhaps be judged—in a hundred years, when the excitement of the discovery of Sharaku is over—to be among his greatest works. When they occur in triptychs, as probably all were originally designed to do, they constitute more harmonious and dramatic units than any of Shunsho's actor-triptychs. The finest, and latest in order of production, are generally those without background; in these, isolated and sublime against an empty universe of yellow tint, rise the supreme evocations of Sharaku's genius.

Great distinction of composition marks all of Sharaku's work. Both the *hoso-ye* and the large bust-portraits are drawn with classic simplicity of

lines and masses. Nothing short of certain of the
Primitives can approach them. Every superfluous
ornament is omitted ; as in Plate 43, each line is
cut down to its meagrest possible limit. But the
expressiveness of the drawing is unsurpassable ;
and the æsthetic effect of the direct composition
grows with every repeated sight. These strange
heads against the dark glimmering backgrounds
seem Titans rooted in the void ; they loom upon
one's vision enormously ; they are overwhelming
with the spiritual greatness of their creator. In
spite of all the disturbing unquietness of their
conflicts, they are charged with a monumental
equilibrium of design, sealed with an exalted
peace of conception, poised as for eternity with the
repose of measureless space and time around them.
At first sight, one would imagine these portraits to
be impossibly restless things to live with ; but greater
familiarity proves them to be like the Sibyls of the
Sistine Chapel—vast and enduring figures, whose
large passion does not obliterate the fundamental
tranquillity of their conception.

The colour which Sharaku employs is of a unique
quality : sombre, with lurid lights ; heavy and opaque ;
nightmare colours, leashed into miraculous and incredible harmony ; things of infernal and dusky
splendour ; "tragic colours," Kurth calls them. The
dark mica backgrounds, which Sharaku is said, without much proof, to have invented, heighten to a
remarkable degree his colour effects. Words and
reproductions are alike powerless to convey any
sense of them ; they hold in store an impressive

sensation for him who has not yet seen them. With them Sharaku takes first rank as a colourist.

Toward the end of his brief career, his portraits became almost too terrible in their savage and tragic irony. In the large double-portraits Sharaku tears the mask of humanity aside and shows the very beast. Yet to call even these most extreme of his productions caricatures is to obscure a subtle spiritual essence by a crude word. They are exactly as comic as the ravings of Lear, as mirth-provoking as the laments of Shylock. They are not the light mocking of a scoffer or a comedian, but the appalling and tortured sneer of a man whose vision of men is coloured by his desire for the gods.

"Because he did not represent reality, but on the contrary painted unnatural figures, the public became hostile toward him." . . . "His figures were too realistic." . . . "He was a bungler in art." . . . From these conflicting criticisms, found in various Japanese authorities, we may gather with what comprehension the public of that day accepted the final work of the great painter; and we may conjecture what neglect and hatred forced him into a never-broken retirement.

Dr. Kurth is of the opinion that, after the year 1795, Sharaku still continued to produce secretly a few prints under the assumed name of Kabukidō Yenkyō, and attempted under this disguise to win back the popularity of his prime. This is an alluring but somewhat fantastic theory, which neither the documentary nor the internal evidence of Yenkyō's work adequately supports. Other authorities believe

Yenkyō to have been an independent artist who was
a pupil of Sharaku. His work strangely resembles
that of Kunimasa I. At the present time it cannot
be said that the question is wholly settled; but it
would be rash to accept Kurth's theory at its face
value.

In conclusion, let us grant that Sharaku is not for
every one. One cannot quarrel with a person who
says, " I understand Sharaku; I see the measureless
depths of his tragic irony, the unique splendour of
his colour, the perfect mastery of his composition.
But I do not like him. I prefer Kiyonaga, just as
I prefer the stately beauty of Keats to the troubled
profundity of Blake." Such a position is comprehensible and impregnable. But he who finds
Sharaku merely grotesque or absurd or repellent
should return to the portraits for further study;
he has not yet reached the immortal heart of
Sharaku's work, and he is missing a memorable
experience.

Exact comparisons are profitless; but most
students of Japanese prints have at certain times
turned from the work of Sharaku with the deep
conviction that this man was the greatest genius
of them all.

Sharaku's output was not large, and his work is
now of the utmost rarity. The Parisian collectors
long ago recognized Sharaku's greatness, and at a
time when Fenollosa was proclaiming Sharaku as
an "arch-purveyor of vulgarities," and Strange was
grudgingly describing him in seven lines as an artist
"of great power but little grace," the collectors of

Paris had already acquired such Sharaku treasures as are now a lavish and deserved reward for their foresight. Perhaps the only collection of Sharaku prints that can rival those of Paris is the notable Spaulding Collection of Boston, which takes high rank.

## CHOKI.

*A Silver Print.*

> The sky, a plate of darkened steel,
> Weighs on the far rim of the sea,
> Save where the lifted glooms reveal
> The last edge of the sun burned free.
> Blood-red, it drops departingly.
>
> And in the nightmare of the hour,
> Against the terrible sea and sky,
> A woman's figure—a strange flower—
> Lingers. Her wearied, curious eye
> Watches the burning world go by.

Though Choki is probably not to be counted as one of the few supremely great artists of the Ukioye School, his fame has been steadily increasing during the last twenty years; and whereas he once held an insignificant place in the esteem of amateurs, he has of late been regarded with an interest and admiration that at times seem almost more than his deserts. Mr. Strange calls him the most graceful of all the figure-designers of his time, and Kurth does not hesitate to deal with him as "mit einem Riesengroszen." I note in Kurth a tendency to exalt an artist because of his proficiency in technical processes, to an extent that I cannot assent to; Choki was superb, but hardly Titanic. It would be difficult to characterize him more justly than in the words of M. Koechlin, "Le plus curieux des petits maîtres." This description certainly does not err on the side of over-enthusiasm ; perhaps these are rather lukewarm words to apply to a grace so exquisite, a precision so sharp, and a spiritual appeal so strangely alluring as that of Choki.

Absolutely nothing is known of Yeishōsai Choki's life ; it is believed that he was a pupil of Sekiyen,  who also taught Utamaro. The Japanese authorities are inexplicably silent about him. Internal evidence, however, tells us that his work lies between the years 1785 and 1805. His earliest designs are strongly after the manner of Kiyonaga, whose feminine types he at first adopted almost literally. These he modified somewhat a little later when he came under the influence of Yeishi, whose slender and delicate figures led him away from the robust ones of Kiyonaga. One of Choki's

CHOKI.

pillar-prints, illustrated in Plate 45, marks an interesting transition stage. The face and figure seem at first sight almost purely of the Kiyonaga variety, but on closer examination differences appear ; and most striking of all is the fact that the colour-scheme is that peculiar combination of yellow, grey, violet, blue, and black which was distinctive of some of Yeishi's finest work. The influence of Sharaku on Choki was at some time

CHOKI: COURTESAN AND
ATTENDANT.

Size 26×4½.
Signed _Choki ga._

SHUNMAN: TWO LADIES
UNDER A MAPLE-TREE.

Size 24×5.
Signed _Kubo Shunman ga._

*Plate 45*

very strong, though the precise date is almost impossible to determine. So great was Choki's admiration for this master that later, when he had arrived at his own distinctive manner, he produced a pillar-print of a girl holding a fan on which appears Sharaku's famous design of "The Man with the Pipe." But Choki followed no one else as badly as he did Sharaku; though he appears to have learned things that were of great value to him later, his immediate imitations of the great ironist reduced the superb effects of the latter to the level of caricatures and dissipated the effect of concentrated force which marks his work. Utamaro proved a more congenial influence; and in Choki's earlier prints there are many traces of the grace, though not of the versatility, of that artist.

About 1790 there came out of this series of imitations a curious blended type, which finally became Choki's distinctive own. This type is a composite of Kiyonaga, Yeishi, and Sharaku, but ultimately unlike any of them in its effect. The lower part of the face is prominent; the neck is elongated and wonderfully delicate; about the eyes there is a narrowing that is unusual. These figures of Choki's are distinguished by a precision in drawing so sharp as to be almost an affectation, and by a grace half of whose unique fascination is produced by some strangeness of gesture, some keenness of characterization, or some unusual angle of vision. Few examples of Choki's work in this manner survive; but they are sufficient to lift his reputation from that of a copyist to that of a notable creator of women's portraits.

Woman was his great theme. "Er hat ihrem Liebreiz das Hohelied der Japanischen Malerei überhaupt gesungen," says Kurth, in a burst of enthusiasm for these subtle designs. His most striking works in this manner, and perhaps the greatest of all his works, are undoubtedly his half-length figures on mica or silver backgrounds. Of the fascination of these rare prints it is impossible to gain any idea from a reproduction. They rise into the world of the miraculous ; they are pure incantations. Such sheets as the famous " Fireflies," or the two women smoking by the river, or the falling-snow scene, or the sunset by the sea, have a beauty as unique as it is haunting. The colours, dull in tone, produce against the metallic sheen of the silver backgrounds unparalleled arrangements that are positively disturbing in their super-refinement.

Choki's blue and silver and red tones seem to pass over into a region where dwell things inexpressible by ordinary pigments. The most sophisticated amateur shivers before some of these colour-harmonies. Choki's characteristic prints are never restful, but always exciting and vibrant ; they are dominated by some hidden instability of equilibrium that reacts on one's nerves like a drug. Their beauty has a certain madness in it, or at least a note of strain and disquietude. Thus in the end, for all his imitative efforts, Choki stands, as did Sharaku, in solitary isolation and impenetrable mystery.

For reasons unknown to us, Choki late in his activity changed his signature to Shiko and produced under this name a small number of prints regarding

CHOKI: A COURTESAN
AND HER LOVER.

Size 24×4½.
Signed *Shiko, hitsu.*

*Plate 46*

CHOKI: A GEISHA AND HER
SERVANT CARRYING LUTE-
BOX.

Size 24×5.
Signed *Shiko, hitsu.*

the quality of which opinions differ. They are all in the manner of Utamaro's later style, and so little resemble the work signed "Choki" that one has to use a distinct effort to restrain one's incredulity, in the face of pretty clear evidence that the two names were used by a single artist. Easily first among these prints are a few splendid pillar-prints; one of these, the two singers with the black box, illustrated in Plate 46, seems to me almost the finest pillar-print post-dating 1795 that I have ever seen. Of this form Choki was a consummate master. But M. Koechlin regards these Shiko prints as mere imitations of Utamaro's period of decadence, and rejoices in the fact that they are so rare. Mr. Arthur Morrison, on the other hand, who points out correctly that Shiko is Choki's late, not his early name (a matter on which most writers have inexplicably gone astray) feels that the Shiko sheets are,

SHIKO.

in the best instances, of more elegance and distinction than anything produced under the Choki signature. I should hardly like to agree with either view, but am content to put the Shiko pillar-prints and the Choki silver-prints side by side, and regard them as the supreme examples of the double talent of this puzzling genius.

All of Choki's work is of great rarity; that signed Shiko is possibly even rarer than that

signed Choki. Rarest and most highly treasured
of all are his silver-prints ; the ordinary collector
will probably never have an opportunity to obtain
one.

NAGAHIDE II and ICHIRAKUSAI NAGAMATSU
(CHŌSHŌ) may be mentioned as followers of Choki.
The fact that we do not know of more disciples
of so brilliant a designer is another one of the
inexplicable things that surround him.

### TOYOKUNI.

*The Pupil of Toyokuni.*

I walk the crowded Yedo streets,
And everywhere one question greets
My passing, as the strollers say—
" How goes the Master's work to-day?
We saw him sketching hard last night
At Ryogoku, where the bright
Trails of the rockets lit the air.
You should have seen the ladies there !
All the most famous of the town
In gorgeous robes walked up and down
The long bridge-span, well-knowing he
Was there to draw them gorgeously.
I'm sure he'll give us something fine—
Dark splendid figures, lights ashine,
A great procession of our best
And costliest Oiran, with the West
Burning behind them.   When it's done,
Pray, of the copies, save me one."

Yes, I am pupil to the great.
How well he bears his famous state !
With what superbness he fulfills
The multitude's delighted wills,
Giving them, at their eager call,
Each play and feast and festival

Drawn with a rich magnificence:
And they come flocking with their pence
To buy his sheets whose supple power
Captures the plaudits of the hour—
Till even Utamaro's eyes
Turn, kindled with swift jealousies.

Strange! that before this crowded shrine
One voice is lacking, and that mine—
I, learner in his lordly house—
I, on whose cold, unwilling brows
The lights of his strong glory burn,
Blinding my heart that needs must yearn
Far from the measure of his state—
I, liegeman to another fate.
Would that some blindness came on me
That I might cease one hour to see,
For all his high, ambitious will,
His is a peasant's nature still. . . .
What utter madness that my thought
Weighs him—I who am less than naught!
Where he walks boldly, there I creep.
Where his assured long brush-strokes sweep
Unhesitant, there I falter, strain
With agony—perhaps in vain—
For some more subtly curving line,
Some musical poising of design
That shall at last, at last express
My frailer glimpse of loveliness.
And yet, for all his facile art,
I hug my impotence to my heart.
For there are things his marching mind
In steady labours day by day
With all its sight shall never find,
With all its craft can never say.
There are lights along the dusky street
That his bold eyes have never caught;
There are tones more luminous, more sweet
Than any that his hopes have sought.
There are torturing lines that curve and fall
Like dying echoes musical,
Or twine and lave and bend and roll,
In labyrinths to lure my soul.

His ladies sumptuous and rare
Move princess-like in proud design
Of glowing loveliness : but where
His bannered pomps and pageants shine,
I feel a stiller, rarer peace,
A cadence breathless, slender, lone.
And where his facile brush-strokes cease
Begins the realm that is my own.

I wander lonely by fields and streams.
I lie in wait for lingering dreams
That brood, a tender-lighted haze
Down the wide space of ending days—
A secret thrill that hovering flies
Round some tall form, some wistful eyes,
Some thin branch where the Spring is green—
A whisper heard, a light half-seen
By lonely wanderers abroad
In crowded streets or solitude
Of hills—to haunt with dim unrest
The empty chambers of the breast.

Perhaps some day a heart shall come,
Like me half-blind, like me half-dumb,
Like me contentless with the clear
Sunlighted beauties men hold dear.
Perhaps he will more greatly prize
My faltered whispers from afar
Than all the Master's pageantries
And confident pomp and press and jar.
Yet, well or ill, how shall I change
The measure doled, the nature given?
Mine is the thirst for far and strange
Echoes of a forgotten heaven.
I listen for the ghosts of sound;
Remote, I watch life's eager stream ;
Through wastes afar, through gulfs profound,
I, Toyohiro, seek my dream.

Utagawa Toyokuni was born in 1768, and early
began his apprenticeship as a pupil of Toyoharu.
From this master he learned the rules of European

perspective—a device which he soon abandoned for the true Japanese convention. He may have studied under Shunyei for a short time. Though he was later to become a fertile producer of actor-prints, he inaugurated his work with the figures of women. His first works imitate the type of face and figure made famous by Shunsho's and Shigemasa's book, "Mirror of the Beautiful Women of the Yoshiwara." Before 1790 he gave up this type for one copied from Kiyonaga, who was at this time at the height of his fame. But Toyokuni was no such draughtsman as Kiyonaga, and his figures in this manner are generally poorly drawn and awkward. At this time he frequently adopted colour-schemes from Shunman. After Kiyonaga's retirement Toyokuni began to use the delicate type made popular by the rising genius of Choki; but after a short interval he went over to Utamaro, who was then coming into supreme mastery.

TOYOKUNI.

Up to 1791, therefore (according to Friedrich Succo, "Toyokuni und Seine Zeit," München, 1913), Toyokuni was exclusively a painter of women. But when in the early nineties the colossal Sharaku brought out his revolutionary actor-portraits, Toyokuni abandoned his old field and adopted, to the extent that a smaller man could, the themes and eventually the manner of this great genius. At first

Sharaku appears to have been an awakener rather than a guide to Toyokuni ; for we find that it was to Shunsho's style that Toyokuni first looked for a model. But when Sharaku's great series of the Ronin bust-portraits appeared, Toyokuni at once responded to them as the strongest influence of his whole life and produced a number of similar portraits in a manner that captures all the eccentricities but little of the strength or insight of Sharaku. A more successful series, also definitely inspired by Sharaku's Ronin busts, was a set of full-length Ronin figures which Toyokuni then brought out. These tall monumental designs, with striking masses of black and deep colour against grey or mica backgrounds, are perhaps the finest actors in the whole long list of this artist's work. Though they never surpass Shunsho's or Sharaku's supreme creations, they are powerful conceptions, and constitute some basis for the claim of Toyokuni's admirers that he was the third-greatest of the actor-painters.

When, about 1794, Sharaku's career came to a sudden and tragic close, Toyokuni turned back from actors to women. Once more he followed Utamaro in the selection of his type, and with greater success than heretofore. To this period belongs the really splendid triptych, " The Journey of Narahira," representing a man on horseback and six attendants, admirably spaced, at the foot of Fuji. In this period also must be placed the series of pillar-prints of unusual width and shortness, very richly printed, representing courtesans and actors together. The print of this series which shows Ichikawa Kōmazō

TOYOKUNI: LADIES AND CHERRY BLOSSOMS IN THE WIND.

Right-hand sheet of a triptych. Size 15×10. Signed *Toyokuni ga*.
Metzgar Collection.

*Plate 47*

pushing back a reed blind to surprise a half-clothed courtesan is a very fine work. These, and other productions of this time, justify us in calling this decade the best period of Toyokuni's activity.

But before 1800 Toyokuni had followed Utamaro in that artist's adoption of the thin necks, enormous coiffures, and distorted bodies which not even Utamaro was always able to handle beautifully. Toyokuni's success was far inferior. The over-ripeness of the type required all Utamaro's subtlety to make it attractive or significant; and Toyokuni was by no means subtle. Therefore it was no loss when he returned to actor-prints shortly thereafter. One print of this, his second actor-period—the savage portrait of Matsumoto Kōshirō, reproduced by Succo—is notable and fine. But on the whole his second period shows Toyokuni as only slightly more original than in the Sharaku period. In his portraits of women at this time he sometimes leaned a little toward the Yeishi type, with Yeishi's stiffness but without his distinction. Many books, from these as well as from other years, bear witness to his industry; he was a veritable geyser of prints of every sort.

In 1804 Toyokuni was obscurely involved in trouble with the authorities over some of his historical prints. This was the time when Utamaro also suffered at their hands. In 1806 Utamaro died; and Toyokuni, who had so long leaned on the greater painter for his stimulus and inspiration, went to pieces like a house of cards. Without a rival to emulate, he was nothing; and we see him, a tragic figure—indisputably the

most famous master then living, who had survived
the great days when he had competed with Kiyonaga, Yeishi, and Utamaro for popular favour—now
alone in a glory which he could not sustain—a master
bereft of those conditions which had once enabled
him to produce almost-masterpieces.

From this time on his work steadily deteriorated.
The raw and over-complicated colours of his designs
of women made a melancholy contrast to the " Narahira" triptych. He abandoned woman-portraiture
about 1810. His actors continued—a mere outworn
formula—awkward, angular creations, with senselessly
crossed eyes, twisted necks, wry mouths—the veriest
parody on those devices which had once been employed by Sharaku for a sublime end. Toyokuni
died in 1825, a man who had outlived himself.

Toyokuni's production had been enormous. The
contemporaneous popularity indicated by this is hard
to understand unless we remember his frequent shift-
ings of style and realize that at every moment he was
ready to throw off his old manner and adopt that of
whatever artist most strongly appealed to the taste of
the hour. He was the most imitative of all artists.
What the mob wanted he gave them unreservedly,
losing his own integrity thereby.

Toyokuni seems to have been without real individuality or individual view-point. He was devoid of
either illusions or insight; and the true artist must
have the one or the other passionately. He drew his
women without enthusiasm and without tenderness.
He conceived his actors without the white-heat of
real artistic creation. There is something rasping

about the greater part of his work ; it seems full of sound and fury, signifying nothing. It is rhetoric, not the profound and tragic poetry of Sharaku, nor the subtle and decadent lyric strain of Utamaro. Rarely did he make an authentic attempt to capture the beauty or wonder or terror of life as he himself saw it. It is always the vision of other men that he is reporting, not his own. He had no vision.

So long as he could attach himself to some productive master, catching that master's feeling and style to a certain extent, he produced creditable works. But when the support was withdrawn he seemed powerless to take another step along that road. Kiyonaga's retirement, Sharaku's downfall, Utamaro's death—each in turn cut short Toyokuni's prosperous career in the footsteps of these masters. When left to himself he had only one thing to revert to—the typical Toyokuni actor at its worst, a thing of common uglincss.

No fame has tarnished more than his with the passing of time. As Sharaku's has brightened, his has dimmed. Once he was esteemed the greatest living print-designer; now I find that many students feel a sense of surprise when occasionally, out of the thousands of Toyokuni's prints, one appears that is really distinguished.

It must, however, be admitted that at certain times Toyokuni's native brilliancy enabled him to create prints that are not surpassed by any of his contemporaries. He did more poor work than any other artist of his time ; but such triptychs as the " Ryogoku Fireworks," in the Kiyonaga manner, the " Bath House," in which shadows appear on the wall, the

" Fan Shop," and the " Ladies and Cherry-blossoms in the Wind," are beyond criticism.

The best Toyokuni prints are very rare; the common ones are to be found plentifully in every print-shop.  His few finest triptychs, such as the " Narahira," or the " Ladies and Cherry-blossoms in the Wind," of which one sheet appears in Plate 47, are among the collector's important treasures.

The beginner should be warned that there were, in all, at least five men who at various times bore the name Toyokuni.  No one of the successors of the first Toyokuni ever produced work comparable with the finest work of Toyokuni I ; but it is a matter of great difficulty, not yet by any means wholly clear, to distinguish between the late inferior work of Toyokuni I and the work of several of the succeeding Toyokunis.  One simple indication may be of service to the inexperienced collector : If the Toyokuni signature is in a red oval or cartouch, it is not by the first master.  This statement cannot, however, be reversed, for the later Toyokunis often signed without the cartouch.

### TOYOHIRO.

*A Group of Ladies.*

> O careless passer—O look deep !
> These forms from near the sea of sleep
> Come hither ; on each forehead gleams
> The phosphorescent spray of dreams.
> They have sailed in from lonely seas
> Cloaked in a haze of mysteries;
> And hither by a lord are led
> Who snared them, pale himself with dread,
> Upon the very shores of sleep.
> O careless passer-by, look deep !

Utagawa Toyohiro, sometimes also called Ichiriusai, was born in 1773 ; he was a brother, fellow-student, and probably pupil of Toyokuni. It is well known that about 1800 these two artists collaborated to some extent. Toyohiro's own chief work—landscapes, book-illustrations not unlike Hokusai's, and figures of women—was done between 1795 and 1820; he died in the year 1828.

TOYOHIRO.

Fate has been unkind to him in associating him with a man tremendously more productive and incomparably more popular in his own day than himself. Even to the present time, the reputation of Toyokuni still overshadows that of his brother. But the close student of Toyohiro's work will probably come to the conclusion that this present difference in fame is due less to difference in merit than to the fact that Toyokuni was enormously prolific, while Toyohiro's work was scanty. The contemporaneous popularity may be ascribed to the ability of Toyokuni to shift and veer with every change in the public taste, while Toyohiro was unable or unwilling to move with these fluctuating winds. It is reported that a serious breach occurred between the brothers because of Toyohiro's refusal to produce actor-prints as the popular taste demanded. His work is, however, coming to be recognized as of a quality at least equal to his brother's, and in some respects finer and more truly the expression of a rare sense of beauty.

We may conjecture that Toyohiro inherited two things from his first teacher Toyoharu. One was a leaning toward landscape drawing. The other was a certain distinction and shy aloofness that marked the older master.

All Toyohiro's work has an aristocratic touch, a fine subtlety of curve and colour, that contrast markedly with the frequently blaring compositions of Toyokuni. He seldom drew actors or courtesans; most of his figures are ladies of birth and breeding. The beautiful spots of black which are important elements in the majority of his compositions are handled with a keen sense of contrast that not even Kiyonaga's surpassed. His brushwork is firm and delicate, but not so sparkling with vitality as that of some of his predecessors. His colours are soft, his figures wonderfully graceful; the impression he produces upon one is that of a subtle and beauty-hungry spirit, detached from the mob by a refinement beyond their comprehension, driven on by a consuming passion, devoted to the quest of a perfection he was able to project but not to realize.

In style, he draws considerably upon Toyokuni's early Utamaro manner; but in spirit he is nearer to Yeishi and Utamaro himself, both of whom must have influenced him somewhat. Not even the work of Yeishi is so saturated with the wistfulness for beauty, the sense of vanishing loveliness, the home-sickness for regions of otherwhere. One of his triptychs, the "Daimyo's Kite Party," reproduced

TOYOHIRO: A DAIMYO'S KITE-PARTY.

Triptych. Each sheet size 15×10. Signed *Toyohiro ga.*

*Plate 48*

341

in Plate 48, so embodies these qualities that it is worthy of special attention.

In a landscape of green hills, where a circle of low slopes encloses a space of level ground, stands, on the rising edge of that natural amphitheatre, a group of noble ladies and children in the soft brightness of festal attire—richly decorated pink, black, white, translucent heliotrope. Below and behind them boys are manœuvring a kite, and older men direct briskly. The ladies for whom this simple and charming pastime is arranged do not seem wholly intent upon it. Their tall slender figures move as if in abstraction, an isolated group in the foreground. One grey cherry-tree, with gnarled branches etched against a clear sky, stands in their midst, bare except for the pink of earliest blossoms; and the pale green of the more distant encircling hills is here and there touched with the same luminous flowers.

Across this landscape the slender figures move in slow procession. Their robes sway about them slowly. These sweeping draperies, which Harunobu would have charged with peace and solemnity, are here touched with the tension of more unquiet curves, restless, troubled with some element of torture in their beauty. These are the lines of the branch and of the wave, bent by the strain of hidden and conflicting forces. The clear festive brightness of pink cherry-blossoms with the light of spring shining through them serves but to accentuate the faint melancholy of the trailing figures on whom lies a wistfulness that no spring can satisfy. They linger, exquisitely aimless; beautiful, and weary for a yet-

unattained beauty; happy, but grave with the shadow
of fleeting happiness; sad, though reconciled by the
knowledge that beauty is half sadness. They have
walked with expectant steps to the edge of the
world; and now they pace, delicately wondering, not
far from the abyss where there is nothing. Autumn
will always be to them cold and unkindred; yet
in the flush of the spring their thoughts will turn
toward death and autumn. One cannot imagine
them wholly joyous. They seem haunted by a
nostalgia for remote delights, unearthly music, secret
and dimly remembered gardens. Strange, late, exotic
flowers are these, whom a pensiveness not known
to simpler and sturdier natures disturbs with futile
dreams.

A similar feeling is so often repeated in Toyohiro's
work that I venture to regard it as the keynote of
his genius.

Toyohiro's landscapes are without notable beauty.
He had a habit of cutting across the middle of his
picture with wide streaks of white mist—an unpleasant device adopted to produce the effect of
distance. He is, however, an historical link of great
importance between his master, Toyoharu, and his
pupil, Hiroshige, the greatest of all landscape
painters. As a conduit of landscape painting at a
time when the Ukioye School was little given to this
as a separate study, Toyohiro's work in this field
may well engage our attention; but one suspects
that it is the fame of his great pupil's landscapes
rather than the intrinsic merit of his own that has
given his their prominence.

Toyohiro produced a few pillar-prints of birds which have great distinction; an almost classic feeling marks some of them.

Toyohiro's prints are not numerous; Toyokuni's outnumber his twenty to one. His pillar-prints are very rare; his triptychs are generally notable. It is necessary to add, however, that poor impressions of his work, printed in poor colours, are more common than any other kind.

# VII

# THE FIFTH PERIOD:
# THE DOWNFALL

FROM THE
DEATH OF UTAMARO
TO THE
DEATH OF HIROSHIGE
(1806-1858)

# CHAPTER VII

## THE FIFTH PERIOD: THE DOWNFALL

WHEN Utamaro died, in 1806, the great days ot the figure-print were ended. There were to be no more Harunobus or Kiyonagas or Sharakus—only a horde of little men whose work retained few traces of the earlier greatness. And our serious interest in the art as a whole must end here. Were it not for the superb renaissance of landscape which this period includes, side by side with the decay of figure-designing, it would be my choice to mark this date as the end of our history.

The causes of the degradation of prints in this period appear to have been of several natures. For one, the accidents that regulate the birth of geniuses operated unkindly, and few artists of first-rate talent came to take the places of the dead masters. Further, the colour-print had gone somewhat out of fashion among its original public, and the people who now bought were chiefly of a lower and more ignorant class than the purchasers of Kiyonaga's day. To the less exacting but eager demands of this class the publishers catered with coarser designs, cruder colours, and more careless printing. Now, in literal truth, the print-designer was the artisan; and amid the vast flood of commonplace productions of the time it is difficult to search out those few works that have a claim to beauty.

It is probable that a general loss in refinement of taste marked the epoch and was reflected in the prints. The uncouth flaring designs of the textiles, the gross overladen coiffures, the excess of decoration that lay like a blight over all the instruments of life at this time, naturally had their influence upon the standards of the artist.

Furthermore, the movement toward realism here reached its climax. Dominated by Hokusai's earlier work, the artists abandoned the old traditional devotion to stylistic restraint and went madly in chase of a distorted kind of literal truth that had no relation to beauty. Men who were too impotent to create visions nobly and too dull to observe reality keenly attempted to conceal their double weakness by a double evasion—spoiling what claim their work had to idealistic imagination by touches of crude realism, and ruining it as realism by the most grotesque aberrations of fancy. In the sphere of erotic prints this was characteristically and repellently manifest. Certain examples of this type, produced in the first quarter of the nineteenth century, surpass in grossness even the most studied of European specimens. In landscape alone has the period something of the highest charm to offer us.

## THE SCHOOL OF TOYOKUNI

As we have seen, Toyokuni's career ended anything but brilliantly. Unfortunately his numerous
followers appear to have been influenced more by his
final work than by the production of his better days.
I do not regard it as profitable to wade, as some
writers have done, through this wearying period of
degenerate production and tabulate every fact
obtainable about every insignificant artist with the
same care that one would bestow upon Kiyonaga.
I shall therefore be content to note down only the
most salient features of this epoch of disintegration.

Following Toyokuni, at least four men used
the name made famous by him. The first of
these, Toyokuni II, was that same Toyokuni
Gosotei of whom we shall treat under the heading
of Landscape. His use of the name Toyokuni
appears to have been between the years 1825 and
1835.

Toyokuni III was better known as Kunisada I;
for though he was born in 1786 and lived until 1865,
he did not adopt the name of Toyokuni until about
1844. He added to our confusion by the fact that
he signed himself "Toyokuni" or "Toyokuni II,"
never recognizing the claims of the real Toyokuni II
to the name. Most frequently Kunisada's Toyokuni
signature is enclosed in a long red cartouch, a device
never used by Toyokuni I. This very undistinguished
artist was one of the most prolific producers of the
school. All that meaningless complexity of design,
coarseness of colour, and carelessness of printing

which we associate with the final ruin of the art of colour-prints finds full expression in him.   Every tourist returning from Japan brings back dozens of crudely coloured prints by him or by the members of his school, under the misapprehension that these are the famous and valuable Japanese prints of which he has vaguely heard.  The only figure work of Kunisada's that I am able to recall with any pleasure is his really notable Memorial Portrait of Hiroshige, a dignified and impressive print.  The few landscapes he produced are of much greater beauty than his figures, and one is inclined to wish that he had done more in this field and less in the other.

KUNISADA.

TOYOKUNI IV was also known as Kunisada II and as Kunimasa II.  Born 1833, he died 1880. His prints, largely executed in cheap analine colours, set one's teeth on edge with some of the most shrieking discords that I have ever encountered. There exists an unfortunate collector who proudly brought back from Japan one hundred and nineteen triptychs by this artist.

TOYOKUNI V was also called Kunisada III and Kunimasa III.  His work was worthless.

KUNIMASA I (1772–1810) was an exceedingly able pupil of Toyokuni, who was influenced by Sharaku.  Some of his work is very fine; he stands out as one of the few notable designers of this group.

KUNINAGA, who died in 1804, was a rare pupil of Toyokuni. His work is pleasant, though it has no great distinction ; but it is far more attractive than the work of most of these men, for the reason that he had the good luck to die before the period of general disintegration began. The Spaulding Collection contains a fine diptych by him, in black and several shades of yellow, in the early style of Toyokuni.

KUNIMITSU was also an early pupil of Toyokuni. His work is agreeable but not notable.

From the vast number of minor followers of the Toyokuni tradition, I select the following as the most common : KUNIYASU I, KUNIYASU II, TOYOKIYO, TOYOHIRO II, KUNIFUSA, KUNIHIRO, KUNITANE, KUNIKATSU, KUNIHISA, KUNI-TERA, KUNITERU, KUNIKANE I, KUNIKANE II, KUNITAKA, KUNIMUNE, KUNIHIKO, KUNITOKI, KUNIYUKI, KUNITSUMA, KUNIKIYO, KUNIHANA, KUNITOHISA, KUNIMICHI I, KUNIMICHI II, KUNIAO I, KUNIAO II, KUNITORA, KUNITAKI, KUNITSUGI I, KUNITSUGI II, KUNITADA, KUNINOBU II, KUNIAKI, KIYOKUNI, KUNIMARU I, KUNIMARU II, KUNI-CHIKA, CHIKASHIGE, YOSHITAKI, YOSHITSURU, YOSHIUME, YOSHITSUNA, YOSHISATO, YOSHIFUJI, YOSHIKAGE, YOSHIKUNI, YOSHICHIKA, YOSHIKAZU, YOSHIHARU, SHUNBENI, YOSHITOMI, YOSHIFUSA, SUGAKUDO, SENCHO, TOMINOBU.

CHIKAMARO is said to be identical with KIOSAI, whose work sometimes resembles Hokusai's. Born in 1831, he died very late in the century. He was a vigorous designer—perhaps the best of all the later men. His crow pictures are famous.

KIKUGAWA YEIZAN, a prolific and undistinguished designer of the first quarter of the century, was a late rival and imitator of Utamaro. He eventually sank even to imitating Kunisada. The flowing draperies of some of his prints of women are at first sight attractive to eyes not accustomed to the finest works in this field ; but the complete banality of Yeizan's powers becomes manifest on more prolonged acquaintance, and any trace of charm disappears.

KIKUGAWA YEIZAN.

FOLLOWERS OF THE TORII SCHOOL.

Here may be mentioned those artists in whom the once-great Torii School came to its inglorious end.

KIYOMINE, the fifth head of the school, sometimes signed himself Kiyomitsu ; his work is easily distinguishable from that of the first Kiyomitsu. He studied under Kiyonaga, and later adopted a style somewhat like that of Toyokuni. His work is graceful, but not distinguished. Prints by him are rather rare. He died in 1868.

KIYOFUSA, who died as late as 1892, was the sixth Torii. He also called himself Kiyomitsu III.

and Kiyosada II. Other late members of this school were: KIYOMOTO II, KIYOYASU, KIYOTADA II, KIYOTADA III, KIYOSADA I.

## THE OSAKA SCHOOL.

In the first half of the nineteenth century there grew into importance in the city of Osaka a group of designers who constituted an exception to the statement made earlier in this book—that the art of colour-printing was exclusively a Yedo art. Hokusai is known to have visited Osaka in 1818; and possibly it was his influence that encouraged the movement. At any rate, a large number of the Osaka group were pupils of Hokusai or followers of his manner.

The school thus entered into real activity at a date when the art was far gone in its decline; and its designs produced no arresting effect. Most of the work of these men is crude. Yet when we look at the products of the second quarter of the century in Yedo, we may very possibly feel that the Osaka output was at least no worse. It included chiefly theatrical portraits, all done with a peculiar hardness of line and cold brilliance of colour, and printed as a rule very skilfully. These by no means approach the works of Shunsho, Shunyei, and Sharaku, after which they were obviously patterned, nor even the works of Toyokuni; but the hard treatment so characteristic of them gives a certain dignity of effect which Kunisada's flowing and formless earthquakes of draperies generally lack.

The school does not call for elaborate treatment;

the following men may be mentioned as among the
best known : HOKUSHU, HASEGAWA SADANOBU,
SADAKAGE, KAGETOSHI, SADAFUSA, SADATORA,
SADAMASA, SADAMASU, SADAHIRO, SADAYOSHI,
ASHIKUNI, ASHIYUKI, HIROSADA, SHUNSHI,
HORAI SHUNSHO II, HOKUMIO, HANZAN,
YOSHIIKU, and RANKO.    Others will be mentioned
later as pupils of Hokusai or as landscape-painters.

THE RENAISSANCE OF LANDSCAPE.

Like a beautiful island in the midst of a sea of
wrecks, the landscape prints of the first half of the
nineteenth century stand apart from the general
debasement of print-designing.    The great days of
the figure-print were over ; but now, into an art filled
with the second-rate followers of Utamaro and
Toyokuni, came the fresh and brilliant landscape
genius of Hokusai and Hiroshige.    Their work did
not share in the general decline ; it must be regarded
as a new shoot sent up by the roots of a tree
whose main trunk had already fallen into irreparable
decay.

Landscape-prints were not a new thing ; Utamaro
and Toyohiro had already produced fine work of
this nature, and interesting examples are to be
found as we look backward through the work of
Toyoharu, Shigemasa, Kiyonobu, and Masanobu—
back, in fact, almost to the beginning of the art.
But these earlier landscapes were, upon the whole,
of subordinate importance ; beside the figure-prints
of the earlier masters, they seem crude and rudimentary.    Previous to Hokusai and Hiroshige, they

were chiefly of topographical, not of æsthetic, intention and interest. In the nineteenth century their importance became paramount.

"Japanese colour-prints devoted to landscape," writes Mr. Strange, "form a class apart in the art of the world. There is nothing else like them; neither in the highly idealistic and often lovely abstractions of the aristocratic painters of Japan, nor in the more imitative and, it must be said, more meaningless transcripts from nature, of European artists. The colour-print, as executed by the best men of the Japanese popular school, occupies an intermediate place; perhaps thus furnishing a reason why we Westerners so easily appreciate it. Its imagery and sentiment are elementary in the eyes of the native critics of Japanese high art. Its attempts at realism are in his eyes mere evidence of vulgarity. On the other hand these very qualities endear it to us. We can understand the first, without the long training in symbolism which is the essential of refinement to an educated man of the extreme East. And the other characteristic forms, in our eyes, a leading recommendation. In short, the landscapes of artists such as Hiroshige approach more nearly to our own standards, and are thus more easily acceptable to us than anything else in the pictorial arts of China and Japan; while they have all the fascination of a strange technique, a bold and undaunted convention, and a superb excellence of composition not too remote in principle from our own."

## HOKUSAI.

Because thou wast marvellous of eye, magic of fancy, lithe of hand,
Because thou didst play o'er many a gulf where common mortals
    dizzy stand,      •
Because no thing in earth or sky escaped the pryings of thine art,
I call thee, who wast master of all, the master with the monkey's
    heart.

Where in the street the drunkards roll—where in the ring the
    wrestlers sway,
Where rustics pound the harvest rice, or fishers sail, or abbots pray,
In rocky gorge, or lowland field, or winter heights of mountain air,
Wherever man or beast or bird or flower finds place—yea, every-
    where
Thou standest, as I fancy, rapt in the live play of mass and line,
Curiously noting every poise; and in that ugly head of thine
Storing it with unsated fierce passion for life's minutest part,
Some day to use infallibly—O master with the monkey's heart!

Where Kanazawa's thundering shores behold the mounded waters
    rave,
And Fuji looms above the plain, and the plain slopes to meet the
    wave,
There didst thou from the trembling sands unleash thy soul in
    sudden flight
To soar above the whirling waste with awe and wonder and delight.
Thou sawest the giant tumult poured; each slope and chasm of
    cloven brine
Called thee; and from the scattered rout one vision did thy sight
    divine,
One heaven-affronting whelming wave in which all common waves
    have part—
A billow from the wrath of God—O monkey with a master's heart!

What mind shall span thee? Who shall praise or blame thy
    world-embracing sight
Whose harvest was each rock and wraith, each form of loathing or
    of light?
Though we should puzzle all our days, we could not know thee as
    thou art,
Nor where the seer of vision ends, nor where begins the monkey's
    heart.

Until rather recently Hokusai was, for European spectators, as isolated and commanding a figure in the domain of Japanese art as Fuji is in the Japanese landscape. He was regarded as the one culminating and all-inclusive genius among Japanese painters and print-designers. At precisely the same time, he was esteemed by Japanese connoisseurs to be a prolific but vulgar artisan, whose mere crafts-man-dexterity could not compen-sate for his lack of lofty feeling and poetic vision.

HOKUSAI.

It is not necessary to quarrel with either of these views. Almost every student of Hokusai passes through three stages. At first, he is overwhelmed by Hokusai's technical skill and imaginative brilliance, and regards him as un-rivalled. Deeper experience brings him the conviction that much of this magical dexterity is some-what in the nature of a juggler's antics in a vaude-ville, and that his first burst of enthusiasm was not wholly warranted. Then, finally, he comes to perceive that there are qualities in Hokusai's work which, in spite of so much that is vulgar, justly entitle this artist to his high fame.

One classes Hokusai as a landscape-artist; yet his work was by no means confined to landscape. He pictured, as M. Théodore Duret wrote, "everything to be seen by the eye or invented by the brain of a Japanese." His "Mangwa," that vast twelve-

volume collection of drawings, includes sketches of
a whole world of varied scenes and objects and
people. The bulk of his production was colossal—
dozens of designs a day throughout most of his
eighty-nine years !

His figures are drawn with a swift and sure
realism that is generally tinged with humour and
often with vulgarity. His vigorous power of ob-
serving and recording faces and attitudes is almost
unparalleled. Fantasy, whimsical conceits, irony,
grotesqueness animate them ; always they have super-
abundant life. The play of his brush is miraculous.

His landscapes are his greatest works. In the best
of these he shakes off his trifling mood, and, as in
Plate 51, creates designs whose stark brilliance and
originality of composition is unsurpassed. And at
least once, in the noblest of his prints—the rare and
monumental series of " The Imagery of the Poets "—
he achieves a high seriousness that will always be
impressive.

Hokusai was born in 1760, the son of a mirror-
maker. He lived to the age of eighty-nine years—a
long life, crowded with privation that wins our sym-
pathy, and with incessant devotion to his art. When
in his seventies, he said : " Ever since the age of six
years I have felt the impulse to draw the forms of
objects. Up to the age of fifty years I made a
great number of drawings ; but I am dissatisfied with
everything that I created prior to my seventieth
year. At the age of seventy-three I, for the first
time, began to grasp the true forms and nature of
birds, fishes, and plants. It follows that at the age

HOKUSAI: FUJI, SEEN ACROSS THE TAMA RIVER, PROVINCE OF MUSASHI.

One of the Series "Thirty-six Views of Fuji." Size 10½×15. Signed *Hokusai I-itsu, hitsu.*

*Plate 49*

361

of eighty I shall have made still greater progress; at ninety I shall be able to create all objects; at a hundred I shall certainly have attained to still higher, unimaginable power; and when I finally reach my one hundred and tenth year, every line, every dot will live with an intense life. I invite those who are going to live as long as I to convince themselves whether I shall keep my word. Written at the age of seventy-five years by me, formerly Hokusai, now called the Old Man Mad with Painting." His dying words were: "If the gods had given me only ten years more—only five years more—I could have become a really great painter!"

Hokusai's education began as an apprentice to a wood-engraver, a valuable experience for his later career. At the age of eighteen he entered the studio of Shunsho and adopted the name of Shunro. Under this name he produced actors in the orthodox Shunsho manner and melodramatic illustrations for the popular romances of the day. About 1786 a quarrel with Shunsho, due to the pupil's insubordination, led to Hokusai's expulsion, and he thereupon launched out for himself, to begin his long life of poverty and madly enthusiastic labour.

His work may be divided roughly into three periods. In the first he followed the traditions of Shunsho, Shunyei, Utamaro, and others of his contemporaries, with great skill but no special originality. His countless book-illustrations of this time were all conceived with lively fancy and vigour; but perhaps the finest works of this, his conventional period, are the very wide prints and surimono in which, against a delicately suggested landscape, move extraordinarily graceful women's figures not unlike those of Utamaro. Already he was a master of drawing; but he kept incessantly at his studies under many teachers, learning, among other things, European perspective from Shiba Kokan. His work was done in this and the following periods under a dozen different names, of which Sori, Kako, Shunro, and Taito are the most important.

In 1812 began his second or realistic period, with the publication of the first book of his fifteen-volume series of drawings, the "Mangwa." In this epoch he turned from the styles of his predecessors and launched into a hitherto unknown journalistic realism. With a lively sense of the comic and the burlesque, and an insatiable interest in the homeliest details of life, he threw overboard all formal stylistic quality and set sail on a riotous voyage of naturalistic discovery.

The "Mangwa," which may serve as a type of his whole production in this realistic period, is praised sometimes as his greatest work. In it we shall find not only his most striking *tours-de-force* as a draughtsman but also the key to his weakness. All existence thrilled him as it did Walt Whitman. and each object on which he turned his eyes stirred him with the desire to record it in his pages. Day after day he worked like a madman, throwing off his sketches of man, beast, and phantom, of rock, river and sea, in endless profusion and with inexhaustible ngenuity. And though we grant our admiration to the enthusiasm, sharp vision, and clever draughtsmanship of these sheets, we may still find in this undiscriminating passion a quality incompatible with the highest reaches of artistic greatness. There is something vulgar, childish, under-developed in the mental attitude revealed; it seems a coarse greed for all experience, unlighted by the power to judge and reject, or by any consciousness of the ranks and hierarchies of beauty. It is a vast and dull enthusiasm; a celebration of the victory of the will to live over the will to perfect; a triumph of meaningless sensation over the just judgments of the discriminating mind. All shapes seem equally interesting and beautiful to it—all smells equally sweet. As Pater writes of Balzac—a man who was in many ways not unlike Hokusai—this artist "had an excess of curiosity—curiosity not duly tempered with the desire of beauty."

I can never look through the "Mangwa" without a sense of distressing chaos and a longing for the purer beauties which more finely organized artists have evoked from the heterogeneous welter of the seen world. But just this welter is at this time Hokusai's theme. "A debauch of sketches," Fenollosa calls it. In this work Hokusai stands beside Harunobu exactly as Whitman stands beside Keats —a more interesting mind but a far less perfect artist.

"Hokusai is incomparable," writes the commentator who furnished the introduction to one of his books. "While all his predecessors were more or less slaves to classical tradition and inherited rules, he alone emancipated his brush from all such fetters, and drew according to the dictates of his heart." True:

and this was his curse.   No man has ever lived with
heart profound and subtle enough for such emanci-
pation.   Nor have the supreme artists ever attempted
it.   In Hokusai's case this upstart-abandoning of all
tradition was an error from which he was able later
to retrieve himself; but so great was the impression
produced  by  his  vulgarities  on  the  mob  that  even
to this day popular Japanese art has remained under
the cloud of it.

Hokusai himself did recover.   In his third period,
the stylistic one, the greatness that was in him tran-
scended his petty interest in the trivial idiosyncrasies
of seen things, and he created those visions which
constitute his lasting glory.   Between 1823 and 1830
he issued  those  series, " The  Thirty-six  Views  of
Fuji,"  " The  Bridges,"  " The  Waterfalls,"  " The
Loocho Islands," and " The Imagery of the Poets,"
in which we hail him as master.   No longer the
dupe of realism, he brings us his dreams.

" The Thirty-six Views of Fuji " stands as one of
his two greatest works.   Here, in the forty-six plates
that constitute the main series and the supplement,
the same motive is treated recurrently, but with
infinite variety.   He depicts Fuji, the sacred mountain, in storm and calm, in mist and sunlight—
sometimes dominating the colossally empty frame of
the design, sometimes receding to a mere speck in
the distance; and around the noble peak beat the
waves of the sea and the foam of the clouds and
the restless stream of human life, in a great epic
of infinite diversity and profound unity.

In this series his trivial realism is forgotten, or

HOKUSAI: FUJI, SEEN FROM THE PASS OF MISHIMA, PROVINCE OF KAHI.

One of the Series "Thirty-six Views of Fuji." Size 11½×15. Signed *Saki no Hokusai I-itsu, hitsu.*

*Plate 50*

employed only in just subordination. Throwing aside his earlier vulgar absorption in the minutiæ of existence, he concentrated his vision on one conception, one chosen impression, so sharply and personally seen that he evoked a new style in landscape. Much it borrowed from tradition; but the flavour was Hokusai's. These designs are, primarily, magnificent studies in linear composition. The great sweep of Fuji's slope is related to the rhythm of every other line in the picture. And the line-dominance is preserved by the use of the simplest and most original of colour-schemes—green, blue, and brown—broadly laid on in large masses. A highly decorative quality and great boldness are the result.

The justly famous "Wave" belongs to this series. Here for the first time in our survey of the prints do we find elemental fury depicted with grandiose eloquence. In the majestic composition of the "Great Tree" (Plate 50) the calm sublimity of nature and the infinitely minute, vermin-like aspect of man is superbly expressed. In the "Tama River" (Plate 49) Hokusai gives us a sweep of wave and shore, mist and mountain, that his great predecessors, the landscape-painters of Sung days in China, might have envied. In all these prints he relates man and nature to each other with a vividness and dramatic power foreign to his great rival Hiroshige.

The world which Hokusai pictures in this series is not the real world, but Hokusai's highly personal translation of it into terms of superb imagination. A thousand memory-stored impressions combine to make the sharp composite of each design; and it is,

to use the term in its technical Platonic sense, the
Idea of the scene that he flashes before us.  Herein
lies the abnormal vitality that emanates from these
pictures.  "We feel," says Mr. Binyon, "that the
world holds more wonders than we dreamed of,
sources of power and exhilaration which Hokusai
has revealed, and which we may go and discover
for ourselves."

Hokusai's other great work was a series of ten
upright prints of very large size, "The Imagery of
the Poets."  It returns in feeling, though not in
technique, to the style of the classic masters ; and
remains, because of its high seriousness of mood
and its sweeping magnificence of composition, at the
very top of all Hokusai's work.  Of all his thousands
of designs, the one that is supreme is probably the
print of this set which depicts the famous Chinese
poet Li Peh beside the chasm and cascade of Luh.

Even his latest years were crowded with continued
efforts.  In 1849, at the age of eighty-nine years,
he died.

Fine and well-preserved Hokusai prints are not
common.  His "Poets" and really brilliant impressions of his "Thirty-six Fuji" are very rare,
particularly the former.  Poor impressions of the
latter are numerous.  Practically all of Hokusai's
most famous prints have been reproduced, and the
collector must be on his guard against these worthless
sheets.  One of the best-known judges in Europe
was recently deceived by a fraudulent set of the
"Poets."  Hokusai's fine bird-and-flower designs
and his large early surimono are rare ; as also are

HOKUSAI: THE MONKEY BRIDGE—TWILIGHT
AND RISING MOON.

Size 14½×6½. Signed *Hokusai ga.*

*Plate 51*

good copies of his famous books, the " Mangwa " and the " One Hundred Views of Fuji." Numerous late blurred impressions of these are extant, and should be avoided. His other books are not uncommon.

## PUPILS AND FOLLOWERS OF HOKUSAI.

Hokusai had many pupils; no one of them equalled the landscape work of the master, though several of them produced designs of great interest. As a body they were distinguished for their matchless work in the field of surimono.

The surimono was a type of print not sold in the market; it was made upon special order of private individuals for use as a festival-greeting, an invitation, a congratulatory memorial, or an announcement. Its size was generally small, about five or six inches square; printed on very soft thick paper, it displayed the utmost complexity of the technique of colour-printing. The number of blocks was lavishly multiplied; the most subtle gradations of colour were contrived; and the effect was heightened by every variety of gauffrage, gold, silver, and bronze powders, and mother-of-pearl dust. Yet in spite of all this effort, the surimono is, in the opinion of many collectors, not as a rule very important as a work of art. In the ordinary surimono the medium employed has outstripped the motive expressed, and what should have been the means has become the sole end. Nevertheless they are unrivalled as specimens of workmanship and printing, and the best of them are highly treasured. Some of Hokusai's pupils excelled their master in this form.

GAKUTEI, who also signed himself Gogaku, produced perhaps the finest surimono of any that we know. His work in this field was voluminous and distinguished. He also issued a few exceedingly decorative landscapes.

GAKUTEI.

HOKKEI stands beside Gakutei as a brilliant producer of surimono, closely in the manner of Hokusai. Some of his landscapes, printed in blue and green, have a curious charm and individuality.

HOKUJU produced landscapes in a strange semi-European style, with angular mountains and unusual cloud effects.

YANAGAWA SHIGENOBU, the son-in-law of Hokusai, copied his master closely; some of his work has great charm. According to some authorities he is the same person to whom Hokusai gave his discarded name, KATSU-SHIKA TAITO. Certain prints signed Taito are still somewhat in doubt, notably the well-known leaping fish and the moon-and-bridge scene, both from the "Hari-maze Han"; Mr. Happer has brought forward evidence that these are by Taito, but many authorities still hold to the idea that

HOKKEI.

they are the work of Hokusai under his early name.

Among the numberless Hokusai pupils may be
named: HOKUBA, HOKUGA, NIHO, SHIGEYAMA,
GOKEI, SHINSAI, ISAI, HOKUUN, HOKUYEI,
HOKUTEI, HOKUTAI, HOKUSUI, TAIGAKU, RENSHI,
JUZAN, YASUMICHI, BOKUSEN, KEIJU, RYUSAI,
GANGAKUSAI, KEIRI, HOKUYO.

## HIROSHIGE.

As merchantmen from Eastern Isles
In caravels of purple came,
With freight that alien heart beguiles,
Incense and cloths of woven flame,

So down the gulfs of elder time
Thy glorious pinions bear to me
Mad treasure from the unknown clime
Of worlds beyond the Western Sea.

Now in my bay the sails are furled.
But I, who guess their native skies,
Henceforth must roam that golden world,
Where strange winds whisper and strange scents rise.—

Immortal Fuji's snowy crown—
Wide seas with sky of amethyst—
A street where torrents thunder down—
Branches that toss against the mist—
Smooth hills and hill-girt plains where run
Streams through the rice-fields steeped in heat—
Pines gnarled above a sunken sun—
Cold heights where cloud and mountain meet.

Now visions enter to my breast
That from thy passion won their birth,
When like a bride in radiance dressed
Before thee glowed the summers of earth.

What magic gave thee to behold
This fairness, secret from our sight,
Where morning walks the world in gold,
Or seas turn grey with coming night?

For thee, as when the South Winds blow,
Lands burst to bloom.　On every shore
Where beauty dwells thou didst bestow
A perilous mortal beauty more.

　　Twilight and morn on Biwa's breast—
　　Harima's sands and lordly pines—
　　White Hira-mountain's winter crest—
　　The low red dusk round Yedo shrines—
　　The moon beneath the Monkey Bridge—
　　The Poisoned River's brooding gloom—
　　Rose-dawn on some Tokaido ridge—
　　Pale water-worlds of lotus bloom.

Our toiling race is with the day
Wearied, and restless with the night,—
Unpausing, on its tombward way,
For fear or wonder or delight,—

Unwatchful, mid the sombre things
That mesh us in a vain employ,
For peace that half of heaven brings,
For beauty that is wholly joy.

Lover for whom the world was wide !
Down lighted pathways thou didst move,
Where hills and seas and cities hide
So much for weary men to love.—

　　The mist of cherry-trees in spring—
　　Ships sleeping on some bright lagoon—
　　A swallow's dusky sweeping wing—
　　Steep Ishiyama's autumn moon—
　　The changing marvels of faint rain—
　　The foam that hides the torrent's stream—
　　The eagle o'er the snowy plain—
　　Sea-twilights haunted as a dream.

　　Speaking, thou laidst thy brush aside—
　　" On a long journey I repair—
　　Regions beyond the Western Tide—
　　To view the wonderful landscapes there."

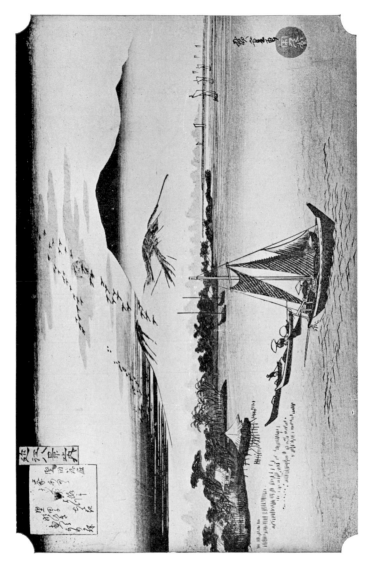

HIROSHIGE: HOMING GEESE AT KÁTADA—TWILIGHT.

One of the Series "Eight Famous Views of Lake Biwa." Size 9×13½. Signed *Hiroshige ga.*

*Plate 52*

Yet, at Adzuma, loosed from all
Thy mortal bonds, made free to roam,
Methinks thou couldst not break the thral
That held thee to thy human home.

Surely no heaven could harbour thee,
Nor other world of keener bliss,
Who didst with such deep constancy
Worship the loveliness of this.

Moon-flooded throngs in Yedo streets—
Dawn-quickened travellers on their road—
Lone ocean-fronting hill retreats—
An Oiran's perilous-sweet abode—
A mighty Buddha by the sea
Where all the wondering pilgrims meet—
Immortal Fuji, changelessly
Watching the world around her feet.

Hiroshige takes rank by unanimous consent as the foremost landscape artist produced by the Ukioye School. His prints, known to every one, have been more greatly admired in Western lands than the prints of any other artist except Hokusai. Hokusai's main concern was with the fundamental architecture of landscape; he outlined the structure of mountains, rocks, rivers, waves, and bridges with a hard and brilliant sharpness; but Hiroshige, less rigid in his treatment, seems chiefly intent upon the more delicate and transitory appearances of cloud

HIROSHIGE.

and mist, rain and snow, sunrise and dusk, that give to a landscape at each moment so much of

18

its specific character. These atmospheric effects of his are justly famous. Few landscape painters of any race have succeeded in rendering so finely the mood of a scene. No one can be insensible to the delicate peace and sweetness of a twilight like that of Plate 52, or the vigorous life of wide sea spaces in Plate 53, or the heavy hush of nightfall over the snow-covered village of Plate 54. Even more impressive are the luminous and solemn dusk on the Sumida River (Plate 55) and the mystery of the print called "The Bow-Moon" which appears as the frontispiece.

*The Bow-Moon.*

Where the torrent leaps and falls,
And the hanging cliffs look down,
Cloven grey and ruddy walls
Each with ragged forest-crown,

There across the chasmèd deep
Spans a gossamer bridge on high ;
And below, from gulfs of sleep,
Mounts the Bow-Moon up the sky.

Blue dusk, thickening whence she rose,
Her abysses veils ; above
Moves she into twilight's close
As faint strains of music move.

On the eastern slope her feet,
White, in trancèd ecstasy,
Climb, a ghost of heaven so sweet
That the spent day cannot die.

Walled by crags on either side
Glimmers forth her figure wan,
Straying like some lonely bride
Through the halls of Kubla Khan.

Pilgrim of the riven deep !
Whereso'er thy lover lie,
Sleep to him is troubled sleep
While his Bow-Moon haunts the sky.

Hiroshige's great strength lay in his genius for strikingly effective composition, and in the skill with which he adapted his designs to the limitations of the colour-print technique. He reduced the pictured scene to a few simple elements of a highly decorative character, and managed to make them so symbolic and suggestive that we do not miss the multitude of details which he purposely omits. A strongly dominant unity of impression is the result. His finest designs convey a sense of personal feeling that even the Barbizon artists at their best do not surpass. With the limited resources of the wood block, he achieved subtle renderings of distance, aerial perspective, atmosphere, and light; and the poetic quality of his designs has endeared him to generations of print-lovers in a way more personal than is the case with any other artist. His work will stand beside the "Liber Studiorum" of Turner; it remains perhaps the most complete and magnificent landscape record that any land has ever had.

One curious characteristic of these prints at once strikes the Western eye—the use of a band of dark colour along the top of the picture, which is shaded gradually down into the clear white of the lower sky. This convention serves several purposes. It provides a mass to balance the colour at the bottom of the design, bringing the whole sheet into the picture and not leaving the upper portion as a mere margin above the landscape proper. It also creates depth and atmosphere, setting the brightest part of the design, the middle, back into the frame created by the upper and lower masses. And finally, it renders with

peculiar accuracy the effect of gradual vanishing
which we actually experience as we look at a
landscape : in our visual field, the sky does
not end in a sharp line, but blurs and darkens
at the upper edge of the space that our eyes
survey.

Hiroshige's bird and flower designs are works of
extraordinary freshness and loveliness ; a unique
and idyllic charm emanates from them, and as
compositions they take high rank (Plate 56).

Alilt against the emerald sky,
A tiny violet songster swings,
Clutching a branch, in ecstasy
Of light and height and skiey things.
Singing, he swings ; and swinging, I
For once am showered with joy of wings.

Keen and pure, of a magic power,
Thy rapture stirs what was never stirred.
Thou hast brought to earth a cloudland dower,
The joy of the small sweet singing bird.
All time is richer for thy hour
Of delicate music, gravely heard.

Does the iris droop beneath the heat ?
Its weariness finds voice in thee.
Does the pheasant run with snow-clogged feet ?
Winter is theirs who thy vision see.
Is summer's glow to the swallow sweet ?
Thou hast captured its summer eternally.

Each thou hast wrought as a lyric note
Pure with one mood of sky and trees
And flowers, and tiny lives that float
Or dart or poise in world of these.
The painter's hand, the thrush's throat—
Which masters best these melodies ?

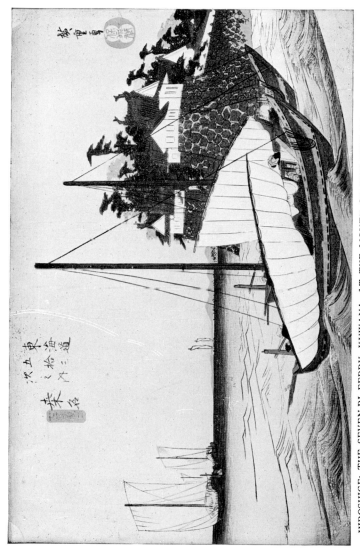

HIROSHIGE: THE SEVEN-RI FERRY, KUWANA, AT THE MOUTH OF THE KISO RIVER—SUNSET.
One of the Series "The Fifty-three Stations of the Tokaido Road." Size 9×14. Signed *Hiroshige ga.*

*Plate 53*

Gusty rain through the tree-tops blown
And a bird that scuds where the grey gusts hiss—
Sapphire wings and a golden crown
Flung skyward in unconscious bliss—
No rare enchanted bird has known
As thou hast known the savour of this !

And winning it, thou hast cast aside
Thy native bonds of mortal birth,
Flinging the spirit-pinions wide
Above this world of weary worth,
To float and poise and skyward ride
With those whose realm is not the earth—

The peacock in his proud repose—
Wild geese that rush across the moon—
The little sleepy owl that knows
The wind-among-the-tree-tops tune—
The kingfisher that darts and glows
Over the reeds of the lagoon—

The flower-lured humming bird that weaves
Spirals more delicate than they—
Sanderlings that on moonlit eves
Over the wave-crest swoop and play—
The crane that shores of sunset leaves
For sunset skies of far away.

Hiroshige was born in 1796, just as the great period of figure-designing was drawing to its close. As a youth he attempted to gain entrance to the studio of Toyokuni; but the fortunate fact that there was no room for him forced him to enter the studio of the less popular but more subtly gifted Toyohiro. Here he studied landscape, a branch in which he was destined far to outstrip his master. That delicate genius which was Toyohiro's cannot but have produced its effect upon the pupil; and it pleases one to fancy that it is some echo of Toyohiro's inarticulate refinement of feeling that gains at last full expression in some of Hiroshige's most beautiful landscapes.

In 1828 Toyohiro died; and Hiroshige became independent. His earliest works probably antedate this time a little ; they consist of a few figures of women and actors, and two very fine horizontal landscape series. These were the " Toto Meisho," or earliest series of Yedo views, distinguished by curious long red clouds in each plate; and the "Honcho Meisho," a group of views of the main island of Japan. Particularly the first of these sets contains work of great beauty.

Shortly after 1830 Hiroshige found occasion to travel from Yedo, the northern capital, to Kyoto, the southern capital, along the great post-road which he has immortalized—the Tokaido. There resulted his series of horizontal plates, " The Fifty-three Stations of the Tokaido," completed about 1834. This remains his best-known and unsurpassed work. Plate 53 is from this series. Each picture records with unfailing vividness and originality some famous scene along the crowded national highway. For reasons unknown to us, Hiroshige prepared new designs for some of the plates after the original publication of the series ; and these variation-plates are of great interest to collectors.

Of the many series that followed, only the most important can be named here. All are of horizontal shape unless otherwise designated.

*Naniwa Meisho*, ten views of Osaka—chiefly crowded wharf and market scenes.

*Kyoto Meisho*, ten views of Kyoto ; a varied and delightful series containing many fine prints.

HIROSHIGE: THE VILLAGE OF FUJI-KAWA—EVENING SNOW.

One of the Vertical Tokaido Series.  Size 13½×9.  Signed *Hiroshige ga.*

Plate 54

*Omi Hakkei*, the Eight Famous Views of Lake Biwa; the most poetic and possibly the greatest of his works (Plate 52).

*Kanazawa Hakkei*, the Eight Famous Views of the Inlet of Kanazawa; distinguished by a fine simplicity of composition.

*Yedo Kinko Hakkei*, the Eight Famous Views of Yedo; a series of masterpieces, of great rarity.

*Chiushingura*, sixteen scenes from the story of the Forty-seven Ronin; fine dramatic compositions, with powerful blacks and greys predominating.

*Toto Meisho* and *Yedo Meisho*, names under which more than fifty different series of Yedo views were issued by different publishers. These sets include many masterpieces.

*Nihon Minato Tsukushi*, ten views of the Harbours of Japan.

*Toto Meisho*, a series of narrow upright panels of Yedo; several are very distinguished.

*Mu Tamagawa*, views of the Six Tama Rivers.

*Series of Fishes*.

*Kwa Cho*, upright panels of birds and flowers, some on full-sized sheets, others very narrow; uneven in quality, some being masterpieces (Plate 56).

*Fan Prints*, with landscapes or bird designs.

In the year 1842 began the so-called Prohibition Period of twelve years, when the sale of actor and courtesan prints was forbidden. The effect of this was to redouble the demand for landscape prints; and Hiroshige was called upon to supply it. This he did by issuing, among others, the following sets :—

*Tokaido Series*, published by Maruzei; next best to the "Great Tokaido Series" of 1834.

*Tokaido Series*, published by Yesaki; slightly smaller than the "Great Series"; when well-printed, which is rare, they take a very high place.

*Tokaido Series*, published by Sanoki, half-plate size; including many charming designs.

*Kisokaido*, the Sixty-nine Stations of the Kisokaido Road between Yedo and Kyoto; a series in which Keisai Yeisen collaborated, producing twenty-three of the seventy plates. Many of the plates are uninteresting; but a quarter of them are superb. The set was reprinted at least twice in inferior editions.

In this, which we may call the Kisokaido Period of Hiroshige's work, he abandoned to a certain extent the delicate drawing of his Great Tokaido and Yedo Period and employed larger unbroken colour masses, aiming at broader effects.

In the fifties, Hiroshige abandoned almost entirely the horizontal or lateral prints of his earlier days and adopted the upright shape. In this form he produced the following series, as well as others not named:—

*Upright Tokaido*, published by Tsutaya, 1855; a fine series when well printed, but the late editions were crude in colour (Plate 54).

*Views of the Sixty-nine Provinces*, 1856; the rare first edition, which is much the finer, is distinguished by having five seals on the face of each plate. It contains a great deal of uninteresting work, but also ten or fifteen masterpieces.

HIROSHIGE: THE OMMAYA EMBANKMENT, ON THE SUMIDA RIVER
AT ASAKUSA—EVENING.

One of the Series "The Hundred Views of Yedo."    Size 13×9.
Sigend *Hiroshige ga.*

*Plate 55*

391

*Three Triptychs.*—The Rapids of Awa No Naruto, Moonlight View of Kanazawa, and Snow Mountains on the Kiso Highway, all dated 1857, and all magnificent.

*Two Kakemono-ye,* very large—the Monkey Bridge and the Snow Gorge of the Fuji River, things of matchless impressiveness.

*The One Hundred Views of Yedo,* 1858; 119 plates, including, besides much rubbish, 25 masterpieces (Plate 55).

*The Thirty-six Views of Fuji,* 1859; inferior, upon the whole, to his earlier work. There are in existence very few well-printed copies.

In the last two or three of these series it is more than probable that Hiroshige was assisted by his pupil Hiroshige II. The finest plates in all these later series are equal to the master's most splendid earlier designs; but certain of the plates are of so banal a character that it is impossible to believe them to be from the great man's hand. Doubtless the distinction between the work of the two artists cannot always be drawn with certainty; but as a general rule we may regard the work as that of Hiroshige II if we find the figures stiff and wooden, if the composition is lacking in any central unity, or if some large ugly object is thrust into the foreground with the hope of thus putting the background into its proper relative place. At this period less care was taken with the printing, and the majority of prints from these later series are miserable impressions that libel Hiroshige's powers. When well printed they can be very fine indeed; but the poor copies outnumber the good a hundred to one.

In the year 1858, just after the publication of the "One Hundred Views of Yedo," Hiroshige died. He did not live to see the plates for his "Thirty-six Views of Fuji" completed. One of the collector's treasures is a striking memorial portrait by Kunisada that was issued shortly after Hiroshige's death. The old man is represented with a finely shaped head, powerful, quiet features, and eyes as piercing as an eagle's.

The number of Hiroshige's different designs runs into at least three or four thousand, not counting his illustrated books; and there must be in existence a hundred thousand prints by him. His work is almost as plentiful as that of all the other artists taken together. In spite of this great abundance, the collector finds it difficult to-day to obtain many really fine prints by him. The prints usually offered are either in bad condition, or they are careless impressions produced without proper attention to the difficult problem of printing. The rush occasioned by Hiroshige's popularity naturally led to slighted work. Even in these poor copies a certain fascination of design generally appears; but it is only in the carefully printed copies, where the register is accurate and the colours are delicately graded, luminous, and soft, that the full beauty of Hiroshige's conception is made clear. Familiarity with the finer impressions forever spoils the attentive observer's taste for the crude ordinary copies. The task of the collector of Hiroshige's work to-day resolves itself

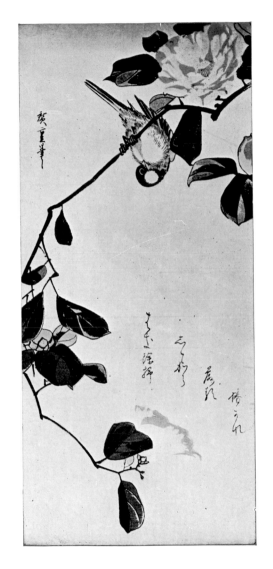

HIROSHIGE: BIRD AND FLOWERS.

Size 15×7. Signed *Hiroshige, hitsu.*

*Plate 56*

into a search for these rare and precious early prints. The collector should lose no opportunity to compare different copies of the same print ; only thus can he educate his eyes sufficiently to appreciate the vast difference between fine and inferior examples. The difference, once grasped, is unforgettable.

The reader who desires detailed information as to the long list of Hiroshige's work is referred to the Sale Catalogue of the Collection of John Stewart Happer (Sotheby, Wilkinson, and Hodge, London), which is the present foundation for any real study of the subject. A valuable article on seal-dates by Major J. J. O'Brien Sexton, in the *International Studio* for May, 1913, should also be consulted by the student.

### THE SECOND HIROSHIGE.

HIROSHIGE II, born 1826, was the adopted son of the great Hiroshige ; as we have seen, he probably assisted in some of the master's last work. After Hiroshige's death the pupil assumed the master's name, previous to that he had been known as Ichiusai Shigenobu. He is not to be confused with Yanagawa Shigenobu, Hokusai's pupil.

It was once thought that Hiroshige II produced all the upright prints signed Hiroshige. Mr. Happer has once for all discredited this idea, and it is no longer held by any one.

Some of the work of Hiroshige II is very good ; upon the accidental destruction of one of the plates of the " One Hundred Yedo Series," he produced a new design that is admirable. But he lacked originality,

SADAHIDE and YOSHIYUKI, both Osaka artists, may be mentioned among the unimportant landscape designers of the second half of the nineteenth century.

To-day the old art of the colour-print is completely dead. But an entirely new school has produced some pleasing though weak designs of birds, flowers, and landscapes ; and some attractive illustrated books have also been issued. The larger part of such work bears the obvious stamp of having been produced for the tourist and the foreign market, and has not a trace of that vigour and integrity which marked the prints of the great masters, whose inspiration sprang from and spoke to the heart of the Japanese people. European influence has produced a bad effect upon the style of these modern prints ; and the weak colour used tends toward prettiness rather than toward beauty.  It is idle to hope that real vitality will ever return to animate this lost art.

# VIII

# THE
# COLLECTOR

work of even great artists, at prices that are within any one's reach. A Yeishi triptych will cost from ten to eighty pounds, but a charming small sheet by Yeishi can perhaps be bought for two. The pleasure which the collector obtains from his collection is not necessarily proportionate to the amount of his expenditure ; and the intelligent lover of beauty can derive lasting satisfaction from his carefully selected but inexpensive little group of Hiroshige landscapes, Shunsho actors, Harunobu book-illustrations, and similar works.

When, however, the owner of some such sheets finds his ambition is growing with his interest, he needs to be somewhat cautious in his effort to extend his collection. A few charming minor prints are a highly desirable possession ; a large collection of them is not. It is easy for the lover of prints who has begun modestly to go on year after year with increasing enthusiasm, piling up numbers of cheap mediocre sheets ; and in the end, after having spent enough money to purchase ten great Kiyonagas, he finds himself the owner of a numerous but undistinguished collection in which there is not a single print of the first rank, nor a single one that will compel the admiration of the connoisseur. It is interesting to have a few prints of each type and period as examples, even though they are not notable works ; but when the collector has a moderate number he will be wise to cease his miscellaneous buying and husband his resources for the occasional purchase of a masterpiece. More pleasure is to be found in acquiring two or three fine sheets a year than from the wholesale acquisition of hundreds of insignificant works.

It is, however, well to define one's limits carefully. If one is not able to expend from ten to a hundred pounds on a single print, one must dismiss from one's mind the idea of owning an important Kiyonaga ; for that is the lowest sum at which one can hope to get it even with luck. If an expenditure of thirty to eighty pounds is impossible, one must put aside all idea of a Sharaku. But lesser treasures at lower prices are to be had ; let the collector only remember to take care that he gets the best things he can afford even though his purchases be few, rather than allow himself to be tempted into buying a great many of a cheaper kind.

Remarkable opportunities to acquire fine prints at low prices sometimes occur, but they are rare. Certain prints may come up for sale only once in a collector's lifetime. These exceptional examples must be seized when they are offered ; one of the characteristics of a great collector is the ability to make these swift and often expensive decisions. He must know the available supply of prints and the probability of having another chance to get this particular sheet ; if he estimates such a recurrence as improbable, and if he esteems the print a masterpiece, he must take it at any price he can afford to pay.

It is, after all is said, the masterpieces that bring the unwaning satisfaction. Most collectors find that the few supreme treasures of their collections give them more pleasure than all their other prints put together. Therefore it is well for the inexperienced collector to bear in mind that quality, not quantity, will prove his most profitable aim. For it is one of the delightful characteristics of collecting that the collector's perception is likely to grow continuously in fineness; and the acquisitions of his earlier years may fail to satisfy his more educated taste of later days. This will sometimes be true of even the prints he once loved best; and much more is it likely to apply to those which he bought merely because they were cheap or would increase the bulk of his collection.

Discrimination is the life-blood of collecting. He who collects everything collects nothing; he is the owner of a scrap-heap or a second-hand shop, not of an ordered series of specimens that illustrate historical or artistic ideas. The true collector would rather have ten selected prints than the whole mass of prints now in existence, if in the latter case he had to keep them all. Many a collection has been improved both in monetary value and in power to give pleasure by merely throwing out of it the second-rate things it contained.

The collector, as a rule, sets out in the beginning with little knowledge and with no very definite notion of what he intends to collect. If he is to profit by his efforts or is to end by having an interesting group of possessions, he must before long define for himself the idea of a collection and the conception which his own is to express. He may decide to obtain at least one representative example of the work of every important artist; or he may prefer to specialize, and assemble all that he can of the works of a single man or a single period. A certain well-known collector has selected Harunobu and Shunsho as his special objects of interest, and has brought together a notable and illuminating series of specimens of their work. Another has chosen Hiroshige, and after many years of effort he can display to the student a fine copy of almost every important print by that artist. A third has especially sought the works of Kiyonaga ; while a fourth has pursued the less costly but very interesting aim of bringing together the sheets of Kuniyoshi. Another is devoted to surimono ; still another, to pillar-prints. The possible list of specialities is inexhaustible. Narrow and exclusive specialization is, however, uncommon among amateurs of Japanese prints ; and even the specialist tries to have in his collection a few representative examples of all important types.

The inexperienced collector may find himself confused, amid so many unfamiliar names, and fail to separate in his mind the notable artists from those of secondary interest. A little study of the following list will perhaps be of assistance. It contains thirty-two names, selected from the three or four hundred mentioned in this book ; each one in the list is important, and a collection that contained even one fine example by each of these designers would represent very fairly the whole scope of the art. In fact, the beginner will not go far astray if at the outset he confines his purchases to the work of the men here listed ; he will at least be saved from the danger of accumulating the productions of unnoteworthy designers.   The names preceded by two stars are the ten outstanding figures whose historical and artistic importance makes it imperative that they be adequately represented in any self-respecting collection.   Thirteen more names, preceded by one star, are of next conspicuousness.   A collection containing a really brilliant example by each of these thirty-two men would cost from three hundred to three thousand pounds to bring together, depending upon the quality and importance of the prints selected.

*List of Principal Artists.*

| | |
|---|---|
| *Buncho | *Shigemasa |
| *Choki | *Shigenaga |
| **Harunobu | *Shuncho |
| **Hiroshige I | Shunko (Katsukawa) |
| **Hokusai | Shunman |
| *Kiyomasu | **Shunsho |
| *Kiyomitsu I | Shunyei |
| **Kiyonaga | Sukenobu |
| *Kiyonobu I | Toshinobu |
| *Kiyonobu II | Toyoharu |
| **Koriusai | Toyohiro |
| *Kwaigetsudō | *Toyokuni I |
| Masanobu (Kitao) | *Toyonobu (Ishikawa) |
| **Masanobu (Okumura) | **Utamaro I |
| **Moronobu | *Yeishi |
| **Sharaku | Yeisho |

Collecting is to a certain extent creative ; for the picture of the art of Japanese prints that a collection presents is almost as definitely an expression of a personal interpretation as is a book on the subject.   What the collectors treasure will be preserved ; what they reject will doubtless perish as valueless.

One of the collector's joys is the sense that he is laying by immeasurable riches for posterity. Much remains for us still to learn from Japanese prints ; and any sheet in a collection may prove to be the key that will some day unlock doors leading to treasure-chambers. Both historically and æsthetically, the field of Japanese prints still offers many undiscovered regions to the explorer. By making available the material for such investigations, the collector performs a valuable service.

The collector's own satisfaction is not dependent upon the fact of possession. To seek, to desire ardently, is not to covet ; and the most eager collectors are the very ones who most thoroughly enjoy a beautiful print owned by another. Possession is an accident ; but enjoyment is a form of genius.

Collecting at its best is very far from mere acquisitiveness ; it may become one of the most humanistic of occupations, seeking to illustrate, by the assembling of significant reliques, the march of the human spirit in its quest of beauty, and the aspirations that were guide. To discover, preserve, relate, and criticize these memorials is the rational aim of the collector. The joy of pursuit which he experiences is a crude but delightful one ; and discovery has the triumphant sweetness of all successful effort. The act of restoring and preserving is a pious service to the future, and a delicate handicraft. To arrange examples in accurate relation to each other, and illustrate a conception of complex history by means of concrete specimens, is a constructive task that involves detailed knowledge and wide vision. And finally, the attempt to appraise the spiritual values of the parts and the whole may be an illuminating achievement, relating all this material to the general stream of cultural development and to the history of the race.

The best way to study an art of the past is to collect examples of it. The collector's historical sense is trained and his discriminative powers are sharpened by his activities. As his education progresses, his chief interest is in works of an ever higher quality. He attempts always to acquire the best, and his knowledge of what is best is always widening. His is the task of judging between degrees of perfection. It differs not so very widely from that desperate search for an ideal fulfilment which is the curse, the inspiration, and the one abiding joy of the artist.

The artist's sense of triumph in an achievement must be only momentary; if he continues long to regard his creation as admirable, he has reached the stagnation of his powers and the end of his career; he must ever hate to-day what he created yesterday, in order that he may be driven on to produce a still finer thing to-morrow. The collector, also, must eventually abandon his present position and move forward; and, tragic to confess, perhaps his ultimate triumph comes on that day when the field he long has loved ceases to suffice his growing sense of beauty, and he sends his collection under the hammer, having mastered it and passed beyond it.

For every collector must in the end transcend his collection, unless he is to perish in it as in some fatal Saragossa Sea.

A collection is a life-estate only, and the important question confronts every collector as to what disposition shall be made of his possessions after his death. My personal feeling is strongly against the bequest of such a collection to a public institution. These prints are inherently suited to private exhibition and not to public display. They must be kept in portfolios, not hung up in galleries, or they fade. They must be examined closely and at leisure; the spectator should be able, seated at ease, to study them as he holds them in his hand. To walk through a gallery of prints is only a slight pleasure; to sit in the library of the collector and inspect and discuss the same prints one by one is a great delight. Further, they require a degree of care that they would not receive in the public institutions. The prints in most public collections are repaired, mounted, and handled with a carelessness that horrifies the collector. That painstaking skill in restoring, preserving, and mounting to the best advantage, which means so much for the ultimate effect of a print, is seldom, if ever, exercised except by the private owner. It may be said that if these treasures are in private hands, the public is deprived of them. This is untrue. The great body of the public would pass them by in a gallery, for this is not a spectacular or obtrusive art like sculpture. On the other hand, any person who gives evidence of a reasonable degree of interest can

not only obtain free and willing access to all the
private collections with which I am familiar, but he
may have at his disposal the services of the owner
of the collection to explain, interpret, and guide.
There are at present scores of highly trained men,
of such cultivation as the museums cannot afford
to employ except in the highest positions, who are
spending weeks and months out of every year in
this unpaid work of serving the public ; while in
the great public collections the ordinary inquirer is
left adrift to find his way as best he can through
the chaos of an improperly arranged exhibit. In
the public collections the prints are of service or
pleasure to almost nobody ; while in the private
collections their service and pleasure to the owner
and his friends is great, and the same opportunities
are easily opened to any one who is qualified to
profit by them.   Therefore it seems better that, upon
the death of a collector, his prints should be sold ;
in order that, as Edmond de Goncourt directed in
the case of his collection, those treasures which have
been so great and so personal a delight to the
owner may pass on into the hands of such others
as will find in them the same satisfaction.   "My
wish is," he wrote in his will, "that my drawings,
my prints, my curios, my books—in a word those
things of art which have been the joy of my life—
shall not be consigned to the cold tomb of a
museum, and subjected to the stupid glance of the
careless passer-by ; but I require that they shall
all be dispersed under the hammer of the auctioneer,
so that the pleasure which the acquiring of each

one of them has given me shall be given again, in each case, to some inheritor of my own taste."

### CONSIDERATIONS GOVERNING THE CHOICE OF PRINTS.

A variety of elements must be weighed in the mind of the collector whenever he decides for or against the purchase of a particular specimen to add to his collection.

**The Artist.**—In the first place, the authorship of the print is an important consideration. If the designer is a very great man like Kiyonaga, or a very rare one like Kitao Masanobu, or both combined like Shigemasa, these facts must be given weight. Other things being equal, a print by an important leader such as Utamaro is more desirable than one by a less original follower such as Banki. A Kiyonaga is a little preferable to an equally beautiful Shuncho, because of Kiyonaga's prime historical importance. The work of certain other men is prized by collectors because of its scarcity; Chincho, for example, would be only moderately valued were it not for the extraordinary rarity of his designs. When rarity combines with greatness, as in the case of Kwaigetsudō, Moronobu, Buncho, and Sharaku, the desirability of the artist's work is naturally doubled in the eyes of the collector.

A print sometimes derives an unusual interest from the fact that it is of a kind seldom produced by the particular artist who designed it. Harunobu and Kiyonaga actor-prints are exceptional things, dating from the early years of these men's careers.

On the other hand, the silver-prints of Utamaro,
the triptychs of Kiyonaga, and the yellow-back-
ground prints of Yeishi are desirable for the opposite
reason ; they represent famous and characteristic
aspects of the work of their respective creators.

**The Quality of the Design.**—The impression produced upon the æsthetic sense of the collector is
the most vital of all the elements that determine his
choice.   The composition, the drawing, the total
beauty of the design, will in each individual case have
their importance ; and upon the collector's estimate
of these qualities will depend his desire to own
the print.   There are some dull and uninteresting
designs by even the most gifted men—work without
charm or life.   Shunsho was a great sinner in this
respect ; so also were Utamaro and Toyokuni.   On
the other hand, men of secondary importance produced occasional triumphs ; a Yeisho or a Yenshi is
sometimes found in which the most brilliant qualities
of composition appear.   Each print must be appraised
on its own merits.

The collector generally passes by all designs in
which clumsiness or awkwardness is evident, and waits
patiently for those in which the force, or grace, or
dignity of the composition proclaims the masterpiece.
Kiyonaga's " Terrace by the Sea," Sharaku's portrait
of the Daimyo Moronao, Hokusai's " Red Mountain,"
and Utamaro's " Firefly Catchers " are examples of
that unsurpassable quality which no experienced
collector willingly lets escape him.

**The Quality of the Impression.**—Different copies of
the same print differ enormously in quality.   The

finest design is of little avail if the work of the printer has not been judicious. Among early prints, before Utamaro, really bad impressions are not very common, although especially fine and brilliant ones are hard to obtain. Later, particularly in the work of Hiroshige, the poor ones much outnumber the good. In a good impression the lines are all sharp and clean : where the hair meets the temples, every brushstroke is clearly defined. The blacks are rich and heavy, not sooty or streaked. The colours must be in perfect register ; that is, each must exactly fill its allotted space without overlapping and without ragged edges. Prints in which these defects occur are either careless impressions or late impressions from worn blocks. Whichever be the explanation, they are not desirable ; the discriminating collector does not care to acquire any but perfectly printed sheets. All the skill and devotion of the printer was needed to make the resulting product a just interpretation of the conception of the designer ; in a bad impression the beauty of the design is ruined.

Prior to the nineteenth century it was the usual practice to give each colour-block a uniform coat of pigment ; thus each separate colour impressed on the paper was completely flat and unshaded. In Hiroshige's time, however, the pigment was often partially wiped from portions of the block, so that in the resulting print the colour shades gradually into the uncoloured white of the paper. Many of Hiroshige's prints derive a considerable portion of their beauty from the subtlety of these gradations.

There are no such things as signed artist's proof-

among Japanese prints; but there is a class of prints
that corresponds to them. They are not labelled ;
nothing distinguishes them from the ordinary copies
except the extreme beauty of the printing. These
rare impressions were probably early ones made
under the eye of the artist. The sharpness of the
lines, the harmony of the colours, and the delicacy
of gradation in any shaded portions are of a perfection
lacking in the ordinary copies. It took much care
and time, and was therefore expensive, to produce
such work ; and probably the majority of purchasers
were unwilling to pay the additional price entailed
by this degree of attention. The few existing copies
of this character are exceptionally prized by the
collector to-day.

The colour-schemes used in printing various
copies of the same print often differ widely, and
there is considerable difference in desirability on this
ground alone. Some of Hiroshige's prints are found
in monochromes of blue or of grey—some of Hokusai's
are in bluish green. These rare and beautiful variations from the normal are highly valued. On the
other hand, the late prints of Hiroshige are generally
printed in raucous greens and reds and purples that
are an offence to the eye ; and only rarely do we find
copies of them in which a soft and harmonious
colour scheme reveals the intention of the artist.
This explains why certain prints from the " One
Hundred Views of Yedo" sometimes bring fifteen
or twenty pounds apiece, though multitudes of
ordinary copies of the identical print can be purchased for a few shillings each. Badly coloured

examples of Hiroshige's work are plentiful and of little value; harmonious and subtly modulated ones are things of unsurpassable beauty, and almost as rare as Kiyonagas. The collector of Hiroshige prints will scrutinize a specimen with the utmost care to determine whether the colour scheme is harmonious, and whether the pigments have been applied in the delicately graded luminous manner that Hiroshige intended. If he finds that the various tones are harsh in quality, or are printed in crude, unshaded masses, he will reject the sheet. Considerable familiarity with really fine impressions is the only safeguard in this matter. The beginner is only too ready to be led astray by the charm of the design, not realizing how much this same design is enhanced if given the expression of appropriate printing; and he is very likely to find himself loaded down with worthless impressions, the very sight of which is repugnant to him after he has become familiar with fine copies of the same prints. Poor copies are worth nothing; but choice ones are never really dear at any price.

In this matter more than in any other a fine collection differs from a poor one, and it is in this that the discriminating collector has his best chance to match his judgment against that of the dealer. Sometimes one can for a few shillings select from a pile of worthless Hiroshiges a notable impression that is worth twenty times the sum asked for it.

A generally accepted classification of prints from the point of view of the quality of the impression would be convenient. There are to-day no recognized terms by which to describe the various grades. I therefore suggest a division into four groups with the following terminology :—

(a) *Artist's Impression.*—Such a print as might have been produced under the eye of the artist himself—every line clear and sharp, every colour delicate and perfectly registered ; the total effect exceptionally luminous and harmonious ; no possible subtlety of technique left to be desired.

(b) *Fine Impression.*—A clear, perfect impression such as a careful printer would normally turn out at his best, but without that inspired fineness in every detail which distinguishes Class (a).

(c) *Good Impression.*—Such a print as would pass muster with the ordinary buyer of that day— good, but not especially fine ; clear, but not notably sharp ; pleasantly enough coloured, but not distinguished in colour scheme. Very slight defects of register or of gradation will not exclude a print from this class.

(d) *Late Impression.*—One in which serious defects appear, such as bad register, raw colour, blurred definition, or any other real error.

Condition.—The state of preservation is one of the most important elements that the collector has to consider. Collectors of Japanese prints do not as a rule pay much attention to questions of margin, but they very properly insist that the effects of time and wear shall not be such as to obliterate or diminish the original beauty of the work itself. The print must not be cut down in size, and its face must be unmarred. Stains, creases, tears, abrasions, discolorations and fading are all defects of a serious nature. Only experience can enable one to judge whether a certain print is of such rarity that one must waive requirements as to condition and accept a defective copy. In the case of the Primitives, flawless examples are so few that one must needs be content with prints that show decidedly the effect of time. The same is true of pillar-prints. On the other hand, there is no reason why one should ever purchase a damaged Hiroshige, unless it be an exceptional rarity like the " Monkey Bridge." On the whole, the experience of collectors is that in every case of doubt the faulty print should be rejected. For as one sees a print repeatedly one's consciousness of the defect increases, and gradually the flaw becomes more obvious to one's observation than anything else in the print.

In many cases prints that are in undamaged condition have nevertheless acquired with age a peculiar deadness that may not be perceptible to the careless eye. If such a print is placed beside a perfectly fresh one, the difference is at once apparent. In the first case, though the surface is unmarred, there is a slight yellowing of the fibres of the paper that prevents their sending out that vibrating luminosity which is a distinctive beauty in the immaculate copy. This absence of luminous quality is so common that I mention it less to caution the collector against it than to bid him be on his guard to seize the few luminous prints that are offered him.

It is against the really brown prints that the

novice should be warned. The difference in market value between a chocolate coloured copy and a brilliantly white copy is enormous, amounting in some cases to a thousand per cent. Brilliant copies are excessively rare ; and since they are the only ones desired by the great collectors, they bring record prices.

The whole question of condition is one of personal taste ; collectors are by no means agreed about it. European collectors have been, as a rule, less insistent upon condition than have the Japanese and Americans. There are collectors—though they grow fewer daily—who positively prefer faded and "toned" prints, because of their softness. This view is an ill-advised one.

I do not say that, if one can have none other, the damaged prints may not give one pleasure and intimations of the original beauty that was theirs ; but I do affirm that such prints are but makeshifts, and that their market value is, and always will be, very slight. When I began collecting many years ago in Japan, I purchased a number of Hokusai prints that were much blackened by exposure. I thought at the time that any trace of the work of so famous a master was worth treasuring. But I have found that my purchase was quite valueless, not only from the commercial point of view, but also from the artistic, since they do not represent the work of Hokusai with the slightest approach to adequacy.

Perfect condition conveys to us perfectly the artist's conception ; anything else obliterates or modifies his design. Though the beauty of faded or damaged prints is often indisputable, and though some prints are so saturated with beauty that a certain charm remains as long as any trace of the printing is visible, yet these wrecks and fragments are not the desirable specimens. The slight softening of the colours that almost always comes with age is perhaps not detrimental ; but when the luminosity of the colours and the brilliant whiteness of the paper is gone, an irreparable loss has been suffered. For the white spaces and the reflective effect of the white fibres under the coloured spaces were integral and vital elements in the artist's design ; and one cannot say that this is not injured when the paper has been turned to a dingy brown.

Further, it is almost childish to prefer the time-changed colours to the fresh ones. For surely, if these prints have any value at all, it is not the kind of value that beautifully weather-marked pebbles have : their significance lies in whatsoever spiritual values their designers put into them. They are not curiosities of nature, but monuments erected by the human spirit in its search for beauty. We go very far astray when we admire what is in fact lamentable disintegration. To delight in the faded tone of a print is like delighting in the cracks of the Sistine Chapel.

The matter can be made clearer if we become specific. A certain blue of Harunobu's changes, with exposure, to yellow; and the yellow sky or river that results is anything but what the designer intended. A certain white of Hiroshige's oxidizes into black ; the effect is unfortunate as, for instance,

in prints where we now see black snowflakes. The
rich orange beloved of Koriusai and Shunsho, and
the delicate pink used by Harunobu, Kiyonaga,
and Shuncho, are transformed in the course of time
into rusty black ; then in the place of the luminous
rooms intended when the artist planned his composition, we see dingy mottled caverns of mud. The
brilliant early purple turns brown; the still earlier rose
colour vanishes entirely. After all these changes, how
is it possible to prefer the faded print to the fresh
one? The resulting accidental effects may happen to
be beautiful, but they have a destructive influence
upon those elements which alone make the prints
worthy of our serious attention as works of art. The
only marvel is that they do not more completely
ruin the beauty of the artist's work.

The chemical disintegrations of which I speak
are sometimes so great that they are very misleading
to the uninformed. A writer in the London *Times*
of November 6, 1913, reviewing the exhibition at the
Albert and Victoria Museum, discovers an amazing
mare's nest. " One colour alone Harunobu neglects
in common with all his predecessors and contemporaries," he says. " It remained for the artists
of the nineteenth century to discover the possibilities
of blue—a curious and hitherto unnoted omission."
Indeed, the omission had not been previously noted—
for the simple reason that it does not exist. Harunobu used blue a great deal, almost always in
depicting water or sky ; Shunsho used it repeatedly
for sky, water, and draperies in the " Ise Monogo-
tari," and as a solid background in certain *hoso-ye*

actor-prints of which two, in their startling pristine brilliancy, are in the Gookin Collection ; Koriusai used blue frequently in combination with his famous orange. But the blue used by the early artists, particularly that of Harunobu and Shunsho, was the most unstable of colours, and it is rare to find it unaltered by time. Generally it has turned to a delicate grey or yellow that is very beautiful, but very far from what the artist meant it to be.

A systematic classification of the various conditions in which a print may be found will perhaps put the matter clearly before the beginner :—

1. *Publisher's State.*—Without the slightest evidence of any change since the hour it was printed ; colours unaltered ; paper absolutely new and sparkling.

2. *Collector's State.*—As a print might be after a few years in the possession of a careful purchaser ; perfect, except for having been mounted or washed, or except for slight chemical change in the colours due to time only and not to damage ; paper white and clear.

3. *Good State.*—Marred only by minor defects that would be unnoticeable to casual observation—small worm-holes, slight tears or creases, moderate fading of colours, or slightly rubbed surface ; paper toned but not brown.

4. *Ordinary State.*—Still retaining its chief beauty in spite of noticeable injury by tears, small stains, worn or faded colours, or other damage ; paper somewhat browned by exposure.

5. *Defective State.*—Such injuries or colour changes

as deprive the print of its significance as a thing of beauty; paper browned or stained.

**Rarity.**—The rarity of a print may be a factor in determining whether or not it should be purchased. Not only does rarity affect monetary value, but it sometimes indicates to the collector that this is perhaps the only opportunity he will ever have to acquire this particular design. The rain scene from Hiroshige's "Yedo Kinko Hakkei" has a higher value than the equally beautiful rain scene from the " One Hundred Yedo Series," for the simple reason that copies of the former are very few, and that many collectors desire it because of its beauty. There is, however, a danger into which many collectors fall, of esteeming rarity as a precious element *per se*. Rarity alone, detached from other elements of value or interest, is perhaps the most ridiculous element that the human race has ever chosen to esteem.

**Associations.**—Certain prints have an historical value that makes them particularly interesting to the collector. For example, there is the well-known triptych by Utamaro which, because of its portrayal of one of the Shoguns in scandalous surroundings, was the cause of the imprisonment and death of the artist. Also there is the famous memorial portrait of Hiroshige by Kunisada, which is an especially desirable possession because of its associations and because the subject is the great landscape painter. Dated prints are of interest by reason of the light they may throw on uncertain points in Ukioye history. Prints that have belonged to famous collectors, Hayashi, Wakai, Fenollosa, and others,

derive a double interest from that fact ; the associa-
tian is interesting, and the previous possession by a
discriminating collector confirms the present owner's
estimate of the high quality of the print. It should
not, however, be forgotten that enterprising Japanese
dealers recognize this fact. A small red stamp can
be made in Japan for about two shillings ; and a considerable number of prints now bearing the Wakai
and Hayashi seals never formed a part of these
collections.

Prices.—The subject of prices is one so complex
and indeterminate that one writes of it only with
hesitancy. That which seems excessive to one
collector will be willingly paid by another. No
stable standard exists ; I have had equally good
copies of certain Hiroshige prints offered me at
prices as various as 10s. and £10. In discussing the
matter, one can give nothing more than an individual
impression of the normal and usual figures at which
prints change hands to-day. Experience is the only
means by which a collector can equip himself on this
subject. He will acquaint himself with the prices
asked by dealers and the prices at which other
collectors have obtained their specimens ; and from
these, together with a careful study of auction
sale catalogues, he forms his judgment. Auction
prices are likely, however, to be misleading unless
one sees the prints sold ; for the fact that a certain
print brought only £3 at Sotheby's is no indication
that another copy of the same print may not be
worth the £30 asked for it. Variations in condition
and quality of impression make vast differences in

value. An Artist's Impression of Hiroshige's famous Tokaido print, "Rain on Shono Pass," might bring £20; a Fine Impression would perhaps sell for half that; a Good Impression would be worth about £4; while a Late Impression would bring less than £2. Similarly a Kiyonaga might vary from £40 to £4 on this account. In the matter of condition there would be parallel differences. A rare Kiyonaga or Utamaro triptych might vary as follows : Publisher's State, £200 ; Collector's State, £100; Good State, £60; Ordinary State, £30 ; Defective State, £5. A great Sharaku might, in the same way, be priced at £100, £70, £50, £20, and £3 ; and a Harunobu at £60, £50, £20, £8, and £3. Pillar-prints in perfect preservation are rare ; therefore the differences would be even greater ; in the case of an exceptional Koriusai, perhaps £30, £15, £10, £3, £1.

The following very rough generalizations may suggest something to the inexperienced collector. Small Primitive sheets in fair condition can seldom be obtained for less than £5 to £15 ; the rare large sheets and Pillar-prints generally bring £20 to £100. These are minimum prices ; for special treasures such as Kwaigetsudō, prices may rise to several hundred pounds.

Harunobu's work in perfect condition brings from £20 to £100. Shunsho actors are sometimes to be had very cheap, for a pound or two ; but the finest designs will bring from £10 to £20. Buncho is rare ; one may expect to pay at least £15 to £40 for a fine example. Shunyei and Shunko are about the same in price as Shunsho. A good Shigemasa is worth £20 to £50.

Kiyonaga is expensive ; an attractive small sheet by him will cost £5 to £15 ; a fine large sheet, £15 to £40; a triptych brings scores or hundreds. Shuncho and the other Kiyonaga followers are only a little less costly. A notable Sharaku is rarely obtainable for less than £40 to £80. Shunman brings almost as much, as also does Kitao Masanobu.

Small or unimportant sheets by Yeishi, Yeisho, Utamaro, Choki, Toyokuni, and Toyohiro can be had for a pound or two. From this level, prices go up to several hundred pounds, which has been paid for Utamaro's " Awabi Shell-Divers." Triptychs, silver-prints, and large heads by these men are especially expensive, rising from £20 to much larger sums.

Two to five pounds will buy a fair Hokusai ; £20 or more may be asked for an unusually fine one, and certain rare treasures bring much more than that. Prices for Hiroshige prints vary so with the quality of the impression that generalizations are impossible. It can only be said that the purchaser who gets a Hiroshige of the highest quality for £5 is fortunate. On the other hand, it must be stated that fine Hiroshige prints are often obtainable for consider-ably lower prices than this.

All these prices apply to the best prints in good condition. Dealers frequently ask unreasonably high sums for second-rate designs or defective copies ; in such cases the collector should refuse to be made a victim.

Experience alone can dictate to a collector what

prices he may prudently pay.  In the most uniformly
fine private collection I know—a collection com-
prising only one hundred and fifty prints, but each
one a treasure—there are few, if any, sheets that
cost less than £5, and many that cost £20 to £40.
Their value ten years from now may very possibly be
ten times those prices, so admirable has been the
taste of this particular amateur in selecting beautifully preserved masterpieces.

These figures need not terrify the beginner whose
means are limited.  Specimens of great beauty may
still be brought together with a small expenditure of
money, if accompanied by a large expenditure of
taste and judgment.  For example, the book-sheets
of Harunobu called "Serio Bijin Awase," the sheets
of Shunsho's "Ise Monogatari," the later upright
prints of Hiroshige, the pillar-prints of Koriusai—all
of them works of admirable quality—may sometimes
be obtained with only a small outlay.  Their intrinsic
proportionate worth, and the certainty of their
advancing in value, are almost as great as in the case
of those rarer treasures of Masanobu, Kiyonaga, and
Sharaku which have been largely pre-empted by the
great collections, and which are now almost pro-
hibitive in price.

Yet it would not be a kindness to hold out to the
novice the hope that, with the expenditure of a few
shillings, he can form an important collection.  Such
a hope is a mistaken one.  Great discretion is
necessary to obtain at a moderate price prints worth
having at all.  The cheap prints are generally either
the late and crude ones, or the badly damaged ones.

Both of these classes lack the one *raison d'être* of collecting—beauty. It is true that, as I have said, a really fine Hiroshige may still sometimes be picked up for a song, but such opportunities are rare ; they must be waited for a long time, and must be seized with instant determination when they come. The collector who is not well informed is more than likely to find, after a short period of triumph over his bargain, that his copy is a late and poor impression, and that even the beauty of composition will not permanently satisfy him in the absence of fine and appropriate printing. In this connection it should be remembered that while the finest prints are generally more valuable than their cost, the second-rate prints are generally worth nothing whatsoever.

If one has adequate experience, one can well hunt for these opportunities of which I speak. Or if one is unable to pay the normal prices for fine works, one is obliged to lie in wait for them. The average collector will, however, find that in the course of years he gains more by paying normal prices to high-class dealers for the best prints than by seeking in the byways for dubious bargains of speculative quality.

It is true that the prices set upon the finest prints are at present high. Recent years have seen an enormous advance in values. For example, I have known £300 to be asked for a copy of the "Monkey Bridge"; £60 for a superb copy of the Kiso Snow Mountains Triptych ; and several other prints by Hiroshige have changed hands at £60 apiece. These prices of course applied only to remarkably,

and perhaps uniquely, fine copies. In the last
edition of his volume, "Japan and its Arts," Mr.
Marcus B. Huish remarks that prints have "risen
to extravagant prices—prices sober-minded people
consider altogether beyond their worth." This is a
matter of individual opinion. A good Hiroshige at
£5, or a Kiyonaga at £20 will seem to many people
less extravagant than a "proof" mezzotint by Smith
from Reynold's "Mrs. Carnac" at seven hundred
guineas, or Rembrandt's etching of "Jan Six" at
£3,000. In fairness to Mr. Huish, however, we must
continue the quotation. "But these prices," he says,
"have been paid by the Directors of Museums and
other astute persons who do not expend the limited
means at their disposal unless they feel well assured
that they (the prints) will in the future be either
unobtainable or at enhanced prices." This is quite
true. There is no indication that the values of
Japanese prints will ever be lower than they are
to-day; on the contrary, they have been rising
swiftly and steadily for twenty years, and great
advances in value may be expected. To these
advances many forces are already contributing.
Every year a certain number of prints are accident-
ally destroyed, decreasing the total available supply.
No further supplies of large numbers can be expected
from Japan, which has been ransacked with all the
thoroughness of skilled searchers armed with the
lure of high prices. In fact, prices in Japan to-day
are probably higher than prices in London; at least,
higher prices are asked for inferior prints. The
finest prints bring about the same price everywhere.

Each year the great museums of the world acquire by purchase or bequest prints which are thus forever removed from the market. Each year the number of persons who appreciate prints is growing; and there is a continual increase in the number of wealthy collectors who can and will pay almost any price to obtain what they desire. One may be prepared to look back, in twenty years, with mingled amazement and regret as he contemplates what will then seem the absurdly low prices asked for the greatest treasures to-day.

Therefore, without serious doubt, the prudent collector will not suffer because of his present acquisitions. It should, however, always be borne in mind that the very finest prints—those which seem most expensive to-day—are the ones that will rise most rapidly in value as time passes. Poor impressions, soiled copies, and second-rate compositions will never be very rare; but the supremely fine sheets—scarce enough now—will grow scarcer with every year.

Nevertheless, collecting as an investment is not advocated. If the collector is not moved by the delight he gets from the æsthetic qualities of the prints, he had far better leave them entirely alone. Nothing but the passion of real enthusiasm and perception will enable him to select the best works; and without this selection his prints are not likely to be of much ultimate value. When, however, the collector makes his acquisitions out of pure love for their beauty, it is right and prudent that he should consider their value in later years. Such a collector need have no fear; what was to him a delight and a dissipation will probably in the end prove to his heirs an investment of profit.

## FORGERIES.

The collector must be constantly on his guard against reprints, forgeries, and reproductions. These are not as common as some writers believe; but they exist.

Reprints are impressions made at a time so long after the original edition that they have not the original colouring. The register of such prints is generally faulty, and the lines are not sharp. So long as the blocks are in existence these reprints are possible. Early reprints are merely late editions of the originals, and are not objectionable if the blocks have not become worn; but late ones are undesirable. A print made to-day from the original blocks of Harunobu, did they exist, would have no value.

Forgeries are works produced in the style and over the signature of some famous artist. Since they have no prototype among the artist's real works, they present difficulties of their own; there is no genuine copy of the same print with which to compare them. They are very rare; their chief occurrence is in the cases of Harunobu and Utamaro.

Reproductions are prints made from new blocks cut in imitation of the original ones. For unknown reasons a second edition of certain prints sometimes was made very shortly after the first, from re-cut blocks. These prints have no necessary difference in beauty or value from those of the first edition.

But such cases are few. Far commoner are the reproductions proper—most of them copies made within the last twenty-five years, sometimes with fraudulent intent, and sometimes merely as honest commercial copies. In either case, they may be used fraudulently by a present owner.

The ordinary modern reproduction is not difficult to detect. It is generally on a harder, brittler paper than a genuine print. The feeling of the paper between one's fingers is more like that of our wrapping-paper than like that of the old soft papers used by the Ukioye artists. Its surface is compact and glassy, not spongy and pliant. It has a starchy stiffness, and lacks the soft, luminous tone of the genuine. Generally the lines of the block are clumsily cut, lacking the grace and strength of the original ; and a careful and minute comparison with an original impression of the same print will invariably show difference in small details of the lines. Even the Japanese are not skilful enough to cut a new block precisely like the old one.

The colours of a reproduction constitute perhaps the most definite danger signal. They are, as a rule, flat and dead, lacking the soft brilliancy of the old colours. Very seldom are they graded with care—a repellent harshness marks them. Particularly does the blue lack the life and depth of the genuine blue ; and the red and yellow are likely to be staring.

Freshness and perfect preservation are never, in the absence of other signs, to be regarded as evidence of recent production. Conversely, it is only the merest bungler who regards worm-holes or faded,

browned, and damaged condition as any evidence
of age. The Japanese use tea-leaves and various
other devices to give this time-worn appearance to
the most flagrant reproductions. For all I know,
they may have trained worms to eat holes. These
damaged, tea-soaked prints would be almost worthless even if they were genuine. The stray tourist
in Japan, however, customarily accumulates a large
number of these soiled tatters, fearing to touch the
fresh-looking copies. And the Japanese willingly
calm his fears by soaking and soiling their reprints.

There are, however, a few reproductions of so fine
a quality that detection is extremely difficult. These
are the sheets over which experts shake their heads
and go away muttering, to return for councils and
deliberations and sometimes total disagreement.
There exists in an American collection a certain
Kiyonaga print which half a dozen experts believe
to be a modern fraud, though another half-dozen are
prepared to defend its authenticity until Judgment
Day. Work of this quality is expensive to produce,
and the price asked for it is therefore always high.

Certain specific reproductions are to be guarded
against. Many fraudulent copies of Hiroshige's
" Monkey Bridge " and " Kiso Snow Gorge " are on
the market ; all those I have ever seen are so poor
in colour and so different in line-details that it seems
incredible that anyone should be deceived. Several
of the Tokaido Set have been imitated, rather poorly;
and also some of the Birds and Flowers. Quite
recently, there has appeared a remarkable Lake
Biwa set, produced with such beauty and skill that

several of the greatest authorities in the world were at first deceived by it. Hokusai's "Imagery of the Poets," "Waterfalls," "Thirty-six Views of Fuji," and "Loocho Islands," have been reprinted; the colours and the lines are a little imperfect ; and no one who uses care need be misled by them. They are, however, good enough to be dangerous to the beginner. Utamaro's most famous works, particularly the "Awabi Shell-Divers" triptych, have been reprinted fairly well. Perilous imitations of several of the Primitives are extant ; the stiff paper is almost the only means of detection. Sharaku has been reprinted dangerously well ; one lately discovered fraudulent print of his sold for a high price at Sotheby's some years ago, and subsequently passed unquestioned through the hands of a dozen English and American experts, until finally an accidental comparison of it with a genuine sheet revealed points of difference. Another copy of this same reproduction remains to this day as the treasured possession of a well-known English collection.

Possibly the most dangerous of all forgeries and reprints are those of Harunobu's small square prints, for they have sometimes been produced with notable skill. Even the greatest experts have been deceived by them. Fenollosa, at No. 131 of the Ketcham Catalogue, describes in the most glowing terms, as "the central point of all Ukioye," a print which its present owner has found to be a reproduction, not thirty years old, and has discarded from his collection.

The reputable dealers, often men of much experience, never offer reproductions for sale, though

they, like any one else, may occasionally be deceived
by the finest of the fraudulent ones. They use their
best skill to protect their customers, and the protection is generally efficient. If, however, a dealer
is unwilling to give assurance in writing that the
print is genuine, or if his stock contains more than
the two or three reproductions accountable for on
the ground of bad judgment, he should be avoided
as untrustworthy.

The experienced collector, who has seen and
handled tens of thousands of prints, becomes accustomed to the texture of the various papers, the
tones of the various colours, and the contours of
line-cutting. His familiarity produces in him a sixth
sense which is his instinctive guide in the detection
of frauds. Later investigation may define his original
impression and prove it to have been correct; but in
the first instance he relies on intuition. The less experienced collector has no such guide; and he should
realize that he has not, and not try to evolve one
from his inner consciousness. Nothing is more ludi-
crous than to see such a person in a print-shop in
Japan. He turns over pile after pile of prints, selecting those which his judgment tells him are "really
old." What he generally means is, "really dirty."
Advice from bystanders is not often welcomed by
him, and the only peaceable thing one can do is
to leave him to his own curious devices. There is
a certain malicious pleasure to be obtained in going
through the piles such a collector has discarded,
and selecting from them, as one sometimes can, a flaw-
lessly preserved copy of some fine print which he

passed by as too fresh-looking to be anything but fraudulent. But when he returns to his hotel at night and exhibits triumphantly the treasures he has garnered during the day, it would be a hard heart that could do anything but keep silent and weep inwardly. The sixth sense can be relied on only if one has had much experience. If one is inexperienced, the safe way is to ask expert advice.

For the experienced collector I venture to suggest only one maxim. If vaguely suspicious of a print, but unable to tell exactly why, discard the print. Your whole accumulated experience is indefinably expressing itself in your suspicion; and nine times out of ten it is right.

## CARE OF A COLLECTION.

When a print is once properly prepared and mounted, it needs no further care except protection from injury. Prolonged exposure to sunlight is not desirable, since fading may result; dampness is to be guarded against because of the danger of mildew, a terrible foe; care in handling must be exercised, so that the print be not rubbed, creased, or torn. But if these elementary precautions are employed, the print will take care of itself.

It may be worth while for the benefit of the beginner to trace the steps that are taken by a collector between the time when he becomes the owner of a new print and the time when he puts it away in his portfolios as an established part of his collection.

The first step is to examine the print with care

and ascertain what, if any, processes are necessary to
prepare it for mounting. If the condition of the
sheet is flawless, nothing is required. If its condition
is in one way or another defective, it is the task of the
collector to determine whether any operation within
his command can remedy the defect, and to decide
how he will accomplish his end.

This is perhaps a proper place to caution the
inexperienced, and in some cases even the experienced
collector, against acts of vandalism. To cut down,
colour, or otherwise mutilate a print, is one of those
unforgivable offences which often demonstrate con-
clusively how easy it is for a fool to destroy in five
minutes the achievement of a genius's lifetime. One
well-known collector, now dead, boiled his Harunobus
in paraffin to give them lustre; another painted
branches into the pillar-prints of Koriusai; another
cut down the size of his Hiroshiges, leaving only
those portions that particularly pleased him. If the
feelings of later collectors have any potency in
heaven, these men are now in hell. Not only is any
attempt to improve upon the artist's work a con-
temptible piece of presumption, but even the mere
effort to repair damages inflicted by time may be an
unwise venture. Frequently such injuries could be
remedied by an expert were it not that some preceding bungler, with the best intentions in the world,
has, out of sheer inexperience, made the injuries
irreparable. For example, if a print comes into the
expert's hands untouched he can literally slice off
a microscopic layer of the paper and thus remove
a bad surface-spot; but if the paper has been

tampered with by ignorant attempts to erase, he is helpless. Tears, stains, abrasions, and chemical decomposition may yield to skilful treatment; but unless one knows with the utmost exactitude what he expects to accomplish and how he intends to proceed at every step, he had best leave the matter strictly alone, or entrust it to other hands.

If the collector will remember that, though he is the present owner of his prints, he is not the final owner, he will be impelled to move with caution in his handling of them. Long after he is dead and forgotten, generations of lovers of beauty will treasure the sheets he once owned, and he will deserve their reproaches or their thanks according to the respect he has shown for these works. He is custodian for posterity, and his trust is one worthy of careful thought. He cannot do better than bear constantly in mind what should be the golden rule for collectors in all fields: Make no repairs, institute no changes, that cannot be altered; never do anything to a work of art that cannot be undone by its next owner.

Trim no margins; it is easy to mat them. Do not try to make more decent the objectionable rendering of a nude; sell the print to some one who does not find this rendering objectionable. If the colour has faded out, do not try to paint it in; possibly some one else may find the mere black-and-white composition beautiful, and he may prefer to see even the faded work of Kiyonaga rather than Kiyonaga plus the improvizations of a doubtless less illustrious designer.

No one needs such cautions as little as do the few

experts whose experience renders them competent to attempt what are almost capital operations. They are, of all collectors, the most reluctant to essay any manipulation whatsoever. To witness the repeated examinations and deliberations which the competent workman expends on so simple a question as whether or not a certain black spot shall be restored to its original orange hue is to learn a serious lesson.

The first of the steps to be taken in improving the condition of a print will generally be washing. If a print is badly wrinkled or creased, or if it appears to have dust and dirt on its surface, a bath is the best possible thing for it. A perfectly fresh print should never be washed ; nothing is to be gained by it, and much may be lost. For in many cases a little of the colour will come out in the course of the process, and the brilliance of the print will suffer slightly. Certain prints should be washed only if it is absolutely necessary. Harunobu prints with transparent red in them, Shuncho's that have purple, and any print that contains a delicate pigment known to collectors as "surimono blue," should be kept out of water if possible. These colours are not fast, and they are likely to go down in tone, or even run over into the adjoining parts of the print. The yellows and greens are as a rule unchanging, but a large number of the other colours are subject to modification, particularly in the work of the Kiyonaga and Utamaro Periods. The prints of Hiroshige and Hokusai generally undergo no change.

Prints with silver backgrounds should not be washed, and pillar-prints that consist of two joined sheets of paper should be kept in water only long enough to become wet through ; longer immersions will cause the sheets to separate, and necessitate troublesome work in rejoining them.

The process of washing is simple. A large vessel —a prosaic bath-tub is as good as anything—is filled with luke-warm water, and the print is put in and allowed to soak for a few minutes. If another sheet of paper has been pasted on the back of the print, this is carefully peeled off after the paste has become thoroughly wet. Adhering daubs of paste may be rubbed off with the fingers. Sometimes a very brown and dirty print can be cleaned a little by spreading it out while wet on a sheet of glass and applying a solution of some good washing-soap. Such a proceeding should be resorted to only in case of extreme dirtiness ; and prolonged soaking in clear water should follow.

When the washing is finished, the print is lifted from the water and allowed to drain for a few seconds, and is then carefully spread face downwards on a fresh sheet of heavy unglazed cardboard of the kind known as " blank." By means of a large damp brush or a delicately handled cloth, the back of the print is smoothed out so that it lies perfectly flat and even. Another sheet of cardboard is then placed on top of it, and the two sheets, with the print between them, are put away under heavy weights, such as two or three portfolios, and allowed to remain untouched for twenty-four hours or more. A good deal of dirt, and unfortunately a little colour, will generally soak out of the print and into the cardboard. When dry, the print peels neatly away from the cardboard, with its surface freshened and smoothed, sometimes almost remade.

Thin, worn, or disintegrated prints are difficult to handle during these processes; when wet, they tear like damp cigarette-paper. Sometimes prints that have been damaged and skilfully mended will float away in two or three pieces upon immersion. These and other possible troubles make it advisable that the inexperienced collector venture not too boldly in trying experiments. At least let him begin on prints of no value.

After the print is dry, worm-holes or tears can be mended either by patching or inlaying. Generally it is best to dampen the paper before attempting this. The simplest form of repair is to paste back of the hole a small piece of paper of the same colour as the print. A collector will have on hand a number of worthless damaged prints of various shades, out of which he cuts pieces for this purpose. Inlaying is more difficult; it involves either inserting a piece of paper cut to match the hole exactly, or inserting loose paper-pulp which is moulded to fill the hole. Both processes require more skill than the average collector can master, and are best left to the expert.

Stains and spots present difficult problems. Some are superficial, and can be gradually sliced off with a very sharp thin knife—an operation that will invariably result in the ruin of the print if tried by a novice. Minute knowledge of the behaviour of the curious fibrous Japanese paper is necessary for success; the expert generally works under a glass and prays continuously while he works. Stains that have soaked deeply into the paper are almost hopeless. Mildew discoloration is ineradicable. Greasespots sometimes yield to ether, benzine, or other common solvents. The use of these is, however, a desperate remedy; they may spoil the print even if they remove the spot.

Certain chemical changes in the pigments can be reversed, and the original colour restored. The blackening of *tan*, that orange pigment used by Koriusai and many other artists, can be removed and the original brilliance brought back. The same is true of a certain white that blackens with time. The processes employed are, however, easily capable of misuse; and the few persons who know the methods prefer not to make them public.

If a portion of a print is missing, due to a tear or to the ravages of moths, it is legitimate and desirable to tint the paper that is used to fill in the hole so that it matches its surroundings. Watercolours and a fine brush are employed. But on no account should the surface of the print itself be painted; if the colour has worn off in spots, any attempt to restore it will merely increase the damage still further.

A very thin print, or one that has been torn in several places, is best treated by pasting on the back of it while damp a dampened sheet of thin, tough Japanese paper. The operation, simple as it sounds, is difficult and requires practice to produce a smooth result.

Some collectors paste down the four edges of

their prints on thin sheets of cardboard to preserve
their flatness. The practice is an undesirable one;
it prevents any examination of the back of the
print; and does not achieve its end, since the print
and the mount expand and contract differently,
and wrinkles are almost sure to appear eventually.
The better practice is to apply a mere touch of
paste to the two upper corners of the print, and
affix these lightly to the mount. Over this is then
placed a mat, with a hole cut to fit the print
exactly, covering and holding down the print's
edges, and protecting it from abrasions. The size
of the mount and mat is determined by individual
taste; 3 or 4 inches margin would seem to be
the minimum desirable. After many experiments
I have adopted $22\frac{1}{2} \times 15\frac{1}{2}$ inches as the size for
my own collection. Mr. Gookin prefers $25 \times 16$;
but he also finds $23 \times 15\frac{1}{2}$ satisfactory if the
economy of space is any object. As to thickness,
tastes also differ; the mount should be at least thick
enough not to bend much with ordinarily careful
handling. Heavy Japanese Vellum makes the best
mats; it is expensive, but it greatly enhances the
appearance of the prints.

For triptychs and pillar-prints, a much larger
and heavier mount is required than in the case of
ordinary sheets. If the collector has only a few
of the former, he may prefer to mount the three
sheets separately, for convenience in storing, and
place the three mounts side by side only when
exhibiting them. If the two end sheets are mounted
so that they come very close to the right and

to the left-hand edges of their respective mounts, the effect of the three assembled is by no means bad ; and the ease of handling them is an advantage. Only the most perfectly matched triptychs can in any case dispense with the necessity of narrow strips left in the mat to cover the junction-edges of the sheets.

Some collectors have card-catalogues in which they keep all information relating to each print. Others use the bottom of the mount under the mat for that purpose. For a large collection the former is preferable ; for a small one, the latter.

The mounted prints are best kept in portfolios or Solander-boxes, laid flat on shelves and protected from dust as much as possible. Within the portfolio or box, the arrangement that is most useful is the chronological one.

There have been in the past several collections, such as the Hayashi and Wakai, whose owners felt it to be appropriate that they stamp their private seals upon the face of each print held by them. It is useless to comment upon the wisdom or unwisdom of their course ; for the thing is done, and many a fine print is now indelibly branded with these insignia. But it may be pointed out that the present practice of reputable collectors does not sanction such acts. Should any collector who happens to read these lines contemplate thus immortalizing himself, I suggest that he seriously consider whether even one small seal is not a disturbing factor when injected into a design so subtly calculated as the finest prints.

Further, if one collector may so stamp his prints, all others surely have a similar privilege ; and if the habit became universal, what would be the appearance of a print which, in the next two hundred years, should pass—as a print might easily pass—through the hands of twenty collectors ? And lastly, is there not a certain betrayal of petty conceit when the mere temporary owner of a great work of art judges the fact of his brief ownership to be of such importance that future generations must be told of it ; and so places his own emblem beside that of the creator of the print—beside the name of the immortal Kiyonaga or Sharaku ?

## CONCLUSION.

The day is coming—perhaps it is already here—when the Japanese Print will become the spiritual possession of a wider circle than that limited group of collectors who have been devoted to it in the past. Alien though this art is, it has power to penetrate to regions of the mind which Western art too often leaves unvisited.

Much is said unwisely about the elevating and educative power of art. The man in the street has come to believe that the elevating force resides in the theme which a work of art presents—that a picture of Galahad riding for the Grail is a lofty thing, and that a picture of the wings of the theatre during a ballet is a base one. Hence has arisen that unspeakably childish modern school of middle-class painters whose "pictures with a story "—generally a sentimental or edifying story—are the terror of the art-lover. After them, no wonder that even the Cubists came as a relief.

As every artist knows, the elevating power that resides in the mere subject of a picture has at best no more force than a moral maxim; the mind may assent to it, but the heart is unmoved. The same may be said in the case of a poem. The glory of poetry is not that it furnishes elevated sentiments in rhyme for public speakers to quote, but that it embodies music and thought combined in so fitly proportioned and expressive a structure that the reader carries away with him a certain acquaintance with perfection and a lasting desire for ideal beauty in everything.

Thus it is only through its power to cultivate the spectator's sense of form that art may be called elevating. Close familiarity with the productions of great artists gradually develops in the spectator an understanding of proportion, harmony, and conscious design, evoking in him the ability to perceive and even create order and freedom.

Because of the fact that the best Japanese prints are so superb an expression of the sense of form, they may be rated high as cultural agents. In them the eye finds little or no distraction occasioned by mere subject. Here speak the pure elements of artistic creation, liberated from combination with elements of accidental and personal charm. They contain the quintessence of all those harmonious and significant qualities which men desire of life. He who really takes them into his consciousness will be repelled by disorder, dullness, and indeterminateness

all his days.    And  probably  the  world  will  be
saved  by  its  hatred  of  these  things.    Therefore the
Japanese  print  cannot  be  regarded  as  primarily  a
pattern  for  future  designers  of  wood-engraving ;  it
appears  to  have  a  far  wider  and  deeper  office  to
perform.

# INDEX

# INDEX